# it

# Joseph Roach

THE UNIVERSITY OF MICHIGAN PRESS   Ann Arbor

2010   2009   2008   2007      4   3   2   1

*A CIP catalog record for this book is available from the British Library.*

Library of Congress Cataloging-in-Publication Data

Roach, Joseph, 1947–
   It / Joseph Roach.
      p.      cm.
   Includes bibliographical references and index.
   ISBN-13: 978-0-472-09936-8 (cloth : alk. paper)
   ISBN-10: 0-472-09936-1 (cloth : alk. paper)
   ISBN-13: 978-0-472-06936-1 (pbk. : alk. paper)
   ISBN-10: 0-472-06936-5 (pbk. : alk. paper)
   1. Theater—Philosophy.   I. Title.

PN2039.R63 2007
792.01—dc22                              2006038425

*for Lyric*

# acknowledgments

The Andrew W. Mellon Foundation has generously assisted my research by funding two projects: first, a summer seminar, "Writing Performance History," that brought together fourteen dissertation-stage students from ten departments at Yale; second, a Distinguished Achievement Award, the terms of which afford wide latitude in conducting research under the aegis of the World Performance Project. In gratefully acknowledging the foundation's support, I also want to recognize the help of colleagues, students, and staff members at Yale and elsewhere. They are too numerous to list here, but I want to name some of them as special benefactors and guides.

The references in the text and notes of *It* can only imperfectly communicate what the presence at Yale of the Paul Mellon Center for British Art (BAC); its staff; and its Director, Amy Meyers, have meant to the inception and completion of this book. In particular, Julia Marciari Alexander of the BAC and Catherine MacLeod of the National Portrait Gallery, London, created the exhibition and catalog of *Painted Ladies: Women at the Court of Charles II,* to which I am variously and generally indebted. In the process of researching pictures and securing permissions for their reproduction here, Anna Magliaro of the BAC made it all seem so easy, as only someone completely knowledgeable and highly skilled can do.

Susan Brady of the Beinecke Rare Book and Manuscript Library at Yale and Margaret K. Powell of the Lewis Walpole Library at Yale are my collaborators in theater and performance research, and I am humbly grateful for their intellectual generosity; professional gifts; and remarkable forbearance, at least so far, with my scholarly idiosyncrasies. A passage in chapter 3 is adapted from an essay published in collaboration with Margaret K. Powell, "Big Hair" (*Eighteenth-Century Studies,* 2004), and it appears here with her permission. Pamela Jordan at the Yale School of Drama, like so many of the librarians at Yale, came through for me when I most needed her help.

My colleagues Claude Rawson, Jill Campbell, Annabel Patterson, Paul Fry, Elizabeth Dillon, Joe Bizup, Jeffrey H. Richards, and Frank Prochaska contributed a variety of helpful suggestions and corrections, but I am responsible for any shortcomings stemming from my failure to capitalize on their excellent advice. That goes for Julia Fawcett, too, who read the whole manuscript through carefully, justly, and tactfully. Felicity A. Nussbaum and J. Paul Hunter serve as inspirational models for doing scholarship in eighteenth-century studies: I hope that they and other admired colleagues in the period will not find that I have presumed too much upon the elasticity of our subject, even as I hope that my interlocutors in the social sciences, including those at the Center for Cultural Sociology at Yale, led by Jeffrey Alexander, will not conclude that my historical approach has unduly constrained the expansiveness of performance theory.

After four decades of receiving guidance and inspiration from my mentor Marvin Carlson, I know that the only way to pay him back even in part is to emulate his example as best I can in working with my own students. These now include Emily Coates, Artistic Director of the World Performance Project, and the members of her growing team of researchers and performers, drawn from the graduate departments of English, American Studies, and African American Studies and the undergraduate Theater Studies program, a recent alumnus of which, Andy Sandberg, provided valuable research assistance early in the project.

LeAnn Fields and the whole editorial team at the University of Michigan Press—led by Marcia LaBrenz, Rebecca Mostov, Anna M. Szymanski, and the two anonymous readers—kept faith with the project and kept me on schedule. I hope that the outcome makes them glad that they did.

The most important of my many citations to Victorian texts and pictures I owe to my partner and collaborator Janice Carlisle, who has generously shared her wide reading in nineteenth-century fiction and nonfiction prose and her extensive knowledge of Victorian art with me. I am grateful for the world of things that she has done to make our life together wonderful, but here I must specifically acknowledge a scholarly debt: it was she who led me to (and through) Walter Bagehot's *English Constitution,* which figures crucially in *It* but also in *Picturing Reform,* her study of the politics of high Victorian visual culture (Cambridge University Press, forthcoming). Readers will have to make do with my secondhand version until her book appears. Our children, Kate and Joseph, who were so good for so long about sharing their time with previous projects, now are both in graduate school, and they have become very good about sharing their ideas, for which I will always be deeply thankful.

Earlier versions of various sections of the introduction and chapters 1, 3, 4, and 5, now revised and dispersed, first appeared in the following publications: *Theatre Journal* 56, no. 4 (2004): 555–68; *Eighteenth-Century Studies* 38, no. 1 (2004): 79–99; *Yale Journal of Criticism* 16, no. 1 (2003): 211–30; *The Global Eighteenth Century,* ed. Felicity A. Nussbaum (Baltimore: Johns Hopkins University Press, 2003), 93–106; *Theorizing Practice: Redefining Theatre History,* ed. W. B. Worthen and Peter Holland (New York: Palgrave, 2003), 120–35; *Theatre and Celebrity in Britain, 1660–2000,* ed. Mary Luckhurst and Jane Moody (New York: Palgrave, 2005), 15–30; *Writing Race across the Atlantic World,* ed. Philip Beidler and Gary Taylor (New York: Palgrave, 2005), 137–52; and *Notorious Muse: The Actress in British Art and Culture, 1776–1812,* ed. Robyn Asleson (New Haven: Yale University Press, 2003), 195–209.

*It* is dedicated to the memory of the actress Lyric Marie Benson (Yale College, class of 2002), who was murdered by her stalker at precisely the moment in her brief career when her image had only just begun to belong to everyone. The growing number of people being helped by her inspiring example (visit www.lyricoflife.org) can now join together in a common bond with those of us who knew her in life: we won't forget her because we can't.

# contents

# abbreviations

**BA**

*The Broadview Anthology of Restoration and Early Eighteenth-Century Drama.* Ed. J. Douglas Canfield. Toronto: Broadview Press, 2001.

**BD**

*A Biographical Dictionary of Actors, Actresses, Musicians, Dancers, Managers, and Other Stage Personnel in London, 1660–1800.* Ed. Philip H. Highfill Jr., Kalman A. Burnim, and Edward A. Langhans. 16 vols. Carbondale: Southern Illinois University Press, 1973–93.

**Pepys**

*The Diary of Samuel Pepys.* Ed. Robert Latham and William Matthews. 11 vols. Berkeley and Los Angeles: University of California Press, 1970–83.

*Something,* whose Truth convinc'd at Sight we find
That gives us back the Image of our Mind.

—Alexander Pope,
*An Essay on Criticism*


I looked under the skin for the flesh and bone,
like you said, and even the marrow and all that,
but I found her in the hat, and the shades, and
the attitude.

—Lyric Benson, on becoming
the character of "Jackie O"

# introduction

I belonged to the Public and to the world, not because I was talented or even beautiful but because I had never belonged to anything or anyone else.

—Marilyn Monroe

There is a certain quality, easy to perceive but hard to define, possessed by abnormally interesting people. Call it "it." For the sake of clarity, let *it*, as a pronoun aspiring to the condition of a noun, be capitalized hereafter, except where it appears in its ordinary pronominal role. Most of us immediately assume that It has to do with sex, and we're right, but mainly because everything has to do with sex. Most of us also think that It necessarily entails glamour, and so it does, but not for long. Most of us think that It is rare, and it is quite, even to the point of seeming magical, but It is also everywhere to be seen. In fact, however elusive this quality may be in the flesh, some version of it will, at any given moment, fall within our direct view or easy reach as a mass-circulation image; if not, a worthy substitute will quickly come to mind, even to the minds of those who, commendably, want to resist generalizations like these, along with the pervasively seductive imposition of the icons that they describe.

Let's not be unduly prim, however. This is the way of the world right now, and it has been so, with increasingly invasive saturation and ingenious manipulation since the seventeenth century, when popular celebrities began to circulate their images in the place of

1

religious and regal icons. Today these totems can pop up anywhere. Just at the limit of my reach, on the magazine table at the
barbershop on the corner of Chapel and High streets in New
Haven, but looking close enough to touch, Uma Thurman returns
my gaze from the cover of *GQ*. It's uncanny. She might, with minor
adjustments perhaps, just as easily be looking up from the cover of
*Cosmopolitan* in the checkout line of Stop & Shop at the Amity Mall,
but here she is, big as life, sitting right beside me at Tony's, mirac-
ulously outshining the lesser deities of *Maxim* and *Esquire.*

Of course she hasn't popped up just anywhere, because there's
history everywhere. In one direction lies the town green, zoned for
sheep and churches by the founders of New Haven Colony in
1638, the same year that the royal surveyor Inigo Jones laid out
Covent Garden Piazza, later to become London's teeming market
of flowers, flesh, and fantasy; in the other direction, three streets—
Dixwell, Whalley, and Goffe—named for the regicides who took
refuge in Connecticut after 1660 to escape the retribution of the
restored king Charles II, who installed his flashiest mistress and
her complacent, papist husband in the very house in King Street,
Westminster, that Major-General Edward Whalley had abandoned
in order to end up hiding out in a cave near here. Taking local
inventory of a still-active front in these long-running culture wars,
there's no doubt which side has pulled ahead on points: mocking
the Puritan heritage that once sheltered and even honored the
most die-hard iconoclasts anywhere, painted harlots now reign like
royals on newsstands everywhere. As *GQ*'s cover girl, Thurman is
fragile of feature—eyelids drooping, lips parted, hair bad—and
negligent of dress, or about to be, the silken filament of one strap
sliding down almost to her right elbow, carrying part of the lace
bodice with it, the rest apparently soon to follow, if the insinuated
narrative of volition or gravity is to keep its eye-catching promise.[1]

Then again, let's not be wholly prurient either. Thurman's
image fascinates, not merely because she looks to be nearly naked,
but also because she looks to be completely alone. Even as her eyes
meet mine as seductively as they must in order to do their work,
her countenance somehow keeps a modicum of privacy where
none seems possible, a discreet veil of solitude in a world brought

into illusory fullness of being by the general congregation of unaverted stares. That countenance, the effortless look of public intimacy well known in actresses and models, but also common among high-visibility professionals of other kinds, is but one part, albeit an important one, of the multifaceted genius of It.

The following account of that genius—including its characteristic manifestations of public intimacy (the illusion of availability), synthetic experience (vicariousness), and the It-Effect (personality-driven mass attraction)—is a highly selective one. In its Anglocentrism, for instance, my account will pass over a densely woven fabric of thousands of different threads to follow one particular strand. That strand, thin but bright, connects the Stuart Restoration and the theater it launched, a marketing revolution within the larger consumer revolution of the long eighteenth century, to Hollywood. Although admittedly self-limiting, this selection is not arbitrary in either its specifics or its generalities, and this introduction will outline the theoretical and historical issues in detail so as to provide a road map for what follows in the rest of the book. These preliminaries include a definition of It as secular magic and a description of the period of It's modern emergence, here called the "deep eighteenth century." They also include a profile of each of the principal authorities in that period, from a Restoration diarist and his charismatic king to a Hollywood maven and her dressmaker sister, and from sex-bombs to Victorian sages, whose words and deeds best explain the hottest sources of mass attraction.

"It" is a very large subject, but this book begins and ends in very specific locations and engages very particular objects and events along the way, starting at Chapel and High. Across the street from the goddess-infested barbershop looms Louis Kahn's suave facade for the Paul Mellon Center for British Art, a North American repository of Tory glamour, with negligently dressed deities of its own à la Sir Peter Lely, a decisive rebuke to the regicides and iconoclasts, and a privileged resource for research into the ideas and techniques behind It. Here primrose-bearing Diana Kirke, Countess of Oxford, for instance (fig. 1), painted *en déshabillé* by Lely in the late 1660s, returns the gaze of the beholder with a publicly

intimate nonchalance that remains both representative of its age
and still syndicated in reruns today. A primary purpose of this
book is to show how the message her look communicates, combining semidivinity with seminudity, found its way to Hollywood in
the 1920s, another colony, like New Haven in the 1660s, for
refugees and exiles, except that those pilgrims came to promote
the mass worship of graven idols, not to smash or exorcise them.
They found the ways and means to spread the It-Effect worldwide,
but they did not invent it. They also did as much as anyone has
ever done to answer the burning question on everyone's lips: What
is It?

## What It Is

The most pertinent usage of the word *it* was coined in 1927 by a
British expatriate, romance-author, and Hollywood tastemaker
Elinor Glyn (1864–1943), writing in the foreword to *It,* one of her
pulpiest fictions, also done into a screenplay for Paramount. A culture-industry insider, she briskly specifies the properties shared by
abnormally interesting people, intervening with an analytic rigor
that shapes up the flabby abstractions with which critical theory
has otherwise weighted down the subject of celebrity. Glyn writes
leanly: "To have 'It,' the fortunate possessor must have that
strange magnetism which attracts both sexes. He or she must be
entirely unselfconscious and full of self-confidence, indifferent to
the effect he or she is producing, and uninfluenced by others.
There must be physical attraction, but beauty is unnecessary. Conceit or self-consciousness destroys 'It' immediately. In the animal
world 'It' demonstrates [itself] in tigers and cats—both animals
being fascinating and mysterious, and quite unbiddable."[2] Setting
a standard of cavalier sangfroid in charismatic demeanor, Glyn
peels away the outer layers of It to discover its basis in an attraction
that, as the oft-heard rationalization goes, "isn't just physical" or,
more plausibly still, is fundamentally polymorphous. Few have It,
but almost everyone wants to get it anywhere he or she can find it.

The intensity of this attraction presupposes a certain element of
danger, however—of rejection at least, if not something even

Fig. 1. Sir Peter Lely, Diana Kirke, later Countess of Oxford, c. 1665–70.
Yale Center for British Art, Paul Mellon Collection.

worse. Glyn had a quirky interest in animal magnetism and a pro-
nounced weakness for alpha predators found in both sexes and all
orientations but only in a few select species. The most interesting
point she makes about It across the animal kingdom concerns the
"unbiddable" nature of tigers and other cats. An air of perceived
indifference counts heavily in the production of this special allure,
which must appear to be exercised effortlessly or not at all. Evidently, dogs try too hard. Although her distinction between physical attraction and beauty seems disingenuous coming from a
knowledgeable moviemaker, she has support from the entry for
*it* in the *OED,* which cites a variety of uses of the word in Edwardian
slang, including Rudyard Kipling's folksy tautology of 1904:

" 'Tisn't beauty, so to speak, nor good talk necessarily. It's just It. Some women'll stay in a man's memory if they once walk down a street."[3]

Glyn royally dubbed silent film star Clara Bow (1905–1965), whose brief but dazzling career epitomized the flapper era, "The 'It' Girl."[4] Bow's explosive rise to stardom exemplifies the disruptive impact, usefully theorized by Michael Quinn, of the It-Effect on the materials of the scripted character, story line, apparatus of production, and public consciousness of the work. "The shift of perception that celebrity allows," Quinn notes, "is a key one, and is extraordinarily powerful: the audience's attitude shifts from an awareness of the presence of fictional illusion to the acceptance of an illusion, however false, of the celebrity's absolute presence."[5] Behind the refractory celebrity of which Quinn speaks lurks the prior condition of It, emerging from an apparently singular nexus of personal quirks, irreducible to type, yet, paradoxically, the epitome of a type or prototype that almost everyone eventually wants to see or be like. In this sense, there was only one Clara Bow, there will never be another, yet even seventy years after her reclusive retirement and forty years after her death, she still remains everywhere to be seen, leaving behind an afterimage, one that persists and even regenerates in the public mind. As Marvin Carlson has shown, a celebrity actor is "entrapped by the memories of the public, so that each new appearance requires a renegotiation with those memories."[6] Carlson calls this phenomenon "ghosting," and it need not end with the retirement or death of the star. An abused dropout with a painful stammer and hole-in-the-bucket self-esteem, Brooklyn-born Bow won a screen test in a contest run by *Motion Picture* magazine and parlayed it into stardom as the rags-to-riches avatar of sexy pluck and smarty-pants, working-girl attitude. Pinned up thereafter in revolutionary haircut and underwear, she was so unforgettably one of a kind that she lost her self forever in the creation of her type. *It*, the 1927 Paramount Bow-vehicle, recently returned in the form of a musical comedy, *The It Girl* (2001), by Paul McKibbins and B. T. McNicholl, which boasted, "She'll Turn Your Sadness into Gladness!" In Carlson's terms, Bow's screen persona was "ghosted" yet again the very next year by the title character in the flapper revival *Thoroughly Modern Millie* (2002), whose promoters breathlessly asked, "Will Millie become this season's 'It Girl?'" She did.

Like a crown, the It-Girl appellation became a transferable title, once openly aspired to by successive generations of Hollywood starlets, now demurely coveted again under the reactionary aegis of stealth postfeminism.[7] But as Glyn's liberally polymorphous definition suggests, men can have It too. In fact, they have had It for millennia. At the Eureka moment when she found her way to the word, just as the talkies were coming in but before her career as an unofficial chargé d'affaires for British culture in Hollywood burned out, Glyn rechristened what was then only the latest and most powerful version of an oft-observed phenomenon known by many aliases in the annals of cultural performance.

How many? For Quintilian, Latin rhetor in the rule of Vespasian, It was *ethos,* the compellingly singular character of the great orator. For Zeami, the Zen-inflected theorist of Noh acting, It was the ninth and highest level of *hana,* "The Flower of Peerless Charm." For Castiglione, It was *sprezzatura,* the courtly possessor of which turned every head when he, and he alone, suavely entered a room. For many religious thinkers, from the biblical prophets and apostles to modern theologians, It was expressed by the word *charisma,* a special gift vouchsafed by God, a grace or favor, which sociologist Max Weber then condensed into a principle of powerfully inspirational leadership or authority.[8] For adherents of science, It was captured by the metaphoric terms of *magnetism* and *radiance,* which, taken together, neatly express the opposite motions instigated by the contradictory forces of It: drawing toward the charismatic figure as *attraction;* radiating away from him or her as broadcast *aura.* Such metaphors well describe the effects of the phenomenon, but they still explain very little of its mystery. No closer today to a satisfactory theory of It, contemporary speakers of proper English employ various synonyms, such as *charm, charisma,* and *presence.* Americans also have recourse to a well-stocked slang lexicon, including *stuff, spunk,* and *moxie,* the latter term suggesting supreme self-possession even at moments of self-abandonment, a kind of psychical extension of exceptional physical courage, undaunted even by the fear of being found objectionable. What has still gone missing, Glyn's pioneering effort from the 1920s aside, is an analysis of precisely what qualities, then and now, make moxie the cat's meow.

"It" is the power of apparently effortless embodiment of contradictory qualities simultaneously: strength *and* vulnerability, innocence *and* experience, and singularity *and* typicality among them. The possessor of It keeps a precarious balance between such mutually exclusive alternatives, suspended at the tipping point like a tightrope dancer on one foot; and the empathic tension of waiting for the apparently inevitable fall makes for breathless spectatorship: hence Glyn's location of a psychological contradiction with reversible polarities like egoless self-confidence or unbiddable magnetism at the source of the mysterious fascination of It. In *The Secret Art of the Performer* (1991), Eugenio Barba explains the success of analogous oppositions in compelling physical performances: "The performer develops resistance by creating oppositions: this resistance increases the density of each movement, gives movement altered intensity and muscular tone."[9] In classical European theater, such oppositions and hence resistance are suggested by the term *contraposto*, which describes a pose in which the performer turns in different directions simultaneously at the knees, the hips, the shoulders, and the head, making an interesting line of the body. *Resistance* is another way of describing the novelty-inducing asymmetries contained—resisted—by the performer even as they register in the mind of the spectator as a miracle of unstable but inevitable harmonies.

This definition of It, paradox-ridden as it is, moves beyond the tautology of innate charm and enters into the realm of theatrical and cinematic technique, though the open question of whether It is a "God-given" gift to the fortunate few or the hardscrabble self-selection of the fiercely driven is yet another mystery that makes It fascinating. Like perfect pitch, which some have and most don't, It makes certain people interesting all the time; others require a lucky break or a lurid calamity—the fortuitous convergence of personality and extraordinary circumstances or efforts—to activate the fickle prurience of the public. In any event, It comes out in the play of suddenly reversible polarities. Like a gestalt switch, during which the vase transforms itself, in the blink of the beholder's eye, into two faces juxtaposed, only to switch back again, reversible polarities appear both to cause It and to assert themselves as its most startling and continuously compelling effect.

Theatrical performance and the social performances that resemble it consist of struggle, the simultaneous experience of mutually exclusive possibilities—truth and illusion, presence and absence, face and mask. Performers are none other than themselves doing a job in which they are always someone else, filling our field of vision with the flesh-and-blood matter of what can only be imagined to exist. But with an intensity of focus beyond the reach of normal people, those with It can project these and other antinomies apparently at will. From moment to moment on the stage or on the set, they must hold them together with the force of their personalities, but in the service of a representation to which their personalities are supposedly excrescent. Such a precarious center, at once self-expression and self-erasure, cannot hold; but for the two-hour traffic of our stage, the contending forces remain in play, while their contingent interaction generates an intense, charismatic radiance that emanates from their fissionable source. They create a continuous category crisis at twenty-four frames per second (or the digitized equivalent of that analogical pace), oscillating between categories in the minds of spectators faster than Faye Dunaway's child does between "sister" and "daughter" in *Chinatown* (Paramount, 1974). As in all melodrama, the outcome of the struggle between implacable opposites must be deferred to maintain suspense, but at the end, a dark secret remains untold, and even in the afterglow of the most illuminating disclosure, there is an uncanny translucence without transparency, a silhouette. Nor do such contentions always unfold as high drama, for in moments of quiet absorption they can also appear as the flickering play of light and shadow barely perceptible as a disturbance in the soul. But in the most sensitive instrument the subtlest turbulence has its effect as well as its affect, and from the perspective of the audience, we find that inchoate urges, desires *and* identifications, have been stirred in us without claiming anything so vulgar as a name. That being the case, we can't take our eyes off of It.

While the phenomenon of It seems to have been noted at many times in history, particular periods shape it to their own purposes and impress it with their own peculiar styles. Ambivalent heirs to the English theater of "the last century," by which commentators from Charles Lamb to Thomas Babington Macaulay meant the era that began with the Restoration of Charles II and continued into the Regency of George IV (1811–20), the Victorians of Elinor Glyn's youth and the Edwardians of her early adulthood well understood the concept of It, whether they approved of it or not. In fact, they understood it as well as she did after seven years in Hollywood and a lifetime of writing "romance." The novelist George Meredith, for instance, wrote a spot-on description of the phenomenon in *Beauchamp's Career* (1876). In the key scene of the novel, Cecelia, an aristocratic English beauty, gazes fixedly on the photograph of her less beautiful but nonetheless apparently invincible rival for the love of novel's hero. That rival is Renée, Madame de Rouaillont, and her image keeps the jealous, fascinated beholder "enchained" along with everyone else who encounters it. Here's why:

> Dark-eyed Renée was not beauty but attraction; she touched the double chords within us which are we know not whether harmony or discord, but a divine discord if an uncertified harmony, memorable beyond plain sweetness or majesty. There are touches of bliss in anguish that superhumanize bliss, touches of mystery in simplicity, of the eternal in the variable. These two chords of poignant antiphony she struck throughout the range of the hearts of men, and strangely intervolved them in vibrating unison. Only to look at her face, without hearing her voice, without the charm of her speech, was to feel it.[10]

Meredith's concluding "it" is It. Cecelia, with her statuesque beauty and considerable fortune, should have It, but the quality possessed by Madame la marquise remains irresistibly "dark" in its superior attraction, unsettling not only to the putative order of romantic inclination and the hierarchy of sexual selection, but also to every other character's peace of mind.

What Meredith calls "poignant antiphony" bestows a preternatural strangeness on It and often a certain social apartness on those who possess it. In children's games, the player ritually chosen to be "it" is simultaneously elected and ostracized. There is a kind of freakishness to having It; and despite the allure, a potential for monstrosity, which haunts the meaning of *it* as the proper neuter pronoun of the third-person singular, used to refer to things without life, of animals when sex is not specified, and sometimes of infants (*OED*). Charles Addams capitalized on this disturbingly elastic sense of the word by naming a beguilingly amorphous character "Cousin It." Stephen King did the same by titling a horror-thriller *It* (1986) and adding a special frisson to the danger by making the eponymous monster a performer: "The face of the clown in the stormdrain was white, there were funny tufts of red hair on either side of his bald head, and there was a big clown-smile painted over his mouth."[11] P. T. Barnum anticipated both Addams and King by billing his leading sideshow geek "What-is-It?" The uncanny allure of It intensifies when a charismatic performer takes over the typifying marks of gender from the opposite sex, ensuring the prominence of transvestism in the greatest theatrical traditions, but also attracting the routine suspicion of the authorities on grounds of ontological subversion. "Unbiddable" as a cat, the Janus-faced quality of It thus manifests itself in expressive behavior that people who don't think of themselves as actors may find off-putting or threatening, even as they crave to experience its seductive glamour and participate in its public adulation. The audience clamors for It and punishes it too, sometimes at considerable psychic cost to the designated paragon, who might at any time bring out in fans the dark underside of the "poignant antiphony" they nurse deeply within themselves like a jealous lover's grudge. Some even resent the iconic few as thieves, who have stolen from them not what they had, but what they always wanted.

Reappearing as it does in some version of itself throughout history, It cannot be discussed intelligibly apart from its social contexts at specified points in its reception. This is particularly so because, as Gordon Rogoff rightly observes, glossing Max Weber: "Charisma is, by definition, a description of shared needs."[12] As charismatics seem to know telepathically who needs them most when they walk into a room, so particular audiences in different times and places have known what they most needed and from whom when they walked into a theater district, which might be called an "It-Zone," serving as the Habermasian public sphere for newly self-fashioning mobs of star-gazers. "It" occupies much the same place in the empathic life of a reception community that "True Wit" does for the readers of the tightly packed couplet in Alexander Pope's *An Essay on Criticism* (1711). Like "Wit," It is

> *Something,* whose Truth convinc'd at Sight we find,
> That gives us back the Image of our Mind.

The implication of the Augustan poet's use of the first-person plural still obtains: images charged with that certain "*Something*" are more alive in us than ever as the open secrets of our waking dreams. With the rise of print-world publicity and its mass-mediated progeny, preconceptions of abnormally interesting personae become more specialized, even standardized as role-icons— "beauty," "femme fatale," "rake," "fop" and "pirate," for instance— only to be jolted from time to time into fads and crazes through novel iterations by exceptional interpreters: "What oft was Thought," as Pope put it, "but ne'er so well Exprest."[13] What marks the emergence of these objects of abnormal interest, now sufficiently pervasive as to seem unremarkable, is an intensified self-consciousness about the social character of what had once looked like miracles. The most fertile historical period for that emergence is very extensive, but it is not boundless.

### The Deep Eighteenth Century

Scholars have accepted the notion of a *long* eighteenth century, pushing the book-ending dates of the period back to 1660 and forward to 1820. They have more recently introduced the idea of a *wide* or "global" eighteenth century, expanding the Eurocentric boundaries of previous research to encompass the four corners of the world.[14] The shift from popular to mass attraction in the expanding English-speaking theater, however, offers but one reason among many to welcome the addition of a *deep* eighteenth century. The deep eighteenth century is the one that isn't over yet. It stays alive among us as a repertoire of long-running performances. In fact, some of them we can't get rid of, hard as we might try: chattel slavery and colonialism, for example, still exist as themselves here and there and as their consequences everywhere. The deep eighteenth century is thus not merely a period of time, but a kind of time, imagined by its narrators as progress, but experienced by its subjects as uneven developments and periodic returns. As Michel Serres and Bruno Latour succinctly put it, "Time doesn't flow; it percolates."[15] The rationale for imagining a newly complicated three-dimensional period, acknowledging the steadily accelerating commercialization of leisure from 1660 as a long but spastic revolution, is in part the consequence of its culturally prescient texts and discourses, but mainly of its prolific performances and behaviors, which constantly mutate but also persist, rolling through the *longue durée* like human waves through crowds of complicit strangers.[16] The unsteady rise of the actress to prominence and professional respectability offers a general example of this genealogy of performance. The constantly returning hit of *The Beggar's Opera* (1728) offers a specific one. Hydra-headed in its modern revivals, knockoffs, and sequels, John Gay's Newgate pastoral has carried forward the It-Effect of glamorized criminality to bring its guilty pleasures to each succeeding generation, epitomizing what John Brewer has so influentially extolled, channeling Joseph Addison, as "the pleasures of the imagination" in the eighteenth century.[17] But the stagy panoply of demimondaines and rakish gallants popularly associated with the hedonistic performances of this period, on the stage and off, complicated its reputation even as their notoriety publicized and extended it.

Victorian and Edwardian appreciations of the staying power of the deep eighteenth century, cited in very different kinds of books, from the fulminations of John Ruskin against the concupiscent frivolity of baroque funerary monuments in *The Stones of Venice*

(1851–53) to the discerning views of Walter Bagehot on the "visible government" of the nostalgically sacred monarchy in *The English Constitution* (1867), show the extent to which the transitional eighteenth century became a touchstone and a hyperbolic mirror, especially with regard to the shape-shifting "Artificial Comedy of the Last Century." A beguilingly wispy essay by Charles Lamb by that title, originally written in 1822, but appended to an anthology of Restoration playwrights published in 1840, argued, inflammatorily as it turned out, that Restoration and eighteenth-century playwrights wrote free comedy. In Lamb's view, the characters of Etherege, Wycherley, and their successors romp harmlessly through inconsequential predicaments, bouncing off one other like inflatable toys in the moral equivalent of zero gravity: "They are a world of themselves almost as much as fairyland. . . .— a Utopia of gallantry, where pleasure is duty, and manners perfect freedom. It is altogether a speculative scheme of things, which has no reference whatever to the world that is." If "we" were to censure this enchanted Cloud-cuckoo-land, Lamb pleads, speaking for the modernizing genius of the new age, "we would indict our dreams."[18] Macaulay answered Lamb directly in his review of the anthology and indirectly in his still hypnotically readable *History of England from the Accession of James the Second* (1848–61). He pointed out severely that the immorality of the characters and their language in the supposedly "Artificial" comedies, populated as he believed them to be by fornicating rakehells and smut-spewing sluts, offer not an escape from but rather a damning documentation of the depravity of the late but stubbornly persistent age. So vehemently indignant that it recalls the classics of antitheatricalist polemic from Tertullian to William Prynne and the Reverend Jeremy Collier, Macaulay's contempt for the allure of the restored dynasty is of a piece with his disgust with the restored stage: "From the day on which the theatres were reopened they became seminaries of vice." Macaulay's view of the actors and actresses is surpassed in opprobrium only by his opinion of the playwriting wits with whom the monarchs and aristocrats consorted and whose borrowings from Shakespeare, Calderón, and Molière indelibly soiled the originals: "Nothing could be so pure or so heroic but that it became foul and ignoble by transfusion through those foul and ignoble minds."[19]

On the face of it, the preeminent Victorian historian of the later Stuarts seems to take self-congratulatory pleasure in denouncing their most glamorous productions. Behind Macaulay's moral outrage at the culture of the deep eighteenth century, however, lurks the iconoclastic fear that the convergent celebrity of actors and kings may reduce substance to image and nothing more. In that, he was writing as both historian and prophet. Anticipating the terms of Edwardian revisionism, which included a revival of the plays of the Restoration and eighteenth century and a runaway enthusiasm for their theatrical history, Macaulay makes an interesting excuse for the libertine excesses of the Restoration as a predictable if tragically regrettable response to the idol-smashing Interregnum that preceded it: "The turpitude of the drama became such as to astonish all those who are not aware that extreme relaxation is the natural effect of extreme restraint, and that an age of hypocrisy is, in the regular course of things, followed by an age of impudence."[20] By the same logic, he might have added that an age of iconoclasm could be expected to yield to an age of icons, which it certainly did, with consequences still widely to be seen and deeply felt.

Today theater practitioners will sometimes speak of the "Restoration comedy of manners" as belonging to something called "period style," signifying the utopian remoteness of the genre from the present, and the results onstage usually confirm their presuppositions. But Norman Holland came much closer to the truth when he called them, in the title of his critical study of the behaviors they represent, *The First Modern Comedies* (1959). "There is nothing in earlier English comedy quite like this," Holland argued,[21] and although not all the reasons he gave then would necessarily be the ones critics emphasize now, his stress on the regulative power of these plays as probative arenas of true attraction and glamour—witty contests between those who have something quite magical about their persons that others obviously lack—sets the scene for subsequent theater historians. They have gone on to explore the intricate relationship between the successes of the characters created by the playwrights and the talents of the sexually self-possessed performers for whom the roles were often specifically tailored.[22] When plays sometimes touted the feature-by-feature attributes of the actresses playing the heroines and when both prologues and epilogues alluded leeringly to their sex lives offstage, the practice of intimacy in public had clearly arrived. Persona and personality oscillated between foreground and background with the speed of innuendo, intensified by the personal chemistry of the starring actors, igniting the precinematic It-Effect and blazing its trail. Herbert Blau puts the case succinctly when he speaks, apropos of the Restoration drama's modernity, of "an economy of pleasure in which sex, matching wits, is the measuring rod, a principle of intelligibility, a critical limit giving the impression that it is the source of pleasure when in actuality it is pleasure's Law, justifying regulation and social control."[23] In the sex battles of the adversary lovers, whose obstacles tend to arise within themselves rather than from the external resistance of blocking characters, fear of self-disclosure sharpens tactics of self-governance, staging erotic play as the most entertaining of all legalities. "Hold!" says the witty Harriet to her lover Dorimant in the famous "proviso scene" of *The Man of Mode; or, Sir Fopling Flutter* (1676), making one of the many profane allusions to religion with which the play abounds, "Though I wish you devout, I would not have you turn fanatic" (5.2.155–56; *BA* 582).

Public intimacy may seem to be a purely modern and secular idea, but it is in fact rooted in traditional religious doctrine and, more deeply and lastingly, in popular religious feeling. In a critique of the Enlightenment shibboleth of disenchantment as the sign and substance of modernity itself, cultural theorists have interpreted the mysterious force of mass attraction as a "reenchantment" of the world.[24] As an instance of temporal "percolation" rather than "flow," reenchantment has doctrinally orthodox beginnings but no end in sight. In order to become enchanted in the first place, saints and martyrs must make themselves tangibly accessible to ordinary mortals even as they communicate with the divine. They must seem at once touchable and transcendent, like movie stars and cover girls, and like them also and for that reason, they very often appear in representation seminude. Their images circulate widely in the absence of their persons—a necessary condition of modern celebrity—but the very tension between their widespread visibility and their actual remoteness creates an unfulfilled need in the hearts of the public. One aspect of this need manifests itself as a craving to communicate with the privately embodied source of the aura, as in the "I and Thou" relationship imagined to exist between a praying supplicant and a god, in which the archaic "*du* form" of intimate second-person address allows the devout speaker to imagine a conversation with an abstract deity personified as if it had a body, a face, and a voice.[25] To be efficacious, the "I and Thou" experience of It requires mental pictures or ideas, not reducible to any single one of the materially circulating images of the celebrity, but nevertheless generally available by association when summoned from the enchanted memories of those imagining themselves in communication with the special, spectral other. An image thus synthesized as an idea, here called an *effigy*,[26] will very likely have only a coincidental relationship to the identity of the actual human person whose peculiar attraction triggered the hunger for the experience in the first place. Typically known to the public, as kings are, by their first names, the effigies produce the uncanny effect of lifelikeness: just because such icons exist only in other people's imagination of them doesn't mean they're unreal. In the extreme case of stalking behavior, the effigy might become more real than anything else, and the celebrity's refusal to conform to the deranged and urgent imperatives of that reality brings the stalker to the door with love on the lips but murder in the heart.

The It-Effect thus often takes on a powerful and sometimes even fearsome religiosity of its own, making everyday experience seem not only strange but also enchanted, as if possessed by the mischievous spirits of portentous little gods. Sociologist Chris Rojek aptly summarizes this theology of pop culture in *Celebrity* (2001), acknowledging the force of the spiritual attraction that drives public intimacy but leaving its source—its It—unnamed and unexamined, except in its idiopathic consequences. "There are many striking parallels between religious belief and practice and celebrity cultures," Rojek writes, citing the fan reception of film idols and rock stars. Indeed, these oft-noted parallels, which include reliquaries, death rites, ceremonies of ascent and descent, shamanic interventions, eucharistic offerings, confessions, resurrections, and promises of everlasting redemption, tend to "reinforce the hypothesis that considerable partial convergence between religion and celebrity has occurred."[27] Rojek makes particularly productive use of *The Elementary Forms of Religious Life* (1912), in which Emile Durkheim slyly but systematically interpreted the structures of his own society in the defamiliarizing light of the animistic beliefs of indigenous peoples. In each case, these structures and beliefs are expressed through "totems," the unifying symbols around which a culture or a people coheres. No matter how "advanced" the members of society may think that their special way of doing things is, their social life is *la vie religieuse,* however secular it may seem and however deeply entrenched its adherents' self-flattering sense of their own rationality may have become. "If the totem is the symbol of both the god and the society," Durkheim asks rhetorically, "is it not because the god and the society are one and the same?"[28]

Two Durkheimian keywords in particular illuminate the history of reenchantment: *manna,* "the Idea of Force," which Durkheim adopted from the Polynesian word for the powers of nature embodied in an object or person; and *effervescence,* which he used to describe the collective experience of religious ecstasy. Speaking for the adepts in any religion that posits some version of manna as the motive force of the spirit world, Durkheim writes: "That it is the soul of so many different things shows how different it is from the beings in which it resides." Durkheim explains effervescence in a way that ought to make sense to anyone who has been part of the crush at a rock concert or other celebrity gala, where the very thought of the proximity of It has triggered the exhilaration of the ensemble and the evaporation of the individual: "The very act of congregating is an exceptionally powerful stimulant. Once individuals are gathered together, a sort of electricity is generated from their closeness and quickly launches them to an extraordinary height of exaltation."[29] The kind of trigger required for an outburst of mass effervescence, when the It-Effect rolls through the culture like an outsized wave, can be illustrated by the peculiarly North American provocation expressed in the title of Marilyn Monroe's collected poems: *My Sex Is Ice Cream* (1996).

For purposes of appreciating the persistence of Durkheim's influence and the attraction of his analysis as the basis for examining the religious dimensions of putatively secular cultures, historians of reenchantment should return as frequently as is necessary to Roland Barthes's *Mythologies* (1957). While divulging the secret paths of meaning that connect sacred totems like "Steak and Chips," "Plastic," and "The New Citroën," Barthes writes an astringent ethnography of public intimacy, synthetic experience, and the It-Effect in "The Face of Garbo": "The name given to her, *the Divine*, probably aimed to convey less a superlative state of beauty than the essence of her corporeal person, descended from heaven where all things are formed and perfected in the clearest light."[30] Greta Garbo famously wanted to be alone, but that pathetic wish succeeded only in summoning millions more to genuflect at her shrine. Consummately unreachable and yet everywhere to be seen, she takes her place in the foremost ranks of the miracle workers who have turned mere bread and wine into bread and circuses.

In an economy inflated by charismatic attractions such as these—and the deep eighteenth century is a mystified economy of guilty pleasures—consumers submit to the caress or the slap of an "invisible hand." Adam Smith's famous phrase from *The Wealth of Nations* (1776) summarizes his insights into the general efficacy of self-interested behavior, celebrated as "rational" in economic theory, but in fact dependent on stupendous leaps of faith. If each participant in an economy is free simply to maximize his own gain ("laissez-faire"), Smith would have everyone believe, the resulting activity will work spontaneously to enlarge the economy as a whole, promoting "an end which was no part of his intention," hence "invisible" to him and the other entrepreneurial participants, but also mutually advantageous to them all.[31] Smith inverts the logic of a gift economy without changing its basis in blind faith. In an economy driven by gift exchange as described by Marcel Mauss, participants work to increase their own aura of prestige by giving away as much as possible—the logic of belief behind traditional potlatch and modern philanthropy. To grasp the applicability of these two economies to a general theory of It, the point to remember is that the medium of exchange (the gift or the money) functions as an accessory to the principal values of the exchange (the obeisant allegiance or the labor). In the memorable chapter "Of Money considered as a particular Branch of the general Stock of Society," Smith describes what he terms "the great wheel of circulation." He emphasizes that money itself is largely worthless *except* as the symbolic instrument that redistributes the value of goods and services vicariously:

> Money, therefore, the great wheel of circulation, the great instrument of commerce, like all other instruments of trade, though it makes a part and a very valuable part of the capital, makes no part of the revenue of the society to which it belongs, and though the metal pieces of which it is composed, in the course of their annual circulation, distribute to every man the revenue which properly belongs to him, they make themselves no part of that revenue.[32]

In the progressive and accelerating metamorphosis of money from precious metal into paper and then into electronic blips, as in the contemporaneous transformation of saints and monarchs into matinee idols, "the great wheel of circulation" requires ever more, not less, readiness on the part of the participants to engage in what Samuel Taylor Coleridge called "the willing suspension of disbelief that constitutes poetic faith" and Walter Benjamin, "reenchantment."[33] Smith's classic has become the holy scripture of the three-dimensional eighteenth century because it promulgates money as the synthetic experience of value, backed, like celebrity, by the full faith and credit of the commonwealth. That's why the authorities stamp the faces of abnormally interesting people on coins and engrave them on bills. The way that Smith uses the word *capital* in *The Wealth of Nations* (money is part of the "capital" but not the "revenue" of society) resembles the way Durkheim uses the word *manna* in *The Elementary Forms of Religious Life* and Barthes uses the word *myth* in *Mythologies:* "the general Stock of Society," the efficacy of manna (which, like Marilyn, belongs to everybody because it belongs to nobody), and the power of myths to turn history into "Nature"—all require some version of the infectious hallucination of the It-Effect.

Again it was a Victorian sage, in this case Matthew Arnold, who most cogently forecast not the outright replacement of religion by the long-running secular productions of the late age, but their surreptitious insinuation into its functions, meeting the spiraling need for more supple and accessible rituals: "There is not a creed which is not shaken, not an accredited dogma which is not shown to be questionable, not a received tradition which does not threaten to dissolve," he wrote of the continuing Enlightenment, adding, "The strongest part of our religion today is its unconscious poetry."[34] As mass culture assumes many of the responsibilities that Arnold formerly assigned to anarchy, however, the Sea of Faith does not so much retreat as turn into soda pop.

### Two New Women

The self-authored myth of Elinor Glyn's life—that of a Victorian Crusoe cast away among flappers—constructs a historical framework for elucidating It by reference to the social attitudes, theatrical traditions, and performance techniques that she inherited from what she lovingly called "Fairy Kingdoms," the unconscious poetry of her national heritage. It also came from her more pragmatic assessment of the liberated sex lives of actresses. Anita Loos, best known as the author of *Gentlemen Prefer Blondes: The Illuminating Diary of a Professional Lady* (1925), described the authoritative way in which Glyn, whose stage idols growing up had included Lillie Langtry and Sarah Bernhardt, "moved in" on the film colony in 1920: "Had Hollywood never existed," Loos wrote in her memoir, "Elinor Glyn would have invented it."[35] Refracting the light of Hollywood star power through the peculiar lens of her romantic and archly royalist understanding of English history and culture, Glyn interpreted modern celebrity as a survival or longed-for revival of what she called the "ancien régime," which for her represented a return of the enchanted and enchanting "noblesse oblige" of monarchy, particularly that of the Stuarts, and above all that of

Charles II, her favorite king. Despite the fact that her historical intuition about the monarchial roots of showbiz can be backed up by good evidence, such as the actual and symbolic durability of the theatrical patents granted during the Restoration, Elinor Glyn branded herself as a proselytizing believer in reincarnation and as an unapologetic snob, so understandably not everyone took her seriously then, and few do today; but in order to make my argument about the urgent role of historic iterations of public intimacy and synthetic experience in the modern creation of It, I must take her any way I can get her, for she understood early on that the most charismatic celebrities are the ones we can only imagine, even if we see them naked everywhere.

Glyn thought of herself as a proper Englishwoman; this meant, of course, that her life was a tangled skein of contradictory idiosyncrasies. Born Elinor Sutherland on Jersey to a relatively well-connected but impecunious family of Franco-Irish-Canadians and raised on both sides of the Atlantic, she believed that she was descended from a titled but attainted follower of the Old Pretender. In 1896, she was presented at court, to Alexandra, Princess of Wales, during the absence due to illness of Queen Victoria herself, in a gown made for the occasion by her elder sister, the exceptionally resourceful couturiere "Lucile," later Lady Duff-Gordon (1862–1935). Both sisters—Elinor, who became a prolific novelist and scriptwriter for Paramount and Metro-Goldwyn-Mayer, and Lucy, who became the most fashionable dressmaker of her time and an innovative costume designer for Florenz Ziegfeld—were born into the middle classes in the middle of Victoria's reign but grew up temperamentally Edwardian as "New Women." As such, each sister maintained a full-time career and multiple sex partners. Each sister also married up, and both remained ambitious trendsetters and tastemakers into the 1920s. Their memoirs, Lucy's *Discretions and Indiscretions* (1932) and Elinor's *Romantic Adventure* (1937), prove that they were also vigilant transatlantic trend-spotters, even from their very early childhood years. These two remarkable women serve as touchstones for most of what follows in this book. They do so in part because both the writer and the designer, particularly the former, had a passionate, if wildly skewed sense of history as the majestic chronicle of lost but redeemable glamour, always driven by the mystical force of "romance," which meant for each sister another way, her own way, of saying "It."[36]

"Romance" for Lucy, who is unfairly more often remembered in connection with her second husband's widely despised conduct as a well-born, adult-male lifeboat occupant during the sinking of the *Titanic* than she is in her own right, meant women's clothes—brilliantly shimmering, diaphanously daring, drop-dead-gorgeous gowns and intimates, which she exhibited and sold in exclusive salons in London, New York, and Paris. As her smart-set clientele would say, "Lucile" frocks were *it*. She called them "emotion dresses," and she gave each one of them its own name, such as "The Liquid Whisper of Early Spring," "Love Will Find Out a Way," or "The Birth of Venus." Among her circle of acquaintances, the theater-loving Lucy particularly enthused over beautiful, celebrated, and liberated actresses who attracted the devotion of both sexes. In *Discretions and Indiscretions,* she remembered calling on the free-spirited Ellen Terry (1847–1928), even after friends warned her that an association with the actress would damage her own reputation. She encountered the star, then appearing in *Faust,* surrounded by a bevy of Sapphic admirers like a romantic queen in her court, gowned, coifed, and accessorized: "I was shown into a room which seemed full of sunlight and flowers, where I found her sitting in the midst of a group of girls who were sewing. She was wearing a flowing robe of blue velvet, and her fair hair was bound round her head like a coronet. She reminded me, in that first glimpse of her in her own home, of a medieval queen seated among her maids of honor." Like both Sarah Bernhardt and Lily Elsie, two other actresses Lucy admired, "Ellen Terry had many men in love with her, but I do not think she cared for any of them seriously." The actresses loved their jobs in a way that "Lucile," the New Woman with her own label, could fully embrace in terms of her own life and presciently on behalf of the flapper generation:

The modern girl has, I think, learnt to look life in the face. She is not afraid of being left unmarried because marriage is no longer vitally necessary to her happiness. So many things are possible to her that were denied to her mother's generation of girls, and she has learnt how to make the most of them. Perhaps she has not the restraint that we, her elders, think she ought to have, but then very few young people have restraint—it is one of the things that the years teach us.[37]

That was "romance" for latitudinarian sister Lucy, Lady Duff-Gordon, who married on a whim twice and cohabited with her husbands as a periodic convenience.

"Romance" for sister Elinor, while deeply spiritual in abstract feeling, also required, for better or worse, behavior, and socially daring actresses proved exemplary for her as well. In *Romantic Adventure,* she recounts her adolescent infatuation with Sarah Bernhardt, a redhead like herself, in language that evokes the seriousness of a first Communion: "I was tremendously stirred by what I saw and heard, and became quite intoxicated with her voice, her marvelous art, and with the realization of a new and undreamt of kind of love—a rather wicked, tigerish, variety."[38] A precocious free-spirit even in her teens, Elinor married well nonetheless; but after fifteen exciting and widely traveled years, Clayton Glyn exhausted both his weak liver and his considerable inheritance (tragically, for her, not in that order). With two children and a slowly dying invalid of a husband to support, she turned her hand to writing romances and snaring extended invitations as a house guest of the rich and famous. One of these, the conspicuously eligible Lord Curzon, the heartbreaking love of her life, kept her on as his mistress for years before wordlessly dumping her to marry an Argentine heiress. Thus twice widowed, in a manner of speaking, Elinor seized the opportunity to invent herself anew.

In the end, both Glyn's writing and her racy lifestyle proved to be good career moves. Her thirty-six novels include *Three Weeks* (1907), a succès de scandale, featuring a memorable scene of erotic encounter, teasingly autobiographical, on a tiger-skin, which led to local ostracism from English society but international

fame. Her purported sexual adventures inspired the epigram, circulated anonymously but attributed by some to George Bernard
Shaw, which to this day literate gentlemen of a certain age will
recite on the slightest pretext while their put-upon wives just roll
their eyes, as if to say, "Oh no, not again":

> Would you like to sin
>   With Elinor Glyn
>   On a tiger skin?
> Or would you prefer
>   To err with her
> On some other fur?[39]

Cecil Beaton read *Three Weeks* on the sly at Eton, recalling that
while "bishops and headmasters inveighed against it, schoolgirls
and schoolboys read it under the bedclothes." He went so far as to
claim that the book and controversy surrounding it made a
significant contribution "in breaking down much of the remaining
Victorian hypocrisy."[40] With over two million copies of this one
book sold, Elinor's stock as an entertaining and decorative house-
guest skyrocketed. Her hosts ranged from the Grand Duchess Kiril
of the Russian empire to William Randolph Hearst of the newspa-
per empire. Celebrity fascinated her at a distance and at close
range, and long before her fateful rendezvous with Clara Bow in
the late 1920s, her way of understanding It percolated through a
number of filters of historical precedent and her own experience,
synthetic and otherwise.

### Samuel Pepys in Hollywood

As a self-fashioning entrepreneur who sincerely believed that
almost everything worth having in life is inherited, Glyn found her
historical imagination excited most vividly by the Stuart Restoration of 1660. Meditating on the extreme carelessness of some
aspects of her otherwise exemplary Victorian upbringing, she
savored the memory of being turned loose at age ten in her step-
father's library, where she found her way to what she called the
"unexpurgated" edition of the *Diary* of Samuel Pepys. In fact,

either one of the two editions that she might possibly have discovered at this date (Lord Braybrooke's of 1825, enlarged in 1848 and 1854, or the Reverend Bright's of 1875–79) was Bowdlerized; nevertheless, much material remained behind that many parents even today would regard as unsuitable for ten-year-olds. Undetected, little Elinor read the *Diary* through with great curiosity and, what is worse, growing comprehension. Among other stimulations, Glyn recounts, "Pepys awakened my great interest in the Charles II period, and strengthened my Stuart proclivities. I wrote under his picture, in a child's illustrated History of England which we had, the words 'Dear Good King' and 'Nasty old Beast!' under the portrait of Cromwell."[41]

Like Richard Eyre's *Stage Beauty* (Lions Gate, 2004), dreamily set at the moment in theatrical history when women replaced female impersonators at the behest of the restored king, Glyn's concept of the romantic genesis of theatrical and cinematic celebrity leans heavily on Pepys's account of the English Restoration's improvisatory mix of theater, politics, religion, careerism, and sex. She cites him on the first page of her memoir as a kindred spirit in practicing, as she tried to do with mixed results, the diurnal ritual of disciplined self reflection that writing a diary requires. She also realized that reading Pepys let her be what she wanted throughout her rebellious childhood—a very naughty Victorian indeed: "Pepys' diary is immortal because it was not intended for other eyes, and is a genuine, intimate chronicle of a very human personality in an important period of History."[42] She rarely capitalizes substantives, but here the oracular voice of "History" speaks to her through the publicly intimate pages of Pepys with a capital *H*.

The affinity of Pepys and Glyn across three centuries was deeper than a shared sense of authorial self-discipline or daring, however, because his *Diary,* which covers ten years in the life of an ambitiously self-fashioning man of affairs, also tracks the diarist's awareness of the rise of synthetic experience. This comes out especially through his account of his preoccupation with celebrity and its role in his prodigious erotic life—vicarious and firsthand—around town, at court, and in the playhouse, predictably enough, but also, even more strikingly, during religious services: "I did entertain myself with my perspective glass up and down the church," he recorded in his entry for Sunday, 26 May 1667, in a passage that ten-year-old Elinor, who even then detested homilies in particular and orthodoxy in general, could have read and might well have underlined, "by which I had the great pleasure of seeing and gazing [at] a great many fine women; and what with that and sleeping, I passed away the time till sermon was done" (8:236). Pepys devoted his fully alert attention to the theater, however; and like Glyn, who decided to go to Hollywood because she believed "a great new art was being born, which would profoundly influence the whole world,"[43] he was present at the founding of a new medium supplied with new techniques, predominantly a producer's or performer's theater, which opened up new places for those who could prove that they had It. And like Glyn, but with a lifetime's worth of more urgently compelling reasons, Pepys preoccupied himself with Charles II, who during the *Diary* years was neither "dear" nor "good" but every inch a king.

Beloved by naval historians as the talented administrator who rationalized the work of the Navy Board as its Clerk of Acts, Pepys imparts to his diary his professional intentions and frustrations, including his complicated feelings toward Charles, the man to whom he is ultimately, if somewhat distantly, accountable. Pepys's ambivalence about this semidivine but all-too-human sovereign comes out in the sexual gossip he retails with mixed disapprobation and envy. His decade-long obsession with the king's most flagrant paramour, for example, opens in 1660 with her installation in the house "which was Whallys; the King and the Dukes there with Madame Palmer, a pretty woman that they have a fancy to make her husband a cuckhold" (1:199). On the one hand, Pepys rode across the Channel at the time of the Restoration with the king's footman, who had charge of one of the royal spaniels, "a dog that the King loved (which shit in the boat, which made us laugh and me think that a King and all that belong to him are but just as others are)" (1:158). On the other hand, he also attended services to watch while Charles, in his office as a consecrated king, laid his anointed hands on his afflicted subjects to cure them of scrofula, "the King's evil" (1:182; 2:74). For his part, the king knew Pepys by name and came to rely on him to improve the management of the largest and most expensive department of his government, but even as Pepys meticulously notes the signs of his growing prosperity and prominence, the reader knows in retrospect what the diarist could not have foretold at the time: that the knighthood he had many good reasons to hope for would somehow slip from his grasp (*Companion* 10:58).

Pepys rose, nevertheless, from a position in household service to professional eminence as a respected public official with servants of his own and the wherewithal to become a careful but highly acquisitive consumer of tangible goods and intangible experiences. He pursued the best of the things and attractions that his age kept in good supply for the improvement and pleasure of the well-to-do: pictures, books, fancy clothes, musical instruments, scientific devices such as telescopes and microscopes, printed ballads, music lessons, dancing lessons, foods and beverages in plenty, plays, operas, tennis, horse-racing, ice-skating, swords, furniture, wigs, pornography, portrait sittings, puppet shows, freak shows, and the punctual submission of compliant subordinates' wives—to list them representatively but not exhaustively. Above all, historians of performance revere Pepys for the record he kept as an indefatigable consumer of the most consequential synthetic experience of the century in which he lived: the theater.

Synthetic experience must answer the human need, regulated by both curiosity and fear, to experience life vicariously as well as directly. Vicariousness suggests the derivative nature of experience from some prior authenticity. The word *vicarious* is cognate to *vicar,* in the sense of one who serves as a substitute, agent or administrative deputy (as in "Vicar of God" for the king of England as head of the church).[44] Professional playwrights and performers manufacture and sell such experiences. Over time, their products have largely displaced, though not wholly replaced others that were once available for free, when amateurs amused one another by performing Mysteries or staging carnivals in the demotic swirl of the public streets. Historians of the "consumer revolution," the origins of which have been variously traced to periods ranging from the Elizabethan age to the eighteenth century, tend to think of commodities as things.[45] Theater historians need to complicate that definition because they know that the experience of attending a performance is not a thing; it is a service of a very dynamic and labile kind. That people would part with good money to experience experience (by vicariously living through someone else's embodiment of it) was a discovery as exciting to some as fire. To them, theatrical performance, like fire— releasing energy from matter that is utterly consumed in the process, disappearing as a condition of its iteration, and leaving behind little trace of itself except the desire for more—roared to life as charismatic attractions on the cusp of medieval vernacular religion and the magic of the market, a revolutionary change in the nature of performances and their reception: hence Shakespeare's famous invocation of "a Muse of fire" in the prologue to *Henry V* (1.prologue.1). Apologizing for the inadequacy of his "unworthy scaffold" to hold the real battle of Agincourt or the warrior-kings and their dragooned armies who fought it, the prologue instead calls upon the audience to experience them through the power of poetic suggestion, specifically stimulated by the trope of staged synecdoche. Like monarchy, synecdoche lets the one stand in vicariously for the many with same celerity as it does the part for the whole:

> O, pardon—since a crooked figure may
> Attest in little place a million
> And let us, ciphers to this great accompt,
> On your *imaginary* forces work.
>     (1.prologue.15–18; emphasis added)

In recompense for these mental labors, the prologue promises the auditors something very special in the flesh: the synthetic experience of public intimacy, face time with an actor who, crooked or not, represents no less than "the mirror of all Christian kings" (2.prologue.6), the victor at Agincourt in propria persona, addressing them just as familiarly within the "wooden O" as he had once showed himself among the "band of brothers" on the eve of battle, "A little touch of Harry in the night" (4.prologue.47), making them confederate in the private travails of "warlike Harry, like himself" (1.prologue.5) and privy to his dynastic love-life as an implacable suitor to Katherine of Valois.

As we shall see, Samuel Pepys had a shockingly intimate public encounter with the remains, imaginary and otherwise, of one of these same royal celebrities. But in the theater, he first met them in the romantic version of their lives and loves dramatized in 1664 by Roger Boyle, Earl of Orrery, and brought to vivid life by the acting of the incomparable Bettertons, Thomas and Mary, "whose parts are most incomparably wrote and done, and the whole play the most full of heighth and raptures of wit and sense that ever I heard" (5:240–41). The limited evidence suggests that the most popular actors in Shakespeare's time enjoyed robust celebrity status, but not under anything like the monarchial mantle that protected the playhouse of Pepys. "The play was Splendidly Cloath'd," noted the old prompter John Downes in *Roscius Anglicanus* (1708) about the production of Orrery's *Henry the Fifth,* and well might it have been: Charles II enhanced the actors' thrilling synthesis of the whole Lancastrian experience by loaning his royal coronation robes to Betterton to wear as a costume, a synecdochical embassy from the ritually sacred past to the vicariously intimate present.[46] "The Cult of Elizabeth" presaged the later political appropriations of traditional devotional practices, but she is not known to have attended the public playhouse. Charles II, by contrast, made attending the theaters, which he also had patented under his own and his royal brother's titles, one of the hallmarks of his reign, along with the prominent display of his other appetites. Given the tabloid-like scrutiny of his personal affairs, it could be argued that the last sacred king was also the first modern head of state, at least on the score of flagrant public intimacy.[47]

## The Last King

When Shakespeare's plays were revived, royalists among the dramatist-adaptors explicitly sought to legitimate them by attaching the Bard to sacral monarchy. While Pepys noted the morale-boosting presence of the king and his whole court on the jam-packed opening night of *The Tempest; or, the Enchanted Island* in

1667 (8:521–22), the adaptors William Davenant and John Dryden set the tone for the occasion by inserting a pointed line into their prologue: "Shakespear's Pow'r is sacred as a King's."[48] While this gestured backward to the precedents of an ancient authority, in practice the Restoration patentees, playwrights, and performers more often had to improvise a new theater out of thin air as well as the bits and pieces of the old repertoire. It is the historic tenacity of that eclectically renovated theater, with its emphasis on the drawing power of celebrity actors and actresses, availability to the general public, and rapidly rotating repertory in two competing patent theaters, that did the most for the theater of the future.

The decade that Pepys's *Diary* documents in flesh-and-blood detail thus began with the official reinstatement of the stage in the repertoire of popular pleasures, but now under the legal and symbolic aegis of the monarchy and with the added attractions of painted scenes and painted women. The overall mise-en-scène became more pictorial, without abandoning the poetic trope of synecdoche in the staging of details (hand props, set pieces, crowd scenes). The successive royal warrants and patents whereby Charles authorized the theaters in 1660–62, which held up in one form or another until 1843 and under which Drury Lane and Covent Garden still legally operate today, specifically encouraged the patentees to cast women in the female roles. In their success, at first evidently uncertain, "the first actresses" eventually superannuated the boy actors, now aging men, who had acted the women's parts before the closing of the theaters. Drawn from working-class or lower-middle-class backgrounds, the Restoration actresses pioneered a new profession that hovered on the cusp of the oldest one, making the path of their ascent one that could and did lead to a zenith of concubinage in the king's own bed and to the ennoblement of the royal bastards they bore him as peers of the realm. These sensational stories should not be allowed to detract from the fact that Restoration actresses, though they generally made less, worked every bit as hard as the actors, that is, very hard indeed: bills changed frequently, often daily, requiring prodigious feats of quick-study memorization, rehearsal, and performance. Some of these actresses played memorable roles in the history of It, and Pepys remains the principal source for the initial effect they had on their contemporaries, which he savored especially when they turned the tables on the transvestite boys and wore tight pants: "I to the Theatre and there saw *Argalus and Parthenia;* where a woman acted Parthenia and came afterward on the Stage in man's clothes, and had the best legs that ever I saw; and I was very well pleased with it" (2:203). Staged synecdoche survives in the totality of illusion so long as there are parts, including parts of the body, which the audience will allow to stand for the whole: hence "britches roles" and later "leg shows." It's untrue to say that in such spectacles nothing is left to the imagination.

The iconic status of the double-bodied king, God's Vicar on Earth and now titular head of the playhouse in the bargain, became ever so much more intimate and therefore problematic in this strange twilight of sacral monarchy, both in the way contemporaries such as Pepys and John Evelyn saw Charles at the time and in the way later historians, particularly the Victorians, judged him in retrospect. Like the best of his actors and paramours, the "Dear Good King" had It, not only on account of his widely reputed personal charm, but also by virtue of his job description, which still empowered him, on the one hand, to cure scrofula by touch and, on the other, to commit serial adultery with social impunity. A number of the most telling episodes of his performance of public intimacy cluster around the theater: carrying on flirtations and even open rows with his mistresses in the auditorium; passing notes with actors and actresses backstage; proposing new plays and translations for the repertoire, and, most remarkably of course, loaning his coronation suit for use as a costume. Wrapped in the theater's cloak of a thousand colors, flaunting his affairs with actresses so notorious that they were popularly known, as he was, by their first names, Charles nevertheless properly signed official documents, including the theatrical patents that legally incorporated the stage into his regime, as "Defender of the Faith."[49]

No wonder Glyn, the coiner of *It*, the royalist spirit-rapper of the old Hollywood Hotel, and a devout believer in reincarnation, found him so attractive across the intervening centuries. "In the theatre of kingship in the age of baroque," writes a modern biographer, "he was a star."[50] Like other Edwardian temperaments in self-conscious rebellion against their immediate predecessors, Glyn used her enthusiasm for Charles II and the Restoration in general as a lever to pry loose Victorian mores, making him the It King of the It Age. In fact, the Victorians themselves used the king they called the "Merry Monarch" as an object lesson, as a touchstone, and as soft-core pornography. Historians ought to try to calibrate the extent to which the prevailing views of the Restoration, our own no less than Glyn's, come down to us filtered either through a layer of yellowing varnish on the history paintings of Augustus Egg or the haze of brimstone lingering from the polemics of Macaulay, who concluded that Charles, though he possessed "some talent for lively conversation," showed alarming deficiencies in every category of moral sentience, his personal sloth and cynicism having grown so all-engulfing as to inure him to the voice of reproach from without or of conscience from within: "Honour and shame were scarcely more to him than light and darkness to the blind."[51] Contrarily, attention should be paid to the extent to which our received opinions show the results of the Edwardians' zealous overcleaning of the reputations of Restoration celebrities by way of reaction, topped off by the bonbon of Shaw's *In Good King Charles' Golden Days* (1939). Shaw portrays the saturnine king forsaking his bed of harlots to make a house call, spaniels in tow, on Sir Isaac Newton to investigate new developments in astronomy and mathematics. Only a touch more plausibly, his most notorious mistresses—Lady Castlemaine (Barbara Palmer), the actress Nell Gwyn, and the Catholic Louise de Kéroualle—follow him there to join animatedly in the intellectual feast.

As do descriptions of any star performer who has It, accounts of Charles II emphasize the contradictions of his character, which still fascinate and disturb his biographers under the aura of what George Meredith called "poignant antiphony." Monumentally selfish, gratuitously treacherous, and vindictively cruel, he nevertheless could, whenever he cared to tilt his head just so and focus his piercing eyes, convince any interlocutor that his or her ideas or qualities interested him more than anyone else's, a sure sign of the strangely empathic presence of It. Part of his celebrity he earned honestly by the sweat of his brow: among his prodigious accomplishments as a divine-right monarch in the rising republican tide must be numbered keeping his head on his shoulders and dying in his bed undeposed, a feat that neither his predecessor nor his successor could manage. Even when ancient ceremonial custom ascribed It to him as a perquisite of office, he could still add to its efficacy by the aplomb with which he conducted the affair: unlike his agoraphobic father, the second Charles seemed to indulge willingly the ritual of curing for the king's evil. Moreover, he was good at it, laying his comforting hands convincingly on tens of thousands of afflicted subjects during his reign, treating up to two hundred in a single ceremony. Pepys recorded that the king did the ancient and holy office "with great gravity" (2:74). John Browne's *Charisma Basilicon* (1684) interprets Charles's gift as presumptive evidence of the divinity of kings, noting that he exceeded all his predecessors in healing as Edward I did *his* ancestors, "which places him on a par with England's last royal saint."[52] The premodern history of the modern It-Effect has few more effervescent rituals, a connection reinforced by the seventeenth-century usage of the word *celebrity* as a sacred performance: a solemn funeral could be performed with "great celebrity" for instance, or a mass could be denominated as "the first Celebrity of Divine Service with organ and Choristers" (*OED*). Haunting the ritual continuity of the reign of Charles II was the memory of his judicially murdered father, reverently apostrophized in the memoirs of the actor Thomas Betterton as "the Royal Martyr."[53] Samuel Pepys's guilty memory of this experience, while consummately theatrical, was not vicarious: as a schoolboy of fifteen, he played truant to watch while the first Charles's head was cut off and held up to the shuddering crowd (1:265, 280).

The legal fiction and symbolic truth that the king had not one but two bodies—the body natural and the body politic—developed out of medieval Christology (the duality of man and God) and into an increasingly pragmatic and secular principle of sovereign succession and legal continuity.[54] The reign of Charles II straddled these two worlds, the one not yet dead, the other stirring

to revolutionary life. The royalist critique of republican government cites the trappings of ceremonial kingship as useful props to
legitimacy when, as so often happens in history, the incumbent
proves personally disappointing. Elinor Glyn, in a moving aside on
the rarity of a great democratic leader like Abraham Lincoln
emerging at precisely the hour of greatest need ("one in a thousand years, I fear"), underlined the importance of the ritual continuity of the body politic in ascribing It to officeholders ex officio
where it cannot be conferred on the merits:

> I am convinced that pageantry is an important part of the life of
> a nation, and should not be given up. The total abandonment
> of all such public functions in America is, I feel sure, one of the
> reasons why the law is held in such little respect there. The sub-
> conscious mind is always impressed by fine ceremonial, just as it
> is by the dignity of complete simplicity; but while the perfection
> of character which commands respect through simplicity is
> rare, the trappings of majesty can maintain dignity even when
> the figure which they clothe is not in itself noble. The respect
> for the Constitution and the traditions engendered by the great-
> ness of one ruler or judge can be perpetuated in the time of a
> less worthy successor by the actual descent of the Prophet's
> mantle upon him in the shape of the Coronation Robes, or full-
> bottomed wig.[55]

Of course Tories historically pride themselves on spotting and ele-
vating truly exceptional talent from outside the birthright of their
immediate tribe, but they also tend to insist, not unreasonably,
that authority must be continuously performed even when it cannot be perfectly embodied. Here ascribed manna has played an
important role: to call this role superficial underestimates what
Glyn terms the "subconscious" impression made by the stylish
pageants of the player-kings.

When Charles II reinforced the unapologetic theatricality of his
reign by loaning his coronation robes to the playhouse, he did not
do so because the staging of symbolic legitimacy severely tested a
nation so freakishly prolific in producing miracle-working actors.
Of Charles Hart's impersonation of Alexander the Great, the

prompter John Downes remembered: "he Acting [the role] with such Grandeur and Agreeable Majesty, That one of the Court was pleas'd to Honour him with this Commendation; that *Hart* might Teach any King on Earth how to Comport himself."[56] Of the whole institution of the stage under the later Stuarts, Charles Gildon, in his *Life of Thomas Betterton* (1710), wrote that it was a "Mimic State."[57] The key element of monarchial government, as Glyn attests, is the public visibility of its sacred head, and His Majesties Servants made their sovereign intimately visible through their daily performances of all genres in his name or his brother's name, not merely on those rare and dangerous occasions when, as in the Exclusion Crisis of 1680–81, they edged too close to current events and seemed to mimic a reigning monarch or his deputies directly and critically. Every performance, except the silenced ones, proceeded with legally explicit royal authorization, like religious services, on every day except Sundays. As increasingly commercial enterprises operating under the variously exercised authority of the state, the "Theatres Royal" enjoyed a long run.

## Mimic State

Celebrities, then, like kings, have two bodies, the body natural, which decays and dies, and the body cinematic, which does neither. But the immortal body of their image, even though it is preserved on celluloid, on digitalized files, or in the memory of the theatergoing public as an afterimage, always bears the nagging reminder of the former. ("She looks great. Isn't she dead by now?") As their sacred images circulate in the vortex of the profane imagination, these double-bodied persons foreground a peculiar combination of contradictory attributes expressed through outward signs of the union of their imperishable and mortal bodies. These include the simultaneous appearance of strength and vulnerability in the same performance, even in the same gesture. Let those marks of strength be called *charismata;* the signs of vulnerability, *stigmata.* They work cooperatively, like muscles in opposable pairs, and their mesmerizing interplay has a long history as well as popular currency as the source of public intimacy.

With or without the Stuarts, the mimic state provided a conduit through which the double body-type of the monarch devolved upon the most famous of his or her subjects. In this expansion of celebrity to a wider aperture of visibility, the stage produced totemic signs, by which the intimate persons of its stars became as familiar to the public as the heraldic trappings of monarchy once were and continued to be. Anne Bracegirdle's white teeth, David Garrick's flashing eyes, and Dorothy Jordan's curly hair, for example, are celebrated *charismata* in English theatrical history. At the same time, Elizabeth Barry's asymmetrical face, David Garrick's short stature, and Sarah Siddons's embonpoint are equally well-known *stigmata*. In the creation of public intimacy, psyche and soma intertwine, and the stigmatizing marks, visible or invisible, leave their emotional trace in every expression, especially the strongest.

As Achilles was a more compelling hero because of his heel, not in spite of it, so Thomas Betterton (1635–1710) became a more effective tragedian in part because his increasingly vulnerable body contrasted so poignantly with his growing moral strength. Except for those by Pepys, who revered him above all other actors at the time, the eyewitness accounts of him come from later in his career, most pertinently Tony Aston's deferential but clear-eyed portrait:

> Mr. Betterton (although a superlative good Actor) labour'd under ill Figure, being clumsily made, having a great Head, a short thick Neck, stoop'd in the Shoulders, and had fat short Arms, which he rarely lifted higher than his Stomach. His Left Hand frequently lodg'd in his Breast, between his Coat and Waist-coat, while, with his Right, he prepar'd his Speech. His Actions were few, but just. He had little Eyes, and a Broad Face, a little Pock-fretten, a corpulent Body, and thick Legs, with large Feet. He was better to meet, than to follow; for his Aspect was serious, venerable, and majestic; in his latter Time a little paralytic. His Voice was low and grumbling; yet he could Time it by an artful Climax, which enforc'd universal Attention, even from the Fops and Orange-Girls.[58]

In many religious traditions worldwide, "shamans, sorcerers, and medicine men" are singled out by extraordinary physical marks or eccentricities of behavior.[59] In modernity, actors are identified in much the same way, even if their oddity is abnormal perfection. Whatever its source, their apartness is no less important than their availability. With Betterton's physical peculiarity came a more powerfully distinguished magic, and contemporaries felt It. Richard Steele's eulogy on the occasion of the actor's burial in Westminster Abbey conveyed the preternaturally vivid presence of the characters he created over a long career, as if he had, before Steele's astonished eyes, actually done the many extraordinary deeds attributed to the heroes and kings he represented and had actually suffered their extraordinary travails. In some sense, he had. In death, Steele realized, Betterton, son of an undercook in the service of Charles I, had officially joined the appropriate assembly in the pantheon of English worthies, avatars of a "Free-born People": "the Sacred Heads which lie buried in the Neighborhood of this little Portion of Earth in which my poor Friend is deposited, are returned to Dust as well as he." Steele further concluded that all differences among living men are "merely Scenical" and "that there is no Difference in the Grave between the Imaginary and the Real Monarch."[60] With growing audacity, performers, whose celebrity was achieved, did not wait for the grave before they claimed their place in the public eye beside aristocrats and royals, whose celebrity was ascribed. This does not mean that they thereby became altogether socially acceptable, but it does mean that they became increasingly interesting.

Above all the other precinematic theatrical attractions of the mimic state in the age of commercialized leisure and celebrity reenchantment was "The Siddons." Like Betterton, whose authority increased with the passing decades, Sarah Siddons (1755–1831) became a more formidable tragedienne with the stigmatizing avoirdupois than without it, for after seven pregnancies, her signature emotions of distressed maternity gained greater conviction as well as gravity. William Hazlitt's famous prayer to Mrs. Siddons as the long-reigning deity of the stage captures both the intensity and the fragility of her charismatic hold on her public. In another place and time, the adulation he reports would be called "Momism." To any Durkheimian, it would qualify as manna. To any sentient manager, it counted as box-office capital:

> The homage she has received is greater than that which is paid to queens. The enthusiasm she excited had something idolatrous about it; she was regarded less with admiration than with wonder, as if a superior order had dropped from another sphere, to awe the world with the majesty of her appearance. She raised tragedy to the skies, or brought it down from thence. It was something above nature. We can conceive of nothing grander. She embodied to our imagination the fables of mythology, of the heroic and deified mortals of elder time. She was not less than a goddess, or than a prophetess inspired by the gods. Power was seated on her brow, passion emanated from her breast as from a shrine. She was Tragedy personified. She was the stateliest ornament of the public mind.[61]

Less often noted is what Hazlitt says he is praying for: he implores Siddons to reconsider her ill-advised return to the stage in 1816, long enough after her retirement that the perfect balance between *charismata* and *stigmata* she had once been able to strike is no longer possible. Slow of speech and largely immobile, she now exhibits vulnerabilities that so surpass her strengths that by coming again upon the boards she risks the almost certain destruction of her hard-won image as an "idol" in the public mind. When *stigmata* so far overrun *charismata,* the embarrassed celebrity becomes too available to the identification of the audience, and that special quality of apartness, which Glyn describes as "unbiddable," disappears, taking It down with it. "Players should be immortal," Hazlitt explains, "if their own wishes or ours could make them so; but they are not."[62]

Apart from the hundreds of roles that Betterton and Siddons each played in their fifty-year careers, many of which they created, these two avatars of the It-Effect also turned themselves into what I am calling *role-icons*. The role-icon represents a part that certain exceptional performers play on and off stage, no matter what other parts they enact from night to night. Betterton's career-long role-icon might be called "the tragedy king"; Siddons's, "the tragedy queen." Other actors may vie for these coveted roles, but the public will usually embrace only one at time. Such role-icons affect box-office receipts because they raise expectations in anticipation of their auratic presence at an event regardless of the other attractions on the bill. The prestige of such role-icons prompted Edmund Burke to cite the tears that Sarah Siddons, along with her precursor David Garrick, one of Betterton's successors as tragedy king, drew from him in connection with his emotional excursus on the sufferings of Marie Antoinette, a truly anointed tragedy queen, in *Reflections on the Revolution in France* (1790). Presciently, Burke went so far as to propose the replacement of religion by the stage, at least for the duration of the emergency: "Indeed, the theatre is a better school of moral sentiments than churches, where the feelings of humanity are thus outraged."[63] As Roland Barthes remarked about such a diffusion or transfusion of manna into modern life, "This mythical character of our kings is nowadays secularized, though not in the least exorcised."[64] In a similar vein of thinking, but with very different politics, Elinor Glyn convinced herself that the Hollywood stars of the 1920s were reincarnated Stuarts, dynastic scions of a second Restoration, and it is the burden of my argument about It to demonstrate the uncanny extent to which she was right: the fact that all the king's men couldn't put Humpty Dumpty back together again did not rule out recycling.

### Bits and Pieces

Like the mythical figure of Pygmalion, who modeled an image with which he promptly fell in love, the consumer of celebrity icons does the work of creating the effigy in the physical absence of the beloved. It's the easiest thing in the world to fall in love with one's own creation, of course, but like the shadow on the wall of Plato's cave, the effigy remains incomplete as a condition of its vicarious advent. That is why the icon that Pygmalion creates, later identified as Galatea, comes to him in parts that can only stand in as surrogates for the whole, not embody it. Book 10 of Ovid's *Metamorphoses,* as translated by John Dryden and printed in Samuel

Garth's edition of 1719, sets up the hero's predicament in a stately couplet, which encapsulates the seductive self-deception at the root of mass attraction:

Pleas'd with his idol, he commends, admires,
Adores; and last, the thing ador'd, desires.

Seeing her form emerge from his sculpting hands with such remarkable lifelikeness, Pygmalion begins to adorn her image further, as he would a living lover, carving in a kind of "madness" to complete the icon, as if completeness will bring her to whole-ness or at least to life. Working synecdochically from the outside in, he creates each part of the image in its turn, as if the whole were ever equal to the sum of its parts, arranging an entire set-ting for it, replete with properties and costumes, starting first with the accessories:

He furnishes her closet first; and fills
The crowded shelves with rarities of shells;
Adds orient pearls, which from the conchs he drew,
And all the sparkling stones of various hue.

After desperately overdoing accessories with parrots and a singing-bird in a silver cage, Pygmalion then moves on to the clothes:

Rich fashionable robes her person deck,
Pendants her ears, and pearls adorn her neck;
Her taper'd fingers too with rings are grac'd,
And an embroider'd zone surrounds her slender waiste.

The addition of clothing and jewelry intensifies his obsession with the texture of her "iv'ry" hair and the "whiteness" of her skin, so smooth to his caress that he can't believe it's not flesh:

Thus like a queen array'd, so richly dress'd,
Beauteous she shew'd, but naked shew'd the best.

Finally, after he takes the statue into bed with him and prays to Venus that his creation may be brought to life as his bride, the goddess relents, and he rapturously kisses the sleeping beauty awake:

Then lips to lips he join'd; freed from fear,
He found the savour of the kiss sincere:
At this the waken'd image op'd her eyes,
And view'd at once the light, and lover with surprize.[65]

With the exception of bone, which has its own honored place among the charismatic dead, Ovid's narration of Pygmalion's creative process, in which the hero fashions It out of his idea, his living dream of it, announces the overall contents of the chapters that follow.

First, they survey representative afterimages of Charles II, beginning with and returning to his royal funeral effigy, an artifact of medieval mortuary ritual, bits and pieces of which appear in each chapter, which also includes readings of the theatrical enterprises set in motion during his reign. Second, they interpret those enterprises in light of the political philosophy of celebrity enchantment that the king's superstitious acolyte Elinor Glyn carried forward from the nineteenth century into the Hollywood dream-factory. Third, they overlay the transformed media of 1920s with those of the 1660s, recognizing that these historical moments cannot possibly be telescoped into one another, but putting them in conversation nevertheless to illuminate public intimacy, synthetic experience, and the It-Effect through the uncanny wormholes opened up by the unique source of Samuel Pepys's *Diary*.

Chapter 1 begins with accessories of Charles's effigy for the same reason that Pygmalion does with Galatea's. In their practical inutility, accessories do the basic symbolic work of propping up the illusion that the role-icon they adorn is complete and completely alive. Pepys takes up wearing a sword, for instance, because that's what the complete "gentleman" wears in the fashion of his time, not because the clerk has any real intention of defending himself or his honor with it. In the overall production of It as social manna, heads of state and actors play a similar role as living accessories to the ensemble of the culture writ large, a point made most incisively by Walter Bagehot in *The English Constitution* (1867) and most pertinently by Elinor Glyn in her asides about royalty, cinematic and otherwise, foregrounding visibility and invisibility as the constitutional antinomy of It. Chapter 2 dresses the effigy with the expert advice of "Lucile," taking as examples the nominated role-icons of the "beauty" and the "rake," both of which provoke struggles between charisma and stigma for control of their afterimage. Chapters 3 and 4 add hair and skin, addressing the role-icons of the tragedy king and the tragedy queen, supplemented by that of the fop for comic relief: Meredith's "poignant antiphony" plays out as a delicate balance of strength and vulnerability, based on the magical properties imputed to hair in four actors and a stateswoman; skin performs magic all its own, following on superstitions of lightness and darkness that surfaced in tragic performances by three tragedy queens—Anne Bracegirdle, Sarah Siddons, and Diana, Princess of Wales. Chapter 5 takes up the similarly touchy issue of flesh, situating its prominence in London's Covent Garden, understood as an "It-Zone," where tangible and intangible goods are exchanged as gifts and commodities, turning on Adam Smith's "great wheel of circulation," which is manna in motion. The role-icon of the Galatea-Cinderella type, which contrasts innocence and experience, famously circulates in Covent Garden, nominated as Eliza Doolittle and embodied by Frances Abington, Mrs. Patrick Campbell, Audrey Hepburn, and, finally, "Barbie": Eliza's metamorphosis from working girl to celebrity icon epitomizes the creation of It out of the energy released by the transformation of a utensil into an accessory.

No doubt any effigy made of It partakes of the character of a fetish object as defined by Freud and even, as commercialized synthetic experience, of the commodity fetish as defined by Marx. But constantly assigning shaming motives to everything becomes tiresome, especially when the assignments might prove accurate in overly obvious ways. Psychoanalytically attuned readers will likely see the relationship between the mental processes discussed here and "transference," the redirection of feelings toward an idealized object, but this is coincidental, as are the connections to the Lacanian mirror stage and *objet petit a*. So in the place of depth psychology, each of the chapters, except the last, offers a case study of surfaces, what Virginia Postrel, writing in *The Substance of Style* (2003), calls "the look and the feel of things."[66] Accessories, clothes, hair, skin, and flesh—each contributes attractive parts with different textures, any one of which might stand for the fugitive whole, which never quite manifests itself satisfactorily, until it disappears forever into bone. As a conciliatory gesture to depth, however, Chapter 6, which juxtaposes the role-icon of the "pirate" with one or two of the most disturbing and bizarre entries in Pepys's *Diary,* will conclude with a brief reflection on the implications of Freud's use of the German *es* as in *Das Ich und das Es* (1923), following a similar use in Groddeck's *Das Buch vom Es,* as the German equivalent of the Latin word for *it,* which is *id* (*OED*). Here, finally, death hovers in poignant antiphony with love, summoning a Nemesis figure from the shadows, a role-icon who both possesses It and relentlessly stalks it too: the charismatic superpredator.

Public intimacy describes the illusion of proximity to the tantalizing apparition; synthetic experience, the consumption of its spun-off products such as plays, magazines, or movies; and the It-Effect, its deifying reception. The It-Effect, in turn, intensifies the craving for greater intimacy with the ultimately unavailable icon. Constructed both through the publicity manipulated by celebrities themselves or their acolytes and through the imaginative contribution of their fans, It patches together a specter more ragtag than any saintly relic: assorted features and body parts, bits of clothes and accessories, briefly glimpsed gestures and expressions—all cohering only in the mass hallucination that everyone either wants to touch or be touched by and no one can either find or forget. It is the *"Something,"* as Pope put it, "That gives us back the Image of our Mind," but maddeningly, never exactly as itself. Historians will rightly decry as presentist those accounts of the past that reduce the long ago and far away to the exigencies of the here and now. What follows attempts to pull hard in the opposite direction, interpreting the present in light of a salient fact about the eighteenth century that historians don't insist on often enough: it isn't over yet.

# 1.

## accessories

Of all the religious and artistic treasures which a visitor may see at Westminster Abbey, the collection of eighteen funeral effigies in the Museum is perhaps the most intriguing. Carved in wood or in wax, these full-sized representations of kings, queens and distinguished public figures, many of them in their own clothes and with their own accoutrements, constitute a gallery of astonishingly life-like portraits stretching over more than four centuries of British history.

—H. R. H. the Prince of Wales

Pray, good people, be civil; I am the protestant whore.

—Attributed to Nell Gwyn

Can only the dead astonish us by seeming "lifelike"? Perhaps even the living can induce this uncanny effect from time to time. Of the eighteen royal funeral effigies in the Norman Undercroft at Westminster Abbey, the one to which the Prince of Wales's description most obviously refers belongs to his predecessor and namesake Charles II, the "Dear Good King" of Elinor Glyn's Tory childhood. The last of its kind, the image was constructed at the time of the king's death in February 1685. Yet Charles's lifelike (and at an imposing six feet, two inches, fully life-sized) effigy played no part in his funeral obsequies, the austerity of which departed from traditional royal mortuary practice, which required the display of a wooden or wax effigy of the monarch along with the corpse, perhaps because rumors of the king's deathbed conversion to Catholicism inhibited the mourners. Whatever economies or sectarian

scruples curtailed the ritual, however, none stinted the craftsman-
ship lavished on the object itself, which crowned a collection of
venerable forebears, going back to the stiff wooden manikin
carved for the burial of Edward III in 1377. Whatever its state of
preservation, each of these icons once materialized in death a well-
known likeness, symbolizing, at a moment of high ritual
expectancy, the general image that all the subjects of a monarchy
might reasonably be expected to hold in their mind's eye, whether
they ever laid eyes on the incumbent or not.

Measured by their success over the long run, the expert artisans
who originally constructed the effigy of Charles II did an excellent
job of making it perform as a vivid afterimage of the charismatic,
stigmatized king (fig. 2). To represent his features as close to life
as possible, they molded the pale skin of his hands and face in wax,
probably working from a life-mask made in anticipation of the
occasion. They fashioned the large, brown eyes from glass and the
pencil-thin moustache and eyelashes from human hair. They fabricated a skeleton from wood and iron wire, fleshing it out with
straw sewn into a canvas skin. Then they dressed the body in the
king's own clothes, from foundation garments to Garter robes—
silk drawers, breeches, stockings, shirt, embroidered doublet,
hood, surcoat, scarlet mantle, cravat. Finally, they topped off the
sumptuous ensemble with accessories: high-heeled shoes, wig,
sword, jewelry, and plumed hat. Except for the sword and the jewels, which were burgled in 1700, the "Dear Good King" stands on
view today pretty much as he has since then, opened out in fourth
position, turned ever so slightly *contraposto* to make an interesting
line of the body; chin up, head back, as if preparing without any
special urgency to step forward and to speak, languidly animated
by the bubble of impudence—astonishingly "lifelike" indeed.[1]

Like the modern It-Effect, the traditional royal effigy made the
monarch seem more mysterious and yet also more available. Withheld from the ritual that occasioned its construction, however, the
discarded effigy of Charles II could do neither, except retrospec-
tively as a historic benchmark in the transmission of public intimacy from sacred to secular icons. As such, it will reappear in this
and subsequent chapters, not only as a relic, a medieval holdover

Fig. 2. Funeral effigy of Charles II, 1685. Westminster Abbey Museum.
Photo by Malcolm Crowthers. © Dean and Chapter of Westminster.

that once stood for the "body politic" of the increasingly superannuated, double-bodied monarch, but also as an instrument that performed a function similar to that which continues to occupy the vast technical capacities of modern media: more colorful than a death mask yet more faithful than a portrait, it attempted to preserve and publicize the image of an individual in the absence of his person.

Some objects do seem to want to speak for themselves. The English royal effigies, even those constructed with far less verisimilitude than that of Charles II, belong to this class of lively artifacts, which trouble the finality they serve to commemorate, giving tangible, nominated form to the imaginative role-icons of "king" and "queen." Their ritualized use died out with the Stuarts; other aristocratic notables in the eighteenth century commissioned their own wax effigies, but the last public figure to be honored in this way was Nelson in 1806. At the moment of the funeral effigy's disappearance from history, however, derivative specters multiplied in public memory and imagination.[2] They anticipated the burgeoning phenomenon described by the word *image* today: the mediatized conception of a person or institution (as in "corporate image"), not reducible to any one of the many icons that publicize it, but rather disseminated pervasively as a ghostly semblance, specific yet intangible, seen by no two people in exactly the same way, yet intelligible to nearly everyone.

This chapter traces the initial path of the afterimage of Charles II, which later fascinated the Victorians who censured it no less than the Edwardians who partially rehabilitated it. As a Victorian, an Edwardian, and a Californian, Elinor Glyn reimagined modern celebrity under the romanticized aegis of Carolean charm, apostrophized in her memory by the beguiling Lely portrait of a female sitter (or knockoff of one) that hung in the drawing room of the rented house on Jersey in which she spent most of her childhood. The inimitable *Diary* of her oracle Samuel Pepys, however, which she also found in that house, offers the best evidence of the early construction of such mental effigies, which endure, then and now, as souvenirs of the passage of exceptional personalities through the imaginative life of their tribes. Confiding intimately to his *Diary*, Pepys calls his secret, masturbatory images of Charles and his women—including Queen Catherine and the whole ensemble of royal mistresses, aristocrats, and actresses alike—"conceits" (9:184). Sometimes these conceits substitute for direct experience in his life, especially when sacred and erotic imagery converge with theatrical representation, as they do in some of the most sensational episodes of personal effervescence he sees fit to record. In them his libidinous urges seem not to negate but rather to intensify his interest in the religious iconology of the painted, sculpted, and engraved role-portraits that proliferated during his lifetime. At other times, Pepys arranges for the practical performance of his pictorial fantasies, even casting his wife Elizabeth as costar or

supernumerary—a human accessory to his ambitiously self-fashioning productions.

Once, when objects such as coins and popular religious icons
alone mediated between relative obscurity and visibility, circulation of personal imagery was restricted to an elite of emperors and
saints. In seventeenth-century England, however, as elsewhere in
early modern Europe, the production and distribution of personal
images underwent an expansion, minor in comparison to what was
to come, yet significant as a harbinger of long-term trends in the
history and culture of celebrity. By the terms of this expansion,
ordinary mortals could reach for the publicity once reserved for
sovereigns or divines. Even as the use of funeral effigies dwindled,
successor forms of lively image-making grew in popularity: full-size
portraits, miniatures, engravings, busts, and statuary, including
many of the monuments that have clogged the aisles of Westminster Abbey and other English places of worship. The marble portrait of Elizabeth Pepys placed by her grieving husband in the
church of St. Olave's, Hart Street, for example, contributes hand-
somely and assertively to this publicly intimate genre of personal
effigy making.

Oft-imitated but unexcelled in the antitheatricality of their views
of the Restoration, Victorian moralists, unsurprisingly, also offer
the most censorious critique of its nonchalant mortuary portraiture. In book 3 of *The Stones of Venice,* John Ruskin contemptuously
traces the path of this "semi-animate type" from Italy to England.
He objects not to the commemorative likenesses per se, but to
their increasingly annoying liveliness. He notes how the corpselike,
piously recumbent effigies on medieval tombs first "raised themselves up on their elbows, and began to look round them." What
they saw must have pleased them, for Ruskin continues:

The statue, however, did not long remain in this partially
recumbent attitude. Even the expression of peace became
painful to the frivolous and thoughtless Italians, and they
required the portraiture to be rendered in a manner that
should induce no memory of death. The statue rose up, and
presented itself in front of the tomb, like an actor upon a stage,

surrounded not merely, or not at all, by the Virtues, but by allegorical figures of Fame and Victory, by genii and muses, by per-
sonifications of humbled kingdoms and adoring nations, and by
every circumstance of pomp, and symbol of adulation, that
flattery could suggest, or insolence could claim.[3]

Ruskin finds unseemly the manner in which the sculptors adorned
the mortuary portraits with frippery, and his censure strikes at
what he sees as the abuse in death of the crucial properties in the
theater of daily social life: accessories. Thus provisioned with the
symbolically indispensable raiment of superfluous things, many of
these new effigies emerged from representations of aristocratic
celebrities and the growing ranks of their social emulators, but
their most consequential innovation was that they no longer
required the death and beatification of their subjects to provide
occasion for their production.

Most vividly, these new effigies came from images of the kind
produced in the studios of portraitists, led in the mid–seventeenth
century by the fashionable Sir Peter Lely (1618–1680).[4] Characteristically showing his sitters in negligent dress or in "role-portraits" as Christian saints or pagan deities and shepherdesses, also
in negligent dress, Lely's heavily accessorized erotic imagery certainly inspired Samuel Pepys. The philandering diarist felt
sufficiently emboldened to propose that Judith Pennington, a
casually willing partner with whom he engaged in his favored flirtatious practice of mutual masturbation (6:310, 318), "undress herself into her nightgown, that I might see how to have her picture
drawn carelessly (for she is mighty proud of that conceit)" (6:335),
and thereafter he arranged for an even more ambitious religious
role-portrait of Mrs. Pepys. Lely's style had a marked effect on the
elite portraiture and decorative schemes of later times and hence
on the tastemakers who grew up with them and in them. Both celebrated and reviled for his series of portraits known as the "Windsor Beauties," so named for the location of many of them and the
eye-candy appeal of their subjects (see fig. 1 in the introduction),
Lely had the misfortune of earning the scorn of William Hazlitt.
Presaging Ruskin's disdain of the mortuary portraits, Hazlitt said

tartly that the Windsor Beauties "look just like what they were—a set of kept-mistresses, painted, tawdry, showing off their theatrical and meretricious airs and graces, without one touch of real elegance or refinement, or one spark of sentiment to touch the heart."[5] Hazlitt loved the theater and wrote idolatrously about the maternal Mrs. Siddons, but here *theatrical* and *meretricious* compete as synonyms for *immoral*. The accumulation of Lely portraits and studio knockoffs later intensified the Victorian association of reprobates and voluptuaries with the Restoration period. This association affords no more telling example than the pervasively imagined afterimage of Nell Gwyn (1650–1687), the most notorious actress of Charles II's reign, the remarkable durability and power of which had much to do with a spate of posthumous misattribution. As David Piper ruefully observes of the connoisseurship on the late-seventeenth-century female subject, "The iconography has been confused almost beyond hope by the continuous baptism of portraits of unknown women of the late seventeenth century with Nell Gwyn's name."[6] And no wonder: as one of the most famous women of this period or of any period, she has attracted more biographers than any of her rivals (*BD* 6:469–70). In many obvious ways, theater earns its clichéd reputation as the most ephemeral of the arts, but more reflective historians understand the uncanny staying power of certain magnetic personalities and types, even—or perhaps especially—when they seem to be playing a merely accessory role in the social dramas of changing times.

What is an accessory? A glance at the decorative appointments to Charles's funeral effigy suggests a preliminary definition of the accessory object, one that by extension discloses the emerging structures of synthetic experience itself. The royal sword-girdle and hanger remain with the figure in Westminster Abbey today, but the sword that they originally held disappeared along with the king's hatband and other baubles. The king's effigy was armed with a rapier, a "civilian sword."[7] Increasingly ornamental rather than practical, the rapier draws attention to a revealing problem of classification: intended for use, a sword is a particular kind of tool—a weapon; intended for show, it is an *objet,* inessential except to add intangible symbolic value to the ensemble. Functioning only as secondary to something else, decorative objects of this kind are classified as accessories. Thus subordinated, they remain accessories even if they once served life-or-death purposes as utensils. Charles, who personally led the desperate cavalry charge into the pikes of the Roundheads at the battle of Worcester, well understood the specialized purposes of edged weapons, and he was proficient in their use; yet for most of his life he wore his sword, when he wore it, symbolically, as gentlemen then increasingly did, to signify their status as gentlemen, not combatants. That the experience of the accessory is synthetic, however, does not mean that it is without meaningful purpose.

On the contrary, to accessorize is to make a useful sign out of a practical superfluity. The word *accessory* suggests not only a surplus or an excess (as in a bejeweled purse too small to hold anything, for instance) but also an oblique yet significant instrumentality (as in an "accessory after the fact"). To accessorize a costume is thus to furnish it with the supplementary but nonetheless telling items that serve to identify or locate the wearer. The less practical the accessory item is, the more it means: even today, a tie—that refunctioned atavism of the nobleman's sword—is required of gentlemen *because* it has nothing useful to do, and no suit, however chic, is proof against a bad one; similarly, the bag lady is known by her bag, not because it contains so many of the things she really needs but so few. Thorstein Veblen's concept of conspicuous consumption illuminates but cannot exhaust the meaning of this transhistorical phenomenon. Today, the world promotes the supplemental everywhere it can, even at the expense of the essential: ever mindful of the power of the right accessory to summarize what really counts, Dooney & Bourke recently touted their knock-off of the Louis Vuitton classic as "The 'It' Bag."[8] Back then, the world was very different in many ways, but not in what really counts in making a fashion statement: the It-bauble.

In the instance of the accessory item, as in so many others, Pepys illuminates the primal social scene with a telling anecdote. Speaking as the candid oracle of vicarious experience among the early modern upper-middle classes, he proudly marks the day when he first walked abroad wearing his newly acquired sword, "as the man-

ner now among gentlemen is" (2:29). That he wears it as an accessory rather than as a weapon Pepys makes clear by his flummoxed
account of the debacle that occurs on the only occasion in the
*Diary* when he acknowledges that he might have put a sword to
practical use: "I was set upon by a great dog, who got hold of my
garters and might have done me hurt; but Lord, to see in what a
maze I was, that having a sword about me, I never thought of it or
had the heart to make use of it" (4:131; see 9:172). Once Pepys
begins to think of himself under the role-icon marked "gentleman" and to perform in fulfillment of its conventional expectations, he doesn't feel well dressed without his sword. He doesn't
think to defend himself with it in an emergency, however, because
that isn't what it's for. It has other work to do. It works as a prop to
support his performance as he fights his way across the threshold
of gentlemanly status and claims the social spaces beyond as his
own. It makes him visible to himself and to others as what he wants
to become. Therein lies its magic. In such charmed rites of passage, accessories are to implements what stages are to altars.

Like stage properties, accessories make meanings under the
ever-useful trope of synecdoche—the part stands in for the whole,
the species for the genus, the one for the many: "since a crooked
figure may / Attest in little place a million" (Shakespeare, *Henry V*,
1.prologue.15–16). Synecdoche shares pride of place in the poet-
ics of performance with her sister metonymy, whereby the word
for one thing stands in for another of which it is an attribute or
with which it is associated, especially when that association occurs
through bodily contiguity or propinquity. Physical objects like
hand props or articles of dress thus make vivid verbal and visual
metonyms, as they do when either *scepter* or *crown*, for example,
stands in synecdochically to name the idea of kingship. Unlike set-
tings, in which *Westminster,* say, would evoke government, or *Bedlam,* chaos, the prop arrives with the performer. When a crown
comes onstage as a visual metonym, it substitutes for many of the
things its wearer would otherwise have to say and do in order to
introduce himself or herself convincingly to the audience. The
same holds true, of course, for the entrance of an actual king, but
the stage accessory can induce the magical It-Effect far less expen-

sively and with a far greater extension of the celebrity franchise to talented aspirants who do not possess It by right of birth. Insightfully tracking the magic of properties in the medieval, early modern, and modern English drama in *The Stage Life of Props* (2003), Andrew Sofer examines the meaning-making virtuosity of the fan, for instance, as a "sexual semaphore" in the Restoration theater. He carefully distinguishes those social and erotic meanings from the religious overtones of the eucharistic wafer, the bloody handkerchief, and the momento mori skull that preceded the fan as the most representative hand props of earlier periods.[9] But Sofer's own data on the effects produced by the fan, which included the gestures of fan-users performing every conceivable behavior except for merely fanning themselves, actually make a strong case for the fan's inclusion on the longer list of enchanted accessories. This list extends the operation of the symbolic host to include the transformative derivation of spiritual presence by collective assent—"effervescence"—from sundry material fetishes. Their efficacy as totems depends on the intensity of consumers' belief in their magic. In that charmed puissance—the power publicly to imagine the whole by making visible the accessorized part—resides the theatrical foundation of modern enchantment.

Accessories thus provide an auspicious place to begin an account of new modes of synthetic experience because their very inutility enchants them. Like the royal effigy itself, which functions symbolically as the durable subordinate to the perishable body of the sacred king, a number of popular accessories derive from or emulate liturgical impedimenta or practices. Ancestor to the decorative parasol, for instance, the medieval *papilionus,* or small umbrella, shaded the pope even during indoor ceremonies, serving as a more mobile supplement to the similarly redundant grand *baldachinum.*[10] This accessory item still performs the importance or holiness of the person walking under it. For nearly a millennium, the *flabellum,* a circular fan, wafted cooling and insect-repelling breezes over the sacred Host during consecration. The fan, of course, later played an expressive role in social communication quite apart from its utility in creating a local breeze. The effects of refunctioned accessories may thus be seen to extend from objects into attitudes and behaviors. The *patin,* or plate, which caught crumbs dropped from the celebration of Eucharist, lent its name to a new variety of vicarious experience, *patina,* which describes the mystical aura that suggestible people perceive radiating from objects that time and reverent use have invested with the grime of antiquity.

Let the quaint effigy of Charles II in the Norman Undercroft of Westminster Abbey, therefore, stand as a representative precursor to role-icons of many other kinds, serving as an example of how the symbolic materials out of which the physical image is fabricated—accessories, clothes, hair, skin, flesh, and bone—in turn construct the kind of mental image that people conjure up as they make celebrities their own in imagination or memory. Beholding these elements synecdochically—seeing them as separate parts made tangibly available from abstracted and elusive wholes—ordinary people can experience a spurious but vivid intimacy with the public figures they represent. They can also put themselves in imaginative touch with the fantastic myths associated with such icons. These specters may then appear to them as "lifelike," sometimes even more so than their living acquaintances, who lack the imaginary body magically conferred on the avatars who have inherited or earned the charismatic offices of It.

In fact, at the juncture of the It-Effect and modern synthetic experience, celebrities themselves became accessories—useless for all practical purposes but symbolically crucial to the social self-conceptions of their contemporaries. Their tribes live vicariously through them, sometimes in their names and even under their names (Luddites, Peronists, Moonies). The more successful ones continue to work their magic on succeeding generations, turning up in the pages of narrative history and the representations of popular culture, first as potentates and saints, then as dictators and divas. Most of them have found what ancient kings already knew, swathed in luxury and placed on high: to have It is to serve no obvious useful purpose for anyone, and thus to be available to belong to everyone.

The most promising place to focus an inquiry into the modern, mass-mediated consequences of such phenomena of the deep eighteenth century is with the received traditions that Elinor Glyn represented to the nascent American dream-factory in its wide-open early years—those she brought with her as baggage from England and those she imagined she had. In her vision of her country and its empire, the constitution of the royal body stood for the national and even racial constitution itself. Raised from childhood to revere the Stuarts for their "noblesse oblige," the perfection of their charm unruffled by effort, she carried the effigy of Charles II with her for the rest of her life, and no mere actual royals then living, certainly not Hanoverians, could surpass in glamour those who reigned in the nostalgic realms predating the French Revolution that Glyn called the "Fairy Kingdoms" of her imagination:

> The outlook and the beliefs impressed upon me by my grandparents, already nearly a century out of date from the contemporary point of view, sank into my mind, and have never been entirely eliminated. They can be seen peeping out of every book I write, even when I fancy that I am being entirely modern. A varied life containing much disillusionment, and which has witnessed the passing of the last vestiges of the *ancien régime* that I was taught so greatly to admire, has not completely removed my childhood's faith in the value of the aristocratic tradition. Even my constant touch with, and ten years' residence in democratic, modern America has not undermined my subconscious belief, born of many fairy tales, that princes and princesses are the natural heroes and heroines of romantic adventures![11]

However much like insupportable guff these notions may seem to some, no one should underestimate their pervasiveness or staying power as articles of a new kind of faith community. The Stuarts reigned in the twilight of sacral monarchy, but today millions of royalists, avowed or circumspect, not all of them British subjects by any means or even Anglophiles, join Elinor Glyn in their unwillingness to acknowledge in their hearts that the sun has ever really set. The public emotion available to be expended from time to time on royal weddings and funerals, for example, attests to the stubbornly enduring magic of the synthetic experience of royalty, especially now when it drapes itself in the weighty mantle of "heritage."

Having arrived fresh out of Canada, descending with her socially pretentious but financially insecure family on Scots-Irish in-laws, Elinor Glyn later recorded her childhood impressions of their hoary residence, Balgregan Castle, identifying herself like any heritage tourist with the historic occupants but specifying her claims on their kinship: "Balgregan had been the scene of some Jacobite plottings, and the whole place was filled with the romantic atmosphere of other days. My mother had told us that we were descended from a follower of the Old Pretender, and I loved to imagine stories of this exciting ancestor." The house on Jersey in which they finally settled in the 1870s and 1880s contained similarly exciting effigies, "fascinating and mysterious, and quite unbiddable," to inspire both the future writer, who would later claim the word *It* for Paramount, and her fashion-designer sister. Of the artwork hanging in the old house, the precocious reader of Pepys's *Diary* later reminisced, "A Lely lady in the drawing room had a romantic air."[12] The spell she cast on the rebellious Sutherland sisters lent the legitimating aura of history (with a capital *H*) to their adolescent apostasy: "I conceived a hatred of Puritanism in all its forms," Elinor wrote in connection with her attraction to the Restoration period during these formative years, "partly based no doubt on my Cavalier and Stuart predilections, but partly too because I felt such an attitude was a blasphemy against the beauty and joy of my romantic dream world."[13] The more down-to-earth Lucy discovered among the artworks in the Jersey drawing room the fashion sense that inspired her future career as "Lucile." During these years she began making clothes for her dolls and then graduated to draping yards of fabric on her sister and herself to create gowns that were both timeless and novel, demonstrably imitative of Lely's painterly way of swathing his sitters in faux-classical drapery or lingerie rather than risk dating their portraits by dressing them in contemporary styles: "I decided to adopt an original style of dress," Lucy wrote, acknowledging the apparent contradiction, "taking my inspiration from the pictures of the old masters."[14]

Elinor Glyn's quixotic childhood identification became the basis of her adult social philosophy, which might be summarized as the

Tory Radical alternative to the revolt of the masses. She attempted
to promote her cause by raising the tone of Hollywood screenplays
in the era of the silent feature film, by tutoring as emerging royalty
the movie stars who acted in them, and by filling the growing number of movie palaces with their adoring subjects, average men and
women who would see their highest aspirations fulfilled synecdochically by the new monarchs of the mimic world: "It is the elevation of all mankind to the rank of princes and princesses in a fairy
kingdom, and not in the abolition of such romantic ideals, and the
degradation of all classes to the level of the sordid, that I see the
future happiness of the world."[15] She envisioned this coming
utopia of democratic romance not as the promised revolution of
the "Bolsheviks," vile regicides that they were, but, dottily enough,
as the long-deferred second restoration of the Stuarts.

With the possible exception of Edmund Burke, no writer has
described the nature of the cultural legacy or burden that Glyn
inherited more cogently than the Victorian journalist Walter Bagehot, author of *The English Constitution* (1867), who cynically anato-
mizes the irrationality of the political structures of the world into
which Glyn and her generation were born. He does so by explain-
ing in more exfoliated detail than Burke provided why the most
prominent people are the ones who serve in the accessory roles.
Woven into the snobbery of his largely persuasive account of the
government and society of Great Britain in the middle of Victoria's
reign is the unspecified but ubiquitous principle of It:

> To state the matter shortly, royalty is a government in which the
> attention of the nation is concentrated on one person doing
> interesting actions. A Republic is a government in which that
> attention is divided between many, who are all doing uninter-
> esting actions. Accordingly, so long as the human heart is strong
> and the human reason weak, royalty will be strong because it
> appeals to diffused feeling, and Republics weak because they
> appeal to the understanding.

Moreover, there is for Bagehot a long-standing religious sanction
to this aggregation of interesting actions in the hands of the illus-

trious one at the expense of the jejune many. This sanction did not lose its efficacy in the 1860s, Matthew Arnold notwithstanding, nor has it entirely since, if religion is to be counted as the communal aspiration to belong to something larger and more important than ourselves. "The English Monarchy strengthens our Government with the strength of religion," concludes *The English Constitution*, with a pointed tautology.[16] One effect of looking at religious faith in Bagehot's sociopolitical way is to imagine a historic move directly from theocratic to theatrocratic rule. It is also to set aside, at least provisionally, the prevailing tendency of the human sciences to see "rationality" and "rational choice" everywhere in the emergence of modern democratic societies. It is to propose instead a lively repertoire of crowd-pleasing romantic comedies and tear-jerking histrionics as an alternative explanation of what passes for popular sovereignty in the age of mass communication, magnetic personalities, and endemic mendacity.

In discussing the sentimental hold of monarchy on the imaginations of the English people, Bagehot's keyword is *visibility*. Royalty, the aristocracy, and the established church (along with anyone else with glamour who might be recruited for the parade) provide the "visible form" of English government, to which loyal emotion is due and by which it is extracted, whereas nameless, faceless bureaucrats provide the "efficient form" of boring—hence invisible—service and regulation, the good offices of which effectively rule but do not reign. Bagehot explicitly compares the visible branch of government to the theater: "A common man may as well try to rival the actors on the stage in their acting, as the aristocracy in *their* acting. The higher world, as it looks from without, is a stage on which the actors walk their parts much better than the spectators can. The play is played in every district, [and] the climax of the play is the Queen."[17] Let it be emphasized that such theatricality does not render the visible branch otiose. On the contrary, one of the great achievements of the English constitution, the most famous document in history never to have been written, is that the visible branch succeeds not only in dramatizing itself, but also in concealing the efficient branch from view, which allows the latter to complete its secret work as if by magic: "The apparent rulers of the English nation are like the most imposing personages of a splendid procession: it is by them that the mob are influenced; it is they whom the spectators cheer. The real rulers are secreted in second-class carriages; no one cares for them or asks about them, but they are obeyed implicitly and unconsciously by reason of the splendour of those who eclipsed and preceded them."[18] Pepys, of course, is often described, and not without reason, as a progenitor to the properly invisible Victorian civil servant whom Bagehot here evokes, modestly deflecting the credit for the success of his department to the ceremonially gifted but notoriously paperwork-averse Charles II: "It had pleased God to give us a King that understood the sea" (10:58). Some of the apparent rulers enjoy their splendor ex officio; their charisma is ascribed. Others have charisma that is attained, promoting them, as their merits deserve, to the ranks of the visible, the celebrated, and the inefficient. Highly visible though they may be, all of the "apparent rulers" perform, in precisely the sense of word used here, as *accessories*.

The narrative of Elinor Glyn's life charts the impromptu extension of the English constitution, with its accessory royalty, to Hollywood, where the visible also works to conceal the efficient. Here, in the magical, rapacious place that has since become the playing fields of Eton for American presidents and governators, Glyn found—and served—a new aristocracy. No wonder that the coiner of *It* believed she had providentially arrived, like Pepys, at the opportune moment of restoration, when new media were expanding monarchial visibility exponentially. She had an ecstatic, religious feeling for the new manna and the new myths. A passionate believer in reincarnation (and for a time, spiritualism) and always a fierce foe of Puritanism of any denomination, Glyn developed her own quirky, quasi-Christian-charismatic, neopagan religion. In the royalist Gospel according to Elinor, social order and aesthetic beauty unite in the ascent to "romance," which was her godhead: "As I see it, the word 'romantic' represents the true opposite of the word 'sordid'; romance is a spiritual disguise, created by the imagination, with which to envelop material happenings and desires, and thus bring them into greater harmony with the soul."[19] She found her special doctrine of "spiritual disguise" revealed in the heroes and heroines she created in fiction or sought out in her journeys, which took on the aura of pilgrimages. Her spiritual quest was for the iconic royals of an imagined dynasty of true glamour and noblesse oblige that ran from her putative Stuart forebears to their modern successors in Tinsel Town. When she unpacked her bags in the autumn of 1920 with a contract in hand from "Famous-Players-Lasky" (later Paramount), she found herself the right person in the right place at the right time: Douglas Fairbanks and Mary Pickford, Glyn recalls, were "the acknowledged King and Queen of the cinema world when I reached Hollywood."[20]

Finding her way as a courtier and advisor to the inner circle of this invented tradition, in which the monarchs were made and not born and reigned only briefly at the height of their glamour, Elinor Glyn served not only as a source of scenarios—as she did in her screenplays for *The Great Moment* (Famous-Players-Lasky, 1920) with Gloria Swanson, *Beyond the Rocks* (Famous-Players-Lasky, 1921) with Swanson and Rudolph Valentino, and *It* (Paramount, 1927) with Clara Bow—but also as a living archive and instant repertoire of cavalier éclat. Lacking a title like her sister's, she styled herself "Madame Glyn" to wow the locals. Madame became a meddlesome but effective consultant to the directors and set-dressers at Famous-Players-Lasky Films and Metro-Goldwyn-Mayer Films on all things English or otherwise beautiful and tasteful. That included advice on how to manage a proper seduction: "American men of those days simply could not make love! Not even the leading screen actors had any idea of how to do it then." It also included the proper appointments and floral arrangements to dress (that is, to accessorize) the sets representing English country houses: "Fine pictures and beautiful ornaments began to replace the dreadful knick-knacks and aspidistras—yes *aspidistras,* which had hitherto been made to sprout in the drawing-rooms of English dukes!"

Madame was on a mission. With the "menace of Bolshevism" threatening to sweep away "the whole beautiful culture of our modern world, with its ancient foundations," she fought back with "the glorification of romance" designed "to stir up the hearts of thousands of little fluffy, gold-digging American girls" with stories and pictures that "are more perfectly English than anything which has been made in this country."[21] Somehow teaching them how to "give" more and "expect" less like proper women would fortify the bulwarks against the Comintern. In recompense, the erstwhile gold-diggers would get American men who knew "how to do it" at last, and also appropriately appointed interiors in which to do it.

In the film version of *Three Weeks,* the 1907 book that had made and ruined her reputation at the same time, Glyn thought she had the cinematic vehicle she needed: with Aileen Pringle, a Glyn look-alike and daughter-in-law of Sir John Pringle, governor general of Jamaica, cast in the leading role, Glyn would make her methods and her doctrine of "spiritual disguise" prevail, resuscitating the ancien régime in the back lot. In *Three Weeks* (MGM, 1924), as in the book, a character known only as "The Lady" and played by Pringle, an exotic, passionate woman of a certain age (precisely Glyn's age in 1907), actually the queen of some unnamed Balkan country traveling incognito, seduces a lad young enough to be her son. Since "Paul" is not in fact her son, however, the properties she uses to effect the seduction shocked the world more than the deed itself. In the shooting script as in the novel, It is all about the accessories. Paul makes his temptress a gift of the pelt of a tiger, and the Lady, like the author, knows how to dress her set with it:

> A bright fire burnt in the grate, and some palest orchid-mauve silk curtains were drawn in the lady's room when Paul entered from the terrace. And loveliest sight of all, in front of the fire, stretched at full length, was his tiger—and on him—also at full length—reclined the Lady, garbed in some strange clinging garment of heavy purple crepe, its hem embroidered with gold, one white arm resting on the beast's head, her back supported by a pile of velvet cushions, and a heap of rarely bound books at her side, while between her red lips was a rose not redder than they—an almost scarlet rose. Paul had never seen one as red before.[22]

With clothes, hair, skin, and flesh all in place on the It-rug, the Lady invites Paul to spend most of the next two hundred pages and nearly the entirety of the three weeks riding the tiger. The rare books add a nice touch, though, complementing the red rose: the Lady also respects Paul for his mind. Glyn herself patiently coached Miss Pringle, who felt uncomfortable, on how to writhe properly on the tiger's skin, just getting by the Hays Office censors with some prim edits. The film version of *Three Weeks* did very well, but Pringle, the debutante, did not produce the hoped-for It-Effect in the role. That would await the rollout of Clara Bow in *It* (1927), a project that would test Madame's ideas and techniques on an untried actress who did not have, in her view, the inborn quality referred to by the word that she sometimes used interchangeably with "It," greatly annoying Anita Loos: "race."²³ But Brooklyn-slum-born Bow did have the aura of the working-class Cinderella-actress about her, a very considerable advantage as it turned out, when added to a ready supply of moxie. In the late 1920s, *Moxie* was the trademark of a popular soft-drink, marketed for its association with vitality and boldness, but its promoters also wanted to link it in the minds of consumers to a kind of self-possessed savoir faire. Consciously or not, they worked in the recognizable stylistic traditions of It.

To understand the making of modern role-icons as accessories—the refunctioning of religious conventions into secular public intimacy—it is necessary to do what Elinor Glyn claimed to have done at an impressionable age: read with care and without embarrassment through the "unexpurgated" *Diary* of Samuel Pepys. Apparently very susceptible to the magic that infuses vicariousness with excitement, Pepys sought it in a variety of venues, including the court, the painter's studio, the theater, and even in his dreams. The most intimate confessions in his *Diary* disclose how synthetic experience emerges from the uneasy play of private desires and the public performance of them—secular rituals for which the theater and the role-portrait offered the models that infiltrated and eventually subsumed those provided by the church.

For both Pepys and his royal sovereign, and not for them alone, the preeminent "It Girl" of the Restoration stage was Nell Gwyn, whose sexuality, in the words of a distinguished historian of the first actresses, "became the central feature of her professional identity as a player."[24] But not the only feature: she also had, *avant la lettre,* moxie—the ability to register self-possession during flights of wild giddiness. Helping to establish the social-historical role-icon—"actress"—that Clara Bow and thousands of performers between the 1660s and the 1920s could step into, Nell Gywn rose up from the bottom of the working class, where she held such humble but useful jobs as tending bar in a brothel and selling oranges in the playhouse, to become a glamorous ornament. She thus pioneered the nominated role-icon of the Galatea-Cinderella type, and the spirited antiphony of her stage persona might be summed up as innocence and experience, a kind of devil-may-care impudence without malice that served her well playing in britches roles. On March 2, 1667, Pepys saw Gwyn in such a part in Dryden's *Secret Love* and recorded what seems to have been a general response to the charismatic intimacy of her public presence, even from women, though the most important spectators at that particular performance the diarist specifically names: "There is a comical part done by Nell, which is Florimell, that I never can hope to see the like done again by man or women. The King and Duke of York was at the play; but so great performance of a comical part was never, I believe, in the world before as Nell doth this, both as a mad girle and then, most and best of all, when she comes in like a young gallant; and hath the motions and carriage of a spark the most that ever I saw any man have" (8:91). That's It—but not nearly all of It.

Historians routinely note how successfully Gwyn attracted men, as she was kept first by the actor Charles Hart, then by Charles, Lord Buckhurst, and finally by King Charles, making him, in her breathtakingly impudent sobriquet, "Charles III" (*BD* 6:463). But she also fascinated women. Aphra Behn, for instance, dedicating *The Feigned Courtesans; or, a Night's Intrigue* (1679) "To Mrs Ellen Gwynn," communicates the magnetism of the abnormally interesting personality of the actress more eloquently than anyone. Even adjusting for the flattery required by the genre of the dedication page, an extraordinary character still shines through—the one in the many and the many in the one:

For besides, Madam, all the Charms and attractions and powers of your Sex, you have Beauties peculiar to yourself, an eternal sweetness, youth and ayr, which never dwelt in any face but yours, of which not one inimitable Grace could be ever borrowed or assumed, . . . but all the world will know it yours; . . . you never appear but you glad[den] the hearts of all that have the happy fortune to see you, as if you were made on purpose to put the whole world into good Humour; whenever you look abroad, and when you speak, men crowd to listen to you with that awful reverence as to Holy Oracles or Divine Prophecies, and bear away the precious words to tell at home to all the attentive family the Graceful thing you uttered.[25]

Behn's emphatic use of religious adjectives—"awful," "Holy," and "Divine"—reveals the peculiarly beatific aura that surrounded Gwyn in her role-icon as the self-described "protestant whore": functionally illiterate but a fluent curser, she was the least sanctimonious person imaginable and the least likely to be officially sanctified, yet she has remained among the most familiarly and quotably revered (*BD* 6:460, 465).

Always ready to ride the cresting wave of a social trend, Pepys recorded something like a conversion experience at a theatrical performance in 1668, a divine apparition resonant of bells and redolent of smells. Supported in full baroque splendor with music and machines, the revival of Dekker and Massinger's *The Virgin Martyr* featured Rebecca Marshall as the saintly Dorothea and Nell Gwyn as her guardian angel:

With my wife and Deb to the King's House, to see *Virgin Martyr,* the first time it has been acted in a great while; and it is mighty pleasant; not that the play is worth much but it is finely Acted by Becke Marshall. But that which did please me beyond anything in the whole world was the wind-musique when the Angell comes down, which is so sweet that it ravished me; and endeed, in a word, did wrap up my soul so that it made me really sick, just as I have formerly been when in love with my wife; that neither then, nor all the evening going home and at home, I was able to think of anything but remained all night transported. (9:93–94)

Nothing exactly like this seems to have to have happened to Pepys in church, though the masturbatory habits he indulged there demonstrate that he felt a certain rapport between his experiences in the two different venues. Apparently driven by the contradictory urges of his para-Episcopal attraction, Pepys went backstage to the dressing rooms after another performance of *The Virgin Martyr*. Here, much to his disillusionment, he found that the painted faces and coarse language of the same actresses now repelled him: "but Lord, their confidence, and how many men do hover about them as soon as they come off the stage, and how confident they [are] in their talk" (9:189). No other detail confirms more decisively the historic emergence of public intimacy than the convention of allowing gentlemen backstage at the playhouse to meet the actresses as they undressed. But it does not diminish the religious force of the impulse Pepys felt at the first appearance of the angel, whose offstage identity he well knew, in a sublime flourish of oboes and the raiment of ecstatic belief. In his voluptuous faith, as in Glyn's, fantasies have the efficacy of prayers, and flesh-and-blood actors, no less than kings, appear in the "spiritual disguise" of gods.

Pepys's *Diary* shows how such sacred and sexual celebrities, never entirely separable as objects of desire, mingled willy-nilly in the secular portraiture, public behavior, and actor-centered dramatic characterizations of the Restoration. As titular head of the theaters and a high-profile audience member as well as the head of the established church, Charles II created an image of sexual celebrity that fascinated and troubled his subjects. Their criticisms forecast and eventually documented the conclusions of the Victorians about the meretricious character of the king. Nowhere was he more disturbingly yet tellingly effigied than by his obscene proxy, Bollixinion, in the demented mock-heroic play *Sodom; or, the Quintessence of Debauchery* (1674),[26] but an equally critical portrait emerged from the far less scurrilous expressions of apprehension and disgust recorded by Pepys and his fellow diarist John Evelyn. Pepys thought that the king "hath taken ten times more care and paines" to reconcile his feuding mistresses "than ever he did to save his kingdom" (8:288). Evelyn confided an epitaph to his diary at the time of the king's burial that illuminates the airy insouciance of the king's effigy: "An excellent prince doubtlesse had he been lesse addicted to Women, which made him uneasy & allways in Want to supply their unmeasurable profusion."[27] Yet in the manipulative negligence of his royal image, which became inseparable from those of the women whose profusion Evelyn could not measure, Charles beguiled Pepys, warming his subject with images of public intimacy and exciting him to remarkable feats of vicarious emulation.

As an inimitable incendiary of mimetic desire, appearing in representation on the cusp of the sacred and the extremely profane, none excelled Barbara Palmer (née Villiers), Countess of Castlemaine and Duchess of Cleveland (1641–1709). As the longest reigning and most fiercely adamant mistress of King Charles II, she once posed along with their bastard son for a role-portrait as Madonna and Child. This blasphemously flattering allegory by Lely later turned up in the chapel of a French convent, where it hung unsuspected above the altar until the nuns finally learned of its objectionable provenance and sent it back. Some of Castlemaine's other transgressions, however, stuck more intractably as motes in the public eye. Her enemies concocted and widely circulated a broadside purporting to represent a petition for redress of grievances from the whores of London addressed to the Countess of Castlemaine as their most distinguished colleague and protector. In a critical climate in which preoccupations with the king's image produced satires as mordant as Andrew Marvell's "Last Instructions to a Painter" (1667), Pepys secured a copy of the anti-Castlemaine screed and remarked on the implications of its popular dissemination: "I wonder it durst be printed and spread abroad—which shows that the times are loose, and come to a great disregard of the King or Court or Government" (9:154). Earlier he recorded the similarly disturbing and wildly titillating testimony of Sir Thomas Crew that Castlemaine had sexually enslaved the king by practicing on him the "postures" of Pietro Aretino, whose manual of positions and techniques rang changes on the possible relationships of organs and orifices. On the scale of mimetic desire, Pepys's comment on the efficacy of the king's participation in "the tricks of Aretin that are to be practiced to give pleasure" scores high in the intensifying category of envy: "in which he is too able, hav[ing] a large ———" (4:136–37).

As long as Castlemaine remained the king's favorite, Pepys continued to record his vicarious erotic obsession with her, and his many references to her chart the nascent production of the celebrity *image* in the "corporate" sense of the word, including the use of accessory items in the manner of a totem or logo. He responds similarly to the persons of other royal mistresses—including the actresses Nell Gwyn and Moll Davis, the flirtatiously elusive Teresa Stuart, Duchess of Richmond and Lennox, and even to the queen herself—but not with the same intensity of feeling or eye for inciting detail. Gaining entry to the privy garden of Whitehall, for instance, he becomes preoccupied with her lingerie hanging out to dry on a laundry line: "the finest smocks and linen petticoats of my Lady Castlemaynes, laced with rich lace at the bottoms that ever I saw; and did me good to look upon them" (3:87). Now to most people undergarments serve as foundations, but to Castlemaine, as to many of the other subjects of the fashionable portrait painters of her day, they were accessories. They notably functioned that way in the role-portraits that combined the sacred and the erotic: fashionable women costumed and accessorized themselves as revered saints to sit for famously expensive painters. The penitent Mary Magdalen, for example, offered a more plausible casting than the Madonna for both Castlemaine and one of two of the other royal mistresses, either Gwyn or Davis.[28] The pictures of these women as the saint look much the same. Tresses undone and spilling over their naked shoulders, smocks fringed with lace and falling open, soft hands cradling the jars of perfumed unguents with which they will offer to bathe their lord, the Magdalens of the Lely type are all made to look as if their intimate services won't end with the drying of their master's feet with their hair.

As he does with most of the important trends of the period 1660–69, Pepys records firsthand the erotic secularization of the sacred effigy in the fashionable female role-portrait. With the advent of Catherine of Braganza as queen, portrait images of fashionable women as the martyred St. Catherine, including several of the inexhaustible Castlemaine, accumulated.[29] Their power to enchant derived in no small measure from the notorious proximity of the sitters to the king's person, and his royal playhouse publicized the trend: speaking the epilogue to John Dryden's *Tyrannick Love* (1669), Nell Gwyn was made to rhyme "St. Cathar'n," in whose tragic story she had just played a role, with "Slater'n," the popularly known role that she was then playing in the royal service (*BD* 6:461). On the stage and on canvas, the saint appeared with her obligatory saintly accessories—the nastily spiked wheel, on which her pagan tormentors broke her body, and the palm frond symbolizing her martyrdom. Socially emulating the glamorous women of the court (and the actresses who were their working-class surrogates or stunt doubles), privileged individuals of lesser rank could aspire to their own performances of mimetic identification and desire—the trickle-down It-Effect. Casting such an alluring role-icon in the expanding repertoire of synthetic experience, Pepys, like a latter-day Pygmalion, nominated his wife as a sainted Galatea.

Sitting for a role-portrait at this time was a performance in itself, and the diarist carefully staged his own role and especially that of Elizabeth Pepys with its sacred accoutrements. After having long admired the Jacob Huysmans portrait of Queen Catherine as St. Catherine (5:254), Pepys is at last able to note his satisfaction in finding in John Hayls an affordable artist of "a very maisterly hand" to paint his wife in a racier version of the same subject. Pepys regards Lely as the better painter but finds him "mighty proud" and no doubt more expensive (8:129). He visits Hayls's studio on St. Valentine's Day, February 14, 1666, and resolves to commission portraits of himself and Elizabeth, perhaps as presents marking the romantic occasion (7:42–43). The first sitting for Hayls takes place the next day. The performance requires mimetically mastering an iconography that has been recycled through the queen and the other painted ladies of the Carolean court. In describing this iconography, Pepys uses the same word for pose—

*posture*—as he had previously in connection with Aretino: "Here Mr. Hales begun my wife in the posture we saw one of my Lady Peters, like a St. Katherine. . . . it did me good to see it, and pleases me mightily—and I believe it will be a noble picture" (7:44). Pepys is clearly aroused at the sight of his wife Elizabeth posing bare-shouldered in the artist's studio for her role-portrait as the Sacred Bride of Christ. To raise even higher the erotic temperature of the studio, he contrives to bring along Mary Knepp, the singer-dancer-actress with whom he is conducting a dalliance. She joins him in song, while together they watch the silent performance of the vulnerable, jealous Elizabeth as she struggles to hold her voluptuous pose with saintly patience and piety (fig. 3). Profaning the altar and mimicking the stage, Pepys synthesizes his own private life in the most publicly intimate way imaginable.

When Pepys says that his wife's portrait will be "like a St. Katherine," which is like Lady Peters, which is like the queen, he effigies her as the latest candidate to claim possession of a venerable role-icon, newly reanimating it by a certain eroticized look. That look is very distinctive. The heavily lidded, "sleepy" eyes, the oval face framed by corkscrew curls, the rouged lips parted slightly, the flushed cheeks, and the emphatic décolleté that characterize the celebrated "Windsor Beauties" also mark the sitters for the religious role-portraits, including the virtuous and long-suffering Elizabeth Pepys. She embodies St. Catherine in the negligent act of losing track of her satin gown at the extremity of her shoulders, even as she artfully displays her pearl-drop earrings and tiara in languorous equipoise. In her hand, she holds the palm of martyrdom. At her side, the menacing rim of the spiked wheel on which St. Catherine was cruelly tortured appears iconically and suggestively. Among other things, it insinuates the sitter's readiness to endure pain, which her guilty husband confessed to having inflicted on her more often than his devoted Christian's conscience could easily bear.[30] In recompense, he might have convinced himself, he liberally adorned her person and her image with a medley of the most fashionable accessories. In so doing, he adorned himself with *her*.

The casual construction of such an effigy in the daily life of his

Fig. 3. James Thomson after John Hayls, Elizabeth Pepys as
St. Catherine, 1825. National Portrait Gallery, London.

marriage illuminates other scenes from Pepys's *Diary* that shock the
reader with their matter-of-fact infusion of the sacred with the sexual in the pursuit of synthetic experience. Paramount among these
must be numbered the several occasions when he confesses his
habit of masturbating in church. Judging from the doubly coded
language of the diary entries recording his intimate practices, masturbating during religious services made Pepys feel more guilty
than usual but also more excited.[31] His giddy diary descriptions of
his onanism, like those of his adulteries, employ not only short-
hand but also a polyglot lexicon combining French and Spanish.
Pepys's keyword is "mi cosa" ("my thing"). Thus, the entry for
November 11, 1666, reads: "Here at church (God forgive me), my

mind did courir upon Betty Michel, so that I do hazer con mi cosa in la eglisa meme" (7:365). Betty Michell was the teenaged daughter of one of Pepys's friends and later the wife of another. Next Christmas Eve, December 24, 1667, he pleasured himself during High Mass in the Queen's Chapel, Whitehall. Though he would not want to have been seen as a papist, the elaborated liturgy and the presence of her most Catholic majesty with her attendants, who included Lady Castlemaine, seem to have inspired him to virtuosic efforts: "The Queen was there and some ladies. . . . But here I did make myself to do la cosa by mere imagination, mirando a jolie mosa and with eyes open, which I never did before—and God forgive me for it, it being in the chapel" (8:588). On May 3 of the next year, he tried it with eyes wide shut, so to speak: "After dinner to church again where I did please myself con mes ojos shut in futar in conceit the hook-nosed young lady, a merchant's daughter, in the upper pew in the church under the pulpit" (9:184).

Like the artisans who crafted the royal effigies, Pepys had techniques to make his dreams astonishingly lifelike. The obligatory element, in expectation and in execution, was the mental image of a woman, sometimes one who was physically present (as with the queen in her chapel and the hook-nosed merchant's daughter); but also one who was absent (as with Betty Michell in the first episode). That the real power resided in the summoned mental image—hence in memory, in performance, in effigy—is suggested by the fact that Pepys closed his eyes to fantasize about the merchant's daughter even though she was then present to his sight in her pew beneath the pulpit. To complete his performance, he turned her into what he called a "conceit," which is itself an accessory before and after the fact of his surreptitious acts. Above all, he seems to have been motivated by a desire not only to have experiences, but also to have the experience of his experiences—hence the nocturnal repetition of the diurnal adventures recorded in his diary; hence the diary itself, unrivaled archive of the early modern It-Effect.

Pepys's encounters in and around London and Westminster provided him with a panoply of potential "conceits" for later use. Their staging can be highly theatrical, replete with dramatic conflict, sets, costumes, and props. Celebrity intensifies their effects, but it also reveals the inner process of making the images whereby It is constructed. On July 13, 1663, for instance, Pepys sees the king, the queen, and Lady Castlemaine taking the air. The king is paying attention to his wife. Castlemaine is in a royal pout. Pepys is captivated not only by the glamour of the queen, but also by the flirtatious play of the court ladies, especially Frances Stuart, who staged an impromptu fashion show, featuring feathered hats. He records: "All the ladies walked, talking and fiddling with their hats and feathers, and changing and trying one another's, but on another's head, and laughing. But it was the finest sight to me, considering their great beautys and dress, that ever I did see in all my life. But above all, Mrs Steward in this dresse, with her hat, cocked and a red plume, with her sweet eye, little Roman nose and excellent *Taille,* is now the greatest beauty I ever saw I think in my life" (4:230). The vaudeville of the hat exchange suggests the fungibility of the painted ladies in the erotic economy of the court, but Pepys puts to work the remembered image of "Mrs Steward," then the chief yet ever-elusive object of the king's sexual designs, and secondarily that of the queen herself to effect the private climax of his mimetic desire, celebrity fantasy, and subsequent auto-performance: "to bed—before I sleep, fancying myself to sport with Mrs Steward with great pleasure" (4:230). Then, two nights later: "to bed, sporting in my fancy with the Queen" (4:232).

Pepys's Mrs. Steward—Frances Teresa Stuart, the Countess of Richmond and Lennox, "La Belle Stuart," the most famously pulchritudinous of all the "Windsor Beauties"—seems to have successfully resisted the advances of the besotted king despite the intervention on his behalf of the supposedly irresistible George Villiers, Second Duke of Buckingham, who amused her by building card castles and letting her knock them down. Intriguingly, she appears in Lely's celebrated Windsor portrait with a bow in hand, evoking the chaste pagan deity Diana. In the same vein, she graces a role-portrait by Henri Gascar as a spear-toting Minerva, and her image was cast in a bronze medal as the similarly armed Britannia. But she does not appear accessorized as a Christian icon, vulnerable in her negligence, suffering, and charity. Frances Stuart, active but not preeminent in Pepys's fantasy life, was the exception that proves the rule of sacred and profane love at the court of Charles II.[32]

Pepys's nocturnal juxtaposition of the images of Queen Catherine and Frances Stuart gives the reader a glimpse into a private nodal point in the larger network of the It-Effect. In this network, the bearers of a certain look and a certain reputation could substitute for one another in the minds of fantasists with even greater celerity than they did in the king's bed. Quite apart from the testimony of Pepys, the strength of that network appears to be confirmed by the physical evidence of the effigies in Westminster Abbey. The wax figure of Charles II is not paired with one in the same style that depicts Catherine of Braganza, his queen, but rather one of Frances Stuart, Duchess of Richmond and Lennox, whose love remained "unbiddable," in Elinor Glyn's term. In a codicil to her will, dated shortly before her death in 1702, she provided for an "Effigie as well done in wax as can be," dressed in the gown she had recently worn at the coronation of Queen Anne (fig. 4). Even then, forty years and a bout with smallpox later, she was remembered by the *Daily Courant* as "that celebrated Beauty," and skilled artisans fixed for posterity her comely image wearing her own clothes and accessories, including her stuffed parrot, a West African gray, the oldest known object of its kind, which became a tourist attraction in its own right later in the eighteenth century.[33] By then the painted ladies had long been collectibles, with a number of sets, called "Beauties Series," turned out by Lely and his staff of copyists, featuring not only celebrated women, but also notorious ones, those whose liaisons with Charles II had marked them in public memory and imagination. Pepys narrates the spectacle of their circulation and implicates himself in it through his ornate fantasies. By 1663, when he swooned over her in her *taille*, "La Belle Stuart" had at least momentarily supplanted Castlemaine as the primary object of the king's extramarital attentions; but Castlemaine quickly returned to the king's favor and perforce to pride of place among Pepys's repertoire of mental images and those of the portraitists. Just as Elizabeth Pepys excited her husband by emu-

Fig. 4 Funeral effigy of Frances Teresa Stuart, Duchess of
Richmond and Lennox, 1702. Westminster Abbey Museum.
Photo: Malcolm Crowthers. © Dean and Chapter of Westminster.

lating Lady Peters emulating the queen as St. Catherine, Castlemaine's return reactivated another erotic trio, wherein, as if at the
Judgment of Paris, Pepys could imaginatively stand in for the king.

The theater offered both the metaphor and the materials for
such dream-state expressions of mimetic desire, and Shakespeare,
more than any other playwright, insinuated his imagery into
Pepys's consciousness of his own sensations. Shakespeare did so,
for instance, in a key passage in which the diarist's imagination
fixes again on Lady Castlemaine, who came to him in a mid-August
night's wet dream in the plague year of 1665. Hamlet's "To be or

not to be" soliloquy, which Pepys had already heard the great actor
Thomas Betterton deliver a number of times, frames the recovery
of his erotic dream as a waking fantasy:

> Up by 4 a-clock, and walked to Greenwich, where called at Cap-
> tain Cockes and to his chamber, he being in bed—where some-
> thing put my last night's dream into my head, which I think is
> the best that ever was dreamed—which was, that I had my Lady
> Castlemayne in my armes and was admitted to use all the dal-
> liance I desired with her, and then dreamed that this could not
> be awake but that it was only a dream. But that since it was a
> dream and that I took so much real pleasure in it, what a happy
> thing it would be, if when we are in our graves (as Shakespeare
> resembles it), we could dream, and dream but such dreams as
> this—that then we should not need to be so fearful of death as
> we are in this plague-time. (6:191)

In a way that recalls the controlling metaphor of Calderón's *La
vida es sueno*—that even dreams are "dreams of dreams," nesting
dolls of consciousness—Pepys enjoys even his own experiences vicariously. Castlemaine, standing in for an actress, exists for him as a
voyeuristic image to be acquired, savored, and refleshed at intervals, most often at the theater, where he noted her presence in the
company of the king (2:80, 164, 174; 3:260; 6:73; 7:347), and at
Whitehall, where a glimpse of her lacy hem sent him into an
ecstasy. As an effect of her celebrity before the age of mass culture,
Castlemaine's image circulated in the absence of her person.
Pepys vowed to obtain a copy of her famous portrait by Lely, and
he did so as soon as it was engraved in 1666. In fact, he bought
three prints, one to be varnished and framed for display, two to be
set aside for private use (7:359, 393; 8:206). He longed not only to
possess her portrait, but also to take his idea of her with him to the
grave. This is the historic, one-of-a-kind effigy multiplied into the
modern It-Effect—the wide circulation of a mesmerizing image of
unobtainable yet wholly portable celebrity, now engraved in the
minds of desiring subjects and consumers, which inspired Pepys
not only to masturbate, but also to shop.

Synthetic experience is that which is fabricated to imitate or replace unobtainable realities, be they threatening or alluring. Its success as a substitute for what passes for real life renders it both a highly marketable commodity, as in the offerings of the commercial playhouse or cinema, and a highly persuasive political technique, as in the vital accessory role played by glamour under the unwritten English constitution, as explained by Walter Bagehot:

> In fact, the mass of English people yield a deference rather to something else than to their rulers. They defer to what we may call the *theatrical show* of society. A certain state passes before them; a certain pomp of great men; a certain spectacle of beautiful women; a wonderful scene of wealth and enjoyment is displayed, and they are coerced by it. Their imagination is bowed down; they feel they are not equal to the life which is revealed to them. Courts and aristocracies have the great quality which rules the multitude, though philosophers can see nothing in it—visibility.[34]

It's magical: visibility increases, and reality vanishes. What Bagehot could be describing with equal familiarity is the relationship between the public and the motion-picture industry in the twentieth century, or between the public and the whole expansive network of mediated spectacles in the twenty-first. If Elinor Glyn's political philosophy can be admitted as evidence of the rise of theatrocracy, the concept of It might then be speculatively assessed as useful to the creation of an invisible British Empire, one that not only survived the Second World War, but actually continues to flourish and grow, as the unwritten English constitution spreads itself worldwide like an oil slick. The suggestive outline of that argument appears in the brief collaboration of two New Women: one, a former bun-slicer at Nathan's on Coney Island, who became suddenly and completely visible; the other, the supposed descendent of the Old Pretender's liegeman, who was born to be efficient.

"American film producers had learnt all that I had to teach them," wrote Elinor Glyn grandly about her departure from Hollywood in 1927, "and I realized that my work was done."[35] But even adjusted to accommodate her vanity, Glyn's work did have consequences. It was she who persuaded earnest set-dressers at Famous-Players-Lasky that Baronial Halls of old English castles ought not to be provided with rows of spittoons. It was she who explained to Rudoph Valentino how to kiss the fleshy inside of a woman's palm instead of the knuckle on the top. And it was she who conjured and honed the image of "The 'It' Girl," who could be plucked out of working-class utility and marketed as an accessory item to the ensemble of American popular culture like "The 'It' Bag." The plan was to make Bow the idea in everyone's mind (fig. 5). Knowing the Coca-Cola-like popularity of just the right antiphony of innocence and experience, not too tart, not too sweet, Paramount wanted Clara Bow to be an American girl next-door, as adorable as Mary Pickford, but also to be self-confidently sexual, as overtly so in her own "aw-shucks" kind of way as the exotic vamp popularized a few years earlier by Theda Bara (a pseudonymous anagram for "Arab death"). This was a tall order, requiring Pygmalion-like finesse, and Glyn set grimly to work.

The publicity department at Paramount arranged for Bow and Glyn to spend time together and to be seen in public doing so. To that end, striking redheads both, they sped around Los Angeles together in a large Packard, accompanied by the actress's great, red chow chow and a redundant driver provided by the studio. Bow, who at best regarded speed limits and traffic lights as advisory, insisted on taking the wheel, while Glyn kept her upper lip stiff in the passenger's seat and the terrorized chauffeur wept and prayed in the back. Both he and the dog were automotive accessories in this carrot-topped road-warrior anticipation of *Thelma and Louise*. The actress was an accessory of a vastly more powerful kind, an ascendant queen of the silver screen, who reigned only briefly, lived very fast, and didn't die young enough: as a producer said of her not long before her contract-ending nervous breakdown, "She had a way of being crazy that photographs pretty well."[36] What intersocietal connection opened up between Glyn and Bow in their work together before that premature retirement cannot be rationally specified, but one did, and it must have had to do with It, which for both of them, in their different genres, meant the ability to stand as if naked in the middle of a crowded room as

Fig. 5. Clara Bow, © Corbis.

if alone. For her part, Bow, a street-wise gamine with the patois of the Brooklyn tenements stenciled on her tongue, suffered icy condescension and impeccably phrased reproof from her mentor. At the same time, Glyn, world authority on gracious living and romance, endured nonstop gum-popping, macaroni and cheese, and the special moniker reserved for her by her tough-cookie tutee: "Shithead."[37]

Looking back, however, Glyn remembered above all else Bow's leonine courage: on location out in the Pacific for the movie version of *It*, shooting a shipwreck scene on a cold day when the shark-infested seas were too high, she watched "The 'It' Girl," who had barely learned to swim, laugh off the stunt double and plunge cheerfully over the side. Nor did Bow ever hesitate to seduce the

Fig. 6. Funeral procession of Diana, Princess of
Wales, 1997, © Getty Images.

men she wanted or apologize for her success in doing so, and Glyn
respected her for that too, rather like something she might have
encountered in the pages of Pepys or, with more demure diction,
in her own novels, where self-assured women politely but decisively
take charge of their erotic fates. Like Steele at Betterton's funeral,
Glyn recalled the actress as having done in life the very deeds she
enacted in representation, and at the end of the day, both women
made their own livings by their talents and their looks, and both
earned enough to well afford the men they supported. Glyn also
believed that Bow's true emotional range was never really tested by
the sexy little comedies in which she was invariably cast. Behind
Bow's freakishly big eyes and brittle laugh, the novelist saw a sor-
row that spoke of the special kind of loneliness peculiar to the age
of public intimacy, when an actress or even a princess might plausibly come to the conclusion that she can belong to the world but
not to anything or anyone else in it (fig. 6).

Glyn rehearsed similarly melancholy and yet elevated thoughts in remembering the state funeral of Queen Victoria in 1901. The three things that struck Glyn most forcefully were first, the tremendous emotion expressed in silence by the bereaved, adoring crowds; second, the resolute fortitude of the men, some of them quite elderly, who followed the gun carriage on foot for the entirety of its long journey; and, finally, the diminutive size, measured against the vast panoply of nation and empire, of "the little, little coffin." At the memory of her sight of this ultimate accessory object, Glyn's thoughts turned again to the irrational but irresistible paradox of the queen's two bodies, the body natural and the body politic, and the visible role that the former plays in creating the invisible dream-works of the latter. In death, her effigy could not have been more lifelike: "This reminder of the smallness, the feminine frailty, of the greatest ruler in the world, brought home to me for the first time the glorious romance of the British Empire, and the greatness of the British race. A sublime spirit of chivalry must be innate in a people whose highest response of loyalty and valour is always made to its Queens."[38] This is Bagehot's "visible government" quaintly working its magic the old-fashioned way, but a century later the anonymous producers of mass spectacle on a global scale continue to take their cue from its elementary but effective prestidigitation: now you see It—hocus-pocus—now you don't.

# 2.

## clothes

For me there was a positive intoxication in taking yards of shimmering silks, laces airy as gossamer, and lengths of ribbons, delicate and rainbow-colored, and fashioning of them garments so lovely that they might have been worn by some princess in a fairy-tale.

—"Lucile"

Posterity interprets the lives of notables in the long eighteenth century in many different and sometimes contentious ways, but everyone can agree that they wore fabulous clothes. Men shared fully in the glamorous bounty, for most of the period falls before the full imposition of what one influential fashion historian has called "the Great Masculine Renunciation."[1] Among other abjurations, they bid adieu to embroidered waistcoats, lace jabots, and exciting colors. In *Men in Black* (1995), John Harvey describes the aggressive metastasis of invisibility that spread from clerical and judicial garments and mourning suits to male attire generally in the nineteenth century, when black became "the colour with which one buried oneself—the colour that, having no colour, effaced and took one's self away."[2] The long-term consequence of this dreary revolution is a far greater uniformity of men's attire and, except in specialized cases, a craven surrender of the most expressive uses of clothing to women. The retention of stylish costumes for all—men and women, rich and poor—in carnival festivity demonstrates by contrast what modern men of different classes and ethnicities have generally resigned to history. Tradition also makes certain exemptions available to men in special categories of role-icon—fops, pimps, rakes, pirates, and gangsters—but important as these specialties are, and they will figure prominently in what follows in this and subsequent chapters, they remain colorful anomalies highlighted against a boring field of black, gray, navy, and brown.

As historic specimens of material culture, the spectacular clothes worn by the effigy of Charles II in the Norman Undercroft of Westminster Abbey likewise confirm by contrast the scope of the loss imposed by the great renunciation. In life they were his personal Garter robes, betokening his office at the head of the Most Noble Order of the Garter, the highest order of knighthood in Great Britain, which took its name and its motto from a legendary incident in the reign of its medieval founder: when a garter worn by Joan, Countess of Salisbury, fell to the floor while she danced with Edward III, the king silenced the snickering courtiers by gallantly picking up the wayward item and by binding it round his own knee, remarking "Honi soit qui mal y pense," or "Evil to him who evil thinks." The tradition thus invented in a moment of public intimacy in 1349 burgeoned conspicuously under the easygoing Charles, when the king and some of his knights even began wearing their robes casually around town, scandalizing Samuel Pepys: "Whereas heretofore their Robes were only to be worn during their ceremonies and service, these, as proud of their coats, did wear them all day till night, and then rode into the park with them on." Pepys deplores the loss of "all gravity" among the knights even as he envies the smashing outfits (8:184–85).

The Garter robes, therefore, must have seemed apposite to the original dressers who costumed the famously accessible monarch's effigy. Working from the canvas skin out, they began very intimately indeed, with the royal underpants, a pair of white silk drawers (fig. 7). As decades or centuries would pass between changes of Charles's linen, only the curatorial experts, successors to the courtiers who personally attended him at his daily *levée* while he lived, can be privy to what the Defender of the Faith wears by way of foundations in perpetuity. But the original artisans clearly wanted the simulacrum of the king's person to be as complete as possible, even the bits that were to remain out of sight. They sewed stockings of bluish-white silk to the drawers. These remain partially visible on the fully dressed effigy. The undergarments are covered by the breeches and a doublet, made from cloth of silver with silver thread and silver bobbin lace, which opens at the neck to reveal a ruffled shirt of white linen, topped off with a cravat (the latter a modern restoration using antique lace). The doublet necessarily follows the English style officially set by Charles in 1661 as an intervention in the excessive reliance on fashions imported from France. A dark blue silk velvet mantle with a standing collar, a red silk velvet surcoat, and red silk velvet hood hang open over the doublet, completing the ensemble except for the missing accessories, which unfortunately include the badge of St. George and other Garter paraphernalia. The napped leather footwear, matching the stockings in color—that is, blue suede shoes—flaunts ribbons for ties, not workaday buckles.[3] The result is very theatrical and much more colorfully personal than a sculpture, for here the clothes literally do make the man.

Concurrent with the rise of synthetic experience but before the great renunciation, the Restoration stage became a site for the wider publicity of fashionable apparel and its uses for men. As a theatrical relic of that time, when sartorial splendor was still normatively hypermasculine, the exchange between Young Bellair, the sympathetic inamorato, and Dorimant, the rake-hero of Etherege's *Man of Mode,* instructively dramatizes the way of the world before the Flood:

> YOUNG BELLAIR. That's a mighty pretty suit of yours, Dorimant.
>
> DORIMANT. I am glad 't has your approbation.

Granted, Dorimant declines to gild the lily by speaking the names of designer labels out loud, as his overdressed foil Sir Fopling does, but he clearly knows what's important to him and why: "I love to be well-dressed, Sir; and think it no scandal to my understanding" (1.1; *BA* 534). At a time when the word *effeminacy* referred to any kind of preoccupation with women, including an

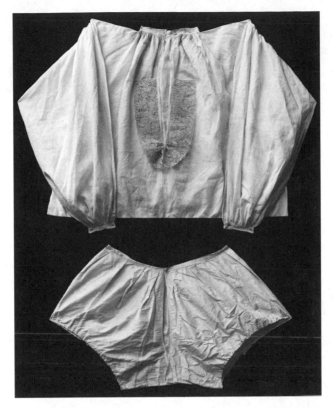

Fig. 7. From the funeral effigy of Charles II, 1685, shirt and drawers.
© V & A Images and Chapter of Westminster Abbey.

excessive desire for them, the playwright juxtaposes and even over-
lays the role-icons of "rake" and "fop."

Etherege explicitly underscores the point by setting the first
scene of *The Man of Mode* in the hero's dressing room, with his
"clothes laid ready" to be put on at leisure as he receives the visits
of his friends and specialist vendors of fruit and shoes. They all
come to *him,* as to a sovereign, and the exposition leaves no doubt
that he has the principal attraction of It, the privileged gift of public intimacy. As Dorimant begins to change out of his "gown and
slippers" and into the ensemble that his young friend admires, cor-
roborating testimony to his prowess accumulates: the audience

learns, for instance, that his list of lovers is currently headed by Loveit, Etherege's aptly named antitype to Southerne's unaccommodated Widow Lackit and Congreve's nostalgic Lady Wishfort. In the course of the scene, which takes up the entirety of the first act, Dorimant completes his "toilet," assisted by his servant, Handy, as a well-attended knight dons armor to do battle. Master and squire thereby mimic the contemporary court ritual of the royal *levée,* the daily ceremonial enrobing of the monarch, in which twelve Gentlemen of the Bedchamber, all of them of high rank, seconded by twelve Grooms of the Bedchamber, men of lesser rank but good connections, took turns handing the king articles of clothing as he dressed for the day. The ritual of putting on clothes did important work to charm the body of the principal as he metamorphosed from private man to public figure. In *The Man of Mode,* the squire must patiently remind his master, who has momentarily rebelled against the necessary ministrations, of the efficacy of the rite: "You love to have your clothes hang just, Sir" (*BA* 534).

Just *so,* Handy might have said. It is true that full-dress military uniforms have partially offset the historic trend toward mediocrity in male attire, but only for those who want to be soldiers, a considerable imposition merely to escape the drab tyranny of the sack suit. Drag is all well and good as far it goes, but the bigoted reception of its performances limits its provisional extension of the franchise.[4] On the one hand, thoughtful critics now understand that the blandness of their dress allows most men to camouflage themselves in the gender wars, thus better to remain, in Peggy Phelan's eye-opening phrase, "unmarked": wearing black, men abjure color but accrue power.[5] On the other hand, less subtle thinkers continue to gloat over the apparent narrowing of rights and privileges imposed by the epochal renunciation. They extol an eloquent rhetoric of fashion, once available to all genders, now spoken fluently only by the lucky ones.

These couture triumphalists field no better-informed spokesperson than Elinor Glyn's elder sister Lucy, Lady Duff-Gordon, the oracular dressmaker "Lucile." Self-proclaimed inventor of "mannequin parades" (runway shows) and the brassiere, she compares her art to depth psychology, which, like Freud's, seeks to educe the disavowed personality of the female subject, but with more tangible and therapeutically beneficial results. "No man," she wrote, "can possibly realize how women are influenced by the clothes they wear." The right gown, she averred, might tease out a version of the It-Effect from even the most unpromising circumstances, transforming neurosis into ordinary human vanity: "Put even the plainest woman into a beautiful dress and unconsciously she will try to live up to it. It is as if for her the designer has created a new personality; her every movement reflects increased self-confidence, a new joy of living."[6] Referring to herself in the third person under her own brand name, Lady Duff-Gordon elaborated on her philosophy, which posits smart clothing, especially the one-of-a-kind "Personality Dresses" and "Gowns of Emotion" in which she specialized, as a repertoire of speech acts, suited to the ethos of the speaker and the pathos of the occasion: "Lucile believes that gowns may express ideas from grave to gay, even emotions and passions. So she has gone to the silent world of desires and temperaments and sensations and translates their secrets into wondrous colors and entrancing forms."[7] Even if fabulous clothes somehow don't add up to the complete language that Roland Barthes claimed for them in *Système de la Mode*,[8] Lucile knew from girlhood that they do make statements. Indeed, they can even make the kind of statements that make things happen. In those instances, they are not mere objects, but rather provocations to enact behaviors or initiate social processes. They *perform,* in a word, and by performing they carry the charismatic potential to turn personalities into events, events into occasions, and occasions into precedents.

This is magic, a physical reenchantment of the social world by means of casting local spells. Clothes can charm the body they adorn, as when, in the practice of witchcraft, the fitting of a garment to an effigy charms the doll and turns it into a powerful idol. Perhaps part of the uncanny allure of fashionable clothing resides in the paradoxical impact of its expressiveness: the act of covering someone up with mere dead matter—cloth, fur, leather, or even metal when it is ingeniously shaped to the purpose—appears to reveal something magical about the life inside. In that expectation, Lucile gave each of her creations a "romantic" name. A soft gray chiffon wrap that veiled an underdress of pink and violet taffeta became, for example "The Sighing Sounds of Lips Unsatisfied." Another, gathering thirty yards of gauze around the hem, debuted as "Love in a Mist." The effigy equivocates, however, because in the beguiling experience of its charm there grows a malignancy of resentment, perhaps rooted in envy of its tangible effects, in fear of its intangible ones, or most likely in some combination of both, hovering ambivalently on the cusp of attraction and aversion. In that spirit, Lucile accepted a commission for one her "Gowns of Emotion," this one daringly draped in scarlet satin, named by the man who was paying the bills for the woman who would wear it for him: "Red Mouth of a Venomous Flower."9

In this context clothes reveal the double-edged nature of the It-Effect in the reception of two nominated role-icons. Despite their obvious differences and separation by two hundred years of social history, their similar fates link the past to contemporary popular culture by passing their images through the moral filter of nineteenth-century publicity: they are the Edwardian "beauty," Lillie Langtry, and the Restoration "rake," Buckingham. In each case, the endurance of the afterimage in cultural memory, like the haunting of Westminster Abbey by its funeral effigies, depends in part on the way in which the icon has been clothed and unclothed. *Clothing* in this usage functions as both noun and verb, as prop and performance, engaging in a double action, each part of which recalls the other as object and subject, which oscillate, adoringly or punitively, between glamour and abjection, *charismata* and *stigmata*. Lest the cultural and social functions of the nominated role-icon seem arcane, let it be recalled that the most ubiquitously available effigy in the late twentieth century, "Barbie," whose global popularity continues undiminished, is also the symbolic object most likely to be made the victim of maimings, burnings, and amputations by the same little hands, overstimulated and vengeful, that lovingly dress her in fabulous clothes.10 To nominate a role-icon is, compellingly, to curse it; and at the same time, but with even more inchoate anger, to curse It.

As a child prodigy designing outfits for her dolls, methodically dressing them up and undressing them and then dressing them yet again, the future couturiere Lucile discovered how clothes not only express but also actively create a persona through the selective revelation or installation of "desires and temperaments and sensations" in the wearer's own mind and in the minds of her beholders. Confirmation of her epiphany came to her in a Pauline encounter with angelic celebrity, when she sought out and found her first real-life doll, one so gorgeously dressed and radiantly animated as to embody the fully blown It-Effect. The fateful meeting happened in part by chance, but mostly by design. Raised on Jersey, Lucy, along with her younger and even more highly impressionable sister, once overheard their parents talking in awed tones about the likely appearance of a famous local beauty at a reception to be given by the governor of that island in honor of her triumphant return home. "It was almost like the arrival of a queen," Lucy recalled of the much-heralded entry.[11]

This demi-royal visitor was, of course, the stunning "Jersey Lily," Lillie Langtry, née Emilie Charlotte Le Breton (1853–1929). In their memoirs, both Lucy, Lady Duff-Gordon, and Elinor Glyn recount their meeting with this auratic celebrity, who would soon transfix the world by becoming the mistress of the Prince of Wales and then truly shock it by going on the stage. The sisters agree on the salient facts of the encounter; they differ on a few small but telling details. Disputed by neither is the importance of the event to both of them as women and as artists. Fascinated by the buzz among all the adults around them, the girls resolved to have a look at Mrs. Langtry in person. They left their dolls in bed at home, snuck under cover of darkness undetected into nearby Government House, and concealed themselves under a muslin-draped dressing-table in the anteroom where the ladies removed their wraps and prepared themselves to be announced at the ball. Their prey entered last of the all the guests and very late, as was her wont, but she did not in any way disappoint her stalkers. Peering out from a peephole, not daring to move and barely allowing themselves to breathe, the future transatlantic tastemakers had their first and probably their most formative encounter with It. Lucy recollected:

I never saw any woman more divinely lovely than [Lillie Langtry] looked in her white dress, with a scarlet flower in her hair nestling against one ear. She came and sat down at the dressing table while she arranged her dress and pinned a beautiful diamond brooch on one shoulder. We were so close to her that we dared not move one inch, for fear of touching her dress and giving away the secret of our presence, but even through the folds of the muslin curtain we could see her perfect beauty. There was an extraordinary radiance about Lily [sic] Langtry that I have never seen in any other woman, and there was something so vital and magnetic in her personality that a room seemed empty when she left it.[12]

The filling up and emptying out of rooms are frequently remarked illusions that accompany the entrances and exits of those who have It. So are the complementary but opposite perceptions of radiance and magnetism. But the crux of Lucile's argument is that duly accessorized clothing gives material shape and emphasis to the flesh that unleashes these apparently metaphysical forces, whose preternatural effects sensitive temperaments don't soon forget, even though they might register them differently.

Elinor also remembered the gown—"a white corded silk dress, with a tight bodice and a puffed up bustle at the back"—but at the same time she recalled with the poignancy of sensation the celebrity's gracious response to the surprise of her ambush by a pair of prepubescent gate-crashers up way past their bedtimes and literally underfoot. Lucy, the designer, who focused her memory entirely on the image of the fashion plate, omitted the detail that their irrepressible giggles gave the girls away, a gap in the narrative remedied by the novelist Elinor, who added that rather than being cross or curt, the great beauty "merely laughed and pulled us out, promising not to give us away." Lillie Langtry behaved, in other words, as beautifully as she dressed, cheerily arranging for the girls to share surreptitiously in the party treats. As the romance author reminisced a lifetime later, reflecting on her childhood glimpse of an apparition that vanished as magically as it had appeared, "I can see her now as she went down the stairs, her wonderfully blue eyes smiling as she kissed her hand to us."[13] It's miraculous. As the room emptied of her vital presence, two very different imaginations filled with her memory. The vivid detail of those impressions remained whether this episode of unauthorized public intimacy happened exactly the way the memoirists said it did or not. "Kind and sweet," Elinor thought, the music of the Jersey Lily's laughter was like a perfume, the *idea* of her lingering, a souvenir for the self-replenishing senses.

Let the trace left behind by the It-Effect be called the *afterimage*. This does not exist as an object, but rather as a sensation that persists even after the external stimulation that caused it has disappeared, like the shape of a flame that lingers in the eye after the candle has gone out. The afterimage appears and endures as the effect of the contrast between light and dark—in the moral as well as the physical sense. "Shades more sweetly recommend the Light," as Pope puts it in an elaboration of the passage in *An Essay on Criticism* about "the Image of our Minds."[14] That is so because the attraction generated by the It-Effect generates an opposing force, its nemesis, no less magical, equally irresistible, and just as crucial to the definition and durability of the image. Whether this darkness originates in an animus projected on the notable figure by the public or in the inevitable exposure of his or her human imperfections to scrutiny and judgment cannot always or even often be known for certain and matters little in the end. What is certain and what does matter is that notoriety inexorably shadows celebrity, as obloquy and abjection wait with predatory patience for the light of glamour to fail in the careers of modern secular idols.

The insidious way in which notoriety stalks modern celebrity appears even in the sisters' charming reminiscences of Lillie Langtry. Both of them, but especially Elinor, turn on her, despite or because of the beauty of her dress, switching their attention from *charismata* to *stigmata* with remarkable alacrity. Lucy was unusual among contemporary and subsequent commentators in omitting from her account explicit mention of the scandal by which Mrs. Langtry is most commonly remembered, cattily choosing instead to link her glamorous clothing and risqué behavior in the thrill of gossipy insinuation: "We were always hearing of what she had worn at the opera, of how she had set the new fashion in hats, and of how often the Prince of Wales had danced with her at the Devonshire House ball."[15] She deferred her final judgment of the beauty to a later chapter of her memoir.

Elinor employed no such circumspection. The future marketer of Clara Bow spoke with severity about the role-icon of "actress," reminding the reader of *Romantic Adventure* that it was at about this time in her Jersey childhood that she had discovered the *Diary* of Samuel Pepys, who chronicled the progress of the first actresses as concubines. Elinor precociously emerged into adult sexual consciousness at a time when Victorian fascination with the excesses of the Restoration court and stage had reached its apogee, as evidenced by stage histories and new editions of the raciest plays, stimulated by Edmund Gosse's 1881 *Cornhill Magazine* article on Etherege. The most memorable appointment of the house in which the sisters grew up was that old Lely portrait of a female sitter, perhaps a knockoff of one of his "beauties," and thus coded, in the late-nineteenth-century scheme of attribution and censure of seventeenth-century glamour, as Cyprian. Role-icons congeal into stubborn expectations. They make even more insistent memories. Observing that "to become a professional actress still entailed an entire loss of caste for any woman of good family," the memoirist rounded out her child's eye view of the star's radiant presence by concluding that "there were plenty of scandals whispered about the 'Jersey Lily,'" the salient one being that she was even then in criminal conversation with the future King Edward VII. Elinor's plummy disclaimer—"But my sister and I would never listen to anything but good of our heroine"—simply draws invidious attention to the other kinds of things people were saying.[16] In the flower symbolism of Lillie's fashionable ensemble, the red rose of passion stigmatized but did not erase the charisma of her lily-white gown, which impressed the girls as exemplary in both its loveliness and its irony. Less abstract than reputation, more fragile than character, and yet always related in some way to both those complex bundles of general association, the ambivalent afterimage of the It-Effect provides the marker under which the public identity of the notable circulates, for better *and* worse.

Likewise, let dishabille or public seminudity, the formal juxtaposition of fabric and flesh, signify the contradictions of the after-image. Nothing intensifies interest in clothes—or in the person wearing them—quite like putting them on or taking them off. The sisters caught Lillie in the act of removing her cloak and fixing her brooch. This enhanced their guilty pleasure. It did so because the act of dressing and undressing transforms clothes into properties and images into actions on the stage of public intimacy. They coalesce into behaviors that invite a play on the word *habit,* which can refer either to garments characteristic of a certain calling, such as the ones that nuns wear, or to an acquired manner of repeating oneself. Habits of both kinds are very informative to observers, but they can work most expressively in ensemble, when the clothes being put on or taken off are those that distinguish a calling in life or a special identity.

"Striptease is identified with a *career,*" Roland Barthes emphasizes in a classic essay on the subject, digressing momentarily on clubs that feature amateur competitions, "and above all, the competitors are socially situated: one is a salesgirl, another a secretary."[17] Striptease is identified with a career because through it the performer can either perpetuate or create a role-icon. A testament to the structural efficacy of the actions of dressing and undressing in this creation is their reversibility: in a popular variant of the genre, the stripper starts completely naked and puts on her clothes as the raison d'être of the dance, typically exiting the dais fully dressed in a tailored business suit, accessorized by eyeglasses, briefcase, and sensible shoes. The point is not mere nudity, then, but enacting the public intimacy of one role-icon, "the professional woman," which in some respects descends genealogically from another, "the actress," by insisting that garments are properties in a spectacle of which flesh is the inciting incident but not the denouement: "Meet the New Boss." The mythologizing scenario of the modern backward striptease thus corresponds structurally with the seventeenth-century royal *levée.* They are both reversible rites of enchantment, and they both assert the identity of the role-icon by the performance of *habits*. It's sorcery: the act of ritualized dressing charms the idol, which may then be despised no less intensely than it is desired.

From 1915 to 1921, Lady Duff-Gordon revolutionized the showbiz pantheon of high-end seminudity, Florenz Ziegfeld's *Follies*, by introducing the "showgirl" there. The showgirl modeled haute couture gowns as she paraded across the stage doing the "Ziegfeld Walk," pelvis forward, shoulder lifted, and gait measured. In contrast to the lot of the chorus girl or "chicken," the Ziegfeld showgirl's role was to be an "A-team" icon, defined by the clothes she put on, not those she took off. Lucile worked extensively in chiffon, however, with wispy foundations or none at all, and so the degree of that distinction depended on stage designer Joseph Urban's light plot.[18] Ziegfeld had attended one of the famous "mannequin parades" performed by "Lucile's mysterious beauties," as Lady Duff-Gordon's runway models in London and Paris were known. Enchanted, the producer proposed to bring the whole show to New York. "But they do not know how to sing or dance, let alone talk," the couturiere cautioned. Ziegfeld replied that all they needed to know was how to walk in Lucile's clothes and smile.[19] The resulting sensation propelled the former typist Kathleen Mary Rose Wilkinson, the greatest "beauty" among Lucile's live mannequins, into major stardom as the nominated role-icon "Dolores." Her statuesque type long outlived her *Follies* appearances through its absorption into Hollywood musicals, featuring majestically beplumed descents down long staircases, and eventually, sans couture, into Vegas-style revues.

Elegant in white, Dolores "ghosted" another beauty. Following the wild success of Lucile's "Empress of Fashion" show for Ziegfeld in 1916, Lillie Langtry came to Lucile's New York studio full of adulation, shopping for a gown like those everyone was raving about. The encounter was extremely awkward, painfully so in contrast to the memory of their first meeting decades before. "I looked at her," Lucy recalls, "and wondered what in the world I could say to dissuade her from having the last dress she ought to wear." The Ziegfeld showgirls were all weighed every week and forbidden to gain even half a pound. "I told her as tactfully as I could," Lucy continues, that the style of dress after which she had inquired was "intended for someone very slim." Whether Lucile's response counted among any of the possible meanings of the word *tact,* what the dressmaker then chose to share with her readers, recounting the occasion when the former beauty, "who belonged to another generation," insisted on and finally was fitted for a Lucile frock, seems almost punitively cruel: "When it was finished she put it on and stood before the glass. I saw the tears were running down her cheeks. 'It makes me look so old,' she said with a smile that was somehow infinitely pathetic."[20] Although the story didn't stay in the fitting room, as it should have, the dress did, and the Jersey Lily never asked for another.

Exactly one hundred years earlier, on the occasion of Mrs. Siddons ill-advised and abortive comeback, Hazlitt had noted that quite beyond celebrities thinking themselves immortal, their adoring fans also wish to imagine them so, but not necessarily because they wish them well. The image that circulates in their name, the one that exists in the minds of their fans and the public at large, builds up a static charge of resentment attributable to the friction caused by its popular mobility. Easily visible everywhere but securely locatable nowhere, It in the fullness of time will inevitably disappoint those who require its perfection *and* its availability, its publicity *and* its intimacy. Under these circumstances, the celebrated image generates an animus of potential aggression not unlike the one described by Sir James Frazer in *The Golden Bough* (1913), when he speaks of sympathetic magic operating through a charm that represents an absent person. He sets his ideas down tendentiously as the "Law of Similarity," whereby like produces like, but his data evince a variety of roughly analogous practices in many different cultures, both historically and ethnographically evoked, that recur willy-nilly under a loosely organizing principle of homeopathic or imitative magic. The charm may be benign, constructed and activated to aid the absent party or to secure his or her happiness at a distance, but more typically and memorably it is anything but:

> Perhaps the most familiar application of the principle that like produces like is the attempt which has been made by many peoples in many ages to injure or destroy an enemy by injuring or destroying an image of him, in the belief that, just as the image suffers, so does the man, that when it perishes he must die.[21]

In *The Power of Images,* David Freedberg produces a number of harrowing illustrations of tortured icons to vivify Frazer's account of this ancient and enduring practice known as *envoûtement.*[22] A so-called Law of Contact or Contagion complements the Frazerian Law of Similarity as the exercise of *envoûtement* through techniques that some people still call "voodoo." This second law accounts for the familiar idea that dressing up the image in clothes associated with the person increases the efficacy of its magic. The charm might be a painted image or an amulet, but more often it takes the form of a doll made from some malleable substance like lead, wax, or straw.

The men who dressed King Charles II every morning, enjoying intimate access to his person but ever resentful of the insecurity of their claims on his fugitive affections, practiced a form of *envoûtement.* The stakes were high, as the body of the king was putatively sacred, a theory that had to be credited as a sociopolitical fact, if not as a religious one, for while he was being dressed, the king was available to be asked favors or to hear complaints that resembled the supplications of daily prayer. Courtiers competed for the chance to offer a range of valet services to the king, who appeared among them in his body natural. These did not approach in pomp the corresponding rites of obeisance performed by and for Louis XIV, who had a designated peer to hold his chamber pot while it was in use, but they did include walking Charles's beloved spaniels—nominated canine role-icons—and procuring women for him. Taking advantage of such publicly intimate contingencies, the Gentlemen of the Bedchamber sought to influence the king's other and more remote corporeality, his body politic. Success must have crowned their efforts often enough to make them seem worthwhile, for as one of the courtiers notoriously wrote of King Charles:

His Scepter and his prick are of a length;
That she may sway the one who plays with t'other.[23]

The contempt with which he was often regarded and sometimes openly treated still shocks readers today, as much as or more than the promiscuous behavior that motivated the derision. He surrounded himself with men of similar tastes and proclivities, men who knew his vices and found them degrading, but also worthy of emulation. The human vulnerabilities they shared made them despise him, as the ancient powers of his office, real and magical, gave them reason to be reverent and afraid. Modern public intimacy has no more evocative progenitor than this particular king's two bodies, and his clothes played a crucial part in punctuating the symbolic highlights of his reign. In 1660, the brilliant raiment that he and his courtiers wore on their sun-drenched triumphal entry into London dazzled the eyes of Samuel Pepys: "So glorious was the show with gold and silver, that we were not able to look at it— our eyes at last being so much overcome with it" (2:83). In 1685, the clothes on his funeral effigy marked his exit with an exclamation point, one that is still here to be seen, as big as life. That these garments once touched warm flesh adds a frisson of the privileged sort, palpable across time, that the Gentlemen of the Bedchamber must have felt now and then as they handed the king—king "by Grace of God of England, Scotland, and Ireland"—his shirt.

No less a luminary than George Villiers, 2nd Duke of Buckingham (1628–1687), the highest-ranking nonroyal peer of the realm, served King Charles II in this personal and self-interested way. The history of public intimacy knows few relationships more exquisitely vexed than theirs. Orphaned as an infant by the assassination of his father, the second duke was raised in the household of Charles I on an equal footing with the royal children, including the future heirs to the throne. This experience added a lifetime of competitive brotherly resentments and obligations to an already complicated dynastic relationship that would prove dangerous enough even without the aggravations of sibling rivalry between two high-born sons of murdered fathers. As sanguine and mercurial as Charles II was phlegmatic and saturnine, Buckingham nev-

ertheless shared many of the king's vices, including a sexual surplus and an attention deficit, without, apparently, ever learning
anything useful from his lord and rival's underlying tenacity and
long-term guile. Variously a devotee to chemistry, stringed musical
instruments, and drama; periodic holder of a number of important offices, military, political, and diplomatic; infamous carouser
and spendthrift; party to the most scandalous act of adultery of the
age, his open cohabitation with Anna Maria Talbot, Countess of
Shrewsbury, the longtime lover whose husband he killed in a duel;
twice a defendant on charges of high treason, and again for
sodomy; the Restoration's greatest clotheshorse, Buckingham did
much on his own pulses to guarantee the notoriety of his afterimage. But he did not work on this extensive project alone. He was
assisted during his own time and in later ones by poets, poetasters,
and painters; and the story of how his role-icon of "rake" became a
self-fulfilling historic prophecy sheds light on the modern It-Effect
and its discontents.

Those most often remembered as "rakes" were more likely to
have thought of themselves as "wits." Intellectuals prefer to call
them "Libertines." Historical personages, such as Buckingham,
have been named as belonging to this role-icon, as have characters
on the Restoration stage, such as Dorimant. Buckingham is usually
joined in the first category by Sir George Etherege; Charles
Sackville, Lord Buckhurst (later, Earl of Dorset); Sir Charles Sed-
ley; and John Wilmot, Earl of Rochester, as members of Charles
II's "merry gang." Representative stage "rakes" include but are not
limited to the legendary Don John in Thomas Shadwell's *The Libertine* (1675), Horner in William Wycherley's *The Country Wife*
(1675), Wilmore in Aphra Behn's *The Rover* (1677), and the nom-
inated-role-icon founder Lothario from Nicholas Rowe's *The Fair
Penitent* (1703).[24] Whatever their personal excesses, the historic
"rakes" all cut literary or theatrical figures, and Buckingham's
most celebrated contribution to their collected works, *The
Rehearsal* (1671), in which he and his collaborators burlesqued
contemporary heroic tragedy, held the stage for the next century.
What the diverse lot of stage characters had in common, a will to
pleasure and power, both philosophical and pragmatic, judicious

and vicious, descends to us filtered through Lamb's gauzy "Utopia of Gallantry," where pleasure was duty, countered by Thomas Babbington Macaulay's veil-rending riposte that the fantasy of abdicated moral duty represented in the plays was all too accurate a reflection of the reality of Restoration society.

As the Victorians excel all other narrators in their elaboration of the human failings of Restoration celebrities, they outdid themselves on the subject of Buckingham's bad habits. His very versatility counted against him as a sign of unreliability. Macaulay waxes eloquent on the duke's character and conduct in the 1660s, when "the immorality which was epidemic among the politicians of that age appeared in its most malignant type":

> Buckingham was a sated man of pleasure, who had turned to ambition as to a pastime. As he had tried to amuse himself with architecture and music, with writing farces and with seeking for the philosopher's stone, so he now tried to amuse himself with a secret negotiation and a Dutch war. He had already, rather than from fickleness and love of novelty than from any deep design, been faithless to every party. At one time he had ranked among the Cavaliers. At another time warrants had been out against him for maintaining a treasonable correspondence with the remains of the Republican party in the city. He was now again a courtier, and was eager to win the favor of the King by services from which the most illustrious of those who had fought and suffered for the royal house would have recoiled with horror.[25]

The historian's Parthian shot alludes to the fact that in his service as a Gentleman of the Bedchamber, Buckingham pimped for Charles with the same savoir faire that he showed in dressing him.[26] He was also, to the king's delight, a spot-on mimic, whose specialty was mock-sermonizing in the style of different religious denominations. Carousing together, they both stood for the prose portrait of Buckingham penned by Samuel Butler: "He was as inconstant as the Moon, which he lives under."[27] But for all the debauched amusements they shared, in the light of day they found each other contemptible, and they acted on these sentiments when opportunities arose. By appealing skillfully to his vanity, for instance, the king duped Buckingham, sending him to France on a fool's errand to negotiate an elaborate public treaty with Louis XIV while the real plenipotentiaries concluded the secret Treaty of Dover on very different terms. Buckingham's seditious ridicule of Charles and his brother the Duke of York got him into deep trouble on more than one occasion, the kind of trouble that his distant but plausible claim on the throne as a Plantagenet scion did nothing to allay and that the Tower of London was kept in good repair to remedy.

A lifetime of finding himself in and out of favor, in and out of office, and in and out of jail made Buckingham cautiously fatalistic. His long-term goal, from which, despite his imputed capriciousness, he never wavered, even in the face of repeated political defeats and eventual ostracism, was to establish freedom of conscience in matters of religion. From the perspective of later times, such a latitudinarian conviction may seem unremarkable; from the perspective of his own, it made Buckingham seem even more eccentric than he already was in the eyes of many and dangerously subversive in the eyes of some. Active in the early formation of Whig politics, Buckingham tried to introduce bills for religious indulgence into Parliament in 1663, 1667, 1672, and 1675. His late essay "A Short Discourse upon the Reasonableness of Men's Having a Religion" (1685) poses its crucial question boldly: "Whether there be anything more directly opposite to the Doctrine and Practice of Jesus Christ, than to use any kind of Force upon Men, in matters of Religion?"[28] In this enlightened cause, he had a skilled polemical ally in the poet Andrew Marvell, who joined the fray over religious toleration with *The Rehearsal Transpros'd* (1672), in which he deployed Buckingham's strategy of burlesque, ridiculing his rigidly pious adversary, Dr. Samuel Parker, by making him look as silly in his own way as "Bayes," the obsessive-compulsive playwright figure in *The Rehearsal.* Buckingham's political career ended for good during the power struggle that ensued from the Exclusion Crisis, in which the sectarian factions had pushed the nation perilously close to civil war over the succession of the Catholic Duke of York as James II and after which the Whigs were temporarily but decisively the losers.

If little of this seems especially apropos to Buckingham's character as a "rake," that is not at all surprising. The genesis of a role-icon requires not the exposition of nuanced positions, in which the shades of gray are duly rendered, but rather the vivid flash of lurid details. Some might say that only the former belongs to proper history; the latter to gossipy memory. The fact is, however, that outside a circle of hyperspecialists on any given topic and sometimes even within it, memory is history, stubbornly ensconced in the popular imagination through the success of eye-catching images or pulse-quickening narrations, salting the record with research-defying anecdotes. The most sharply affecting memorial details from the life of the staged role-icon that was George Villiers, 2nd Duke of Buckingham, concern his clothing. For the coronation of Charles II, an ordinarily reliable biographer reports, the duke spent "£30,000 on his equipage—a sum likely enough when men outdid women in jewels, feathers, and finery."[29] That sum hardly seems likely at all, even before the great male renunciation and even allowing for the notorious wastrel's rapid progress through his fortune, but since relative monetary values are difficult to assess across time, a glimpse into Buckingham's contemporary accounts is instructive: once, in the same week, he paid thirteen pounds to "Gallamoy for a periwig" and settled a salary payment in arrears to "Edward Jones running porter for two years wages and three quarters in full £10."[30] Such a contrast in value between a commodity and labor certainly suggests one good reason why a well-dressed gentleman turned heads, prompting fantastic stories to circulate.

The most vivid anecdote concerning Buckingham's clothing, however, has little to do with fashion, and it involves the expenditure of blood, not money. His biographers, notably the exceptionally proficient Edwardian amateur Winifred Burghclere, cannot resist the melodrama attached to Buckingham's fatal duel with the Earl of Shrewsbury, his mistress's long-suffering husband. "According to Lord Peterborough," Burghclere relates, "the miserable woman, who was the cause of the catastrophe, watched the butchery, disguised as a page, and holding her lover's horse. Nay more, 'to reward his prowess, she went to him in the shirt stained with her husband's blood.'"[31] Although the breathless narration does not make clear who ended up wearing the bloody shirt—a Victorian version of Burnet exclaims, Buckingham "passed the night with the duchess in the shirt stained by her husband's blood!"—the favored reading of the story puts the garment not on her ladyship, who was in the event busy holding the horse, but on the duke, who, by all accounts, though bleeding from his own wound, ran the hapless cuckold straight through the right lung at close quarters.[32] Whichever lover ended up dressed in the bloody shirt, all versions agree, the act he or she then performed in it involved them both. Like Etherege's naturalistic stage direction in *The Man of Mode*, "Handy tying up linen," which follows Dorimant's deflowering of Bellinda (4.2; *BA* 570), Buckingham's bloody shirt emblemizes an icon, which, like Caesar's red cloak, attracts sensational images and anecdotes to itself as a magnet draws iron filings, whether the nominated figure, the "rake" in this instance, is historic or fictive.

The cataclysm that ends *The Libertine* (1675), Shadwell's Anglicization of the Don Juan legend, fills the stage with "Devils," who drag the still-defiant title character over to the trapdoor stage-center and down to a flaming Hell for all eternity. In Restoration comedy, by contrast, the rake in the end typically gets the richest beauty. Retrograde as Shadwell's revival of medieval staging conventions may seem, dredging up, as he does, the damned hero-villain and divine retribution from the mythopoetic substrate, *The Libertine*'s fifth-act apocalypse actually points the way forward to the later bourgeois construction of the role-icon of "rake." The word *rake* is short for *rakehell*, and in the middle-class morality plays of the eighteenth and nineteenth centuries, the punitive violence of the denouement pitches itself shamelessly to the audience's love of retributive justice, however beguiling the object of their wrath may have appeared to them through the previous five acts. Such a scenario comes with powerful and contradictory expectations: that It will be savored and punished in the same action. As theatrical prologues for William Hogarth's definitive treatment of the moralized "rake" narrative in *A Rake's Progress,* John Gay's glamorous and defiant Macheath barely escapes with a reprieve in *The Beggar's Opera* (1728) only to be summarily gibbeted in *Polly* (1729), while George Barnwell sincerely repents and hangs anyway in George Lillo's *The London Merchant* (1731). The print set of *A Rake's Progress* dates from 1735, etched and engraved from a series of eight paintings completed in the previous year. Hogarth's bathetic tableaux dramatize "Tom Rakewell's" incremental descent from glamour to abjection. His disintegration is both symbolized and embodied by his climbing in and out of elegant clothes and then falling into almost total nakedness—a morally uplifting striptease.

In plate 1, the handsome young legatee is being fitted for a mourning suit in anticipation of his miserly father's funeral. In plate 2, garbed, like Dorimant, in a dressing gown and slippers for his morning reception, Tom receives not his friends, but a crowd of avaricious tradesmen and charlatans, all too eager to strip him of his new fortune. In plate 3, the oft-reproduced orgy scene, a bevy of prostitutes and posture molls (ecdysiasts who danced tabletop sans underwear on highly polished plates) skillfully remove not only their own clothes but also Tom's, beginning with his watch. In plate 4, the rake has dressed himself to the nines, as befits a fashionable beau on his way to try to win back his losses at White's gambling den, but he is being arrested on the street for debt, while at his feet his predicament is both mimicked and foreshadowed by a bare-chested bootblack, who, having gambled away everything but his cap and his pants, is about to lose those on the next throw of the dice. In plate 5, Tom, discovered at church in a wedding suit, attempts to repair his fortunes by marrying an aging widow, who presents herself lasciviously and ill-advisedly décolleté. In plate 6, the profligate gambler, head bare and garments disarrayed, has lost both his second fortune and his wig. Plate 7 finds him in a daze and in Fleet, the debtor's prison, a rejected playscript, his last forlorn attempt to raise money, crumpled at his side. By plate 8, like Shadwell's Don John, he plays the fifth-act denouement of the tragedy he himself has authored, although the

Hell down to which he is dragged is not the traditional eschato-logical one (fig. 8).

The place is Bedlam, fitting locale for Tom's climactic mad scene, which is also a nude scene. Crazed, manacled, and naked, the rake laughs maniacally and claws at his exposed and bleeding skin. A gaping wound in his side suggests a more ambitious attempt at self-mutilation. His ravings titillate two well-dressed female spectators, tourists taking in the attractions of London, of which the famous madhouse was the most popular and the most indescribably lurid in its attestation to the magical appeal of pub-lic intimacy.

With such an intensified punitive scenario attaching itself to the role-icon of "rake," the odds were against Buckingham's afterim-age passing through the eighteenth and nineteenth centuries unmoralized, and it did not. The most widely publicized tribunal was convened by the Victorian artist Augustus Egg, R.A., in *The Life and Death of Buckingham,* two pictures painted between 1853 and 1855. Intended to be displayed together in a single frame as one work, Egg's narrative is Hogarthian in its clarity, but even more economical than *A Rake's Progress* in its means, compressing Hoga-rth's eight-part drama of moral and physical dissolution into two scenes (figs. 9 and 10). These starkly juxtaposed tableaux insist on the contrast of night and day, life and death, superfluity and want, dress and undress. They schematize a life into "before" and "after." Before, Buckingham presides over a well-attended bacchanal in his honor; after, his solitary corpse sprawls unattended across a dirty bed in a meanly furnished room. Before, gilded mirrors fes-toon brocaded wallpaper; after, decaying lath uncovers wattle and straw. Before, the dinner plates are filled with delicacies; after, the sickroom dish is emptied even of its sponge. Before, clothes make the man; after, they unmake him: in life, at night, wax candles and moonlight glamorize the well-dressed revelers as they toast the apparently well-loved grandee, whose flesh glows under a blond periwig, set off by white satin sleeves adorned with threads of gold; in death, the yellow light of day cruelly exposes the tattered gar-ments stripped from the wasted body of the prodigal, whose blue velvet Garter and George now mock his ignoble demise.

Fig. 8. William Hogarth, from *A Rake's Progress,* 1735, Plate VIII (Tom in Bedlam). Private Collection. The Bridgeman Art Library International.

Various identities have been proposed for the other figures seated and standing around the table in *The Life,* in which Egg ironically cites *The Last Supper,* dividing his twelve revelers, as Leonardo divides the twelve Apostles, into four groups of three, arranged more or less symmetrically on either side of the central diner. The Countess of Shrewsbury, his illicit love, bends over the honoree to deliver her toast, her hand holding a glass, but appearing to place a crown on his head, which actually belongs to the fretwork of the chair in which the duke is seated. Behind him and to his right, in the spot where Leonardo places John (or Mary Magdalen, for adherents of revisionist pop Christologies) stands the swarthy king. Black wig above blond, his sovereign gaze comes to rest on the empty site of the spurious crown. His expression is unreadable, but

Fig. 9. Augustus Egg, *The Life Buckingham*, 1853–55.
Yale Center for British Art, Paul Mellon Collection.

clearly not communicative of unalloyed enthusiasm for the success
of Buckingham's star turn among the royal mistresses. The seated
woman in the foreground on the lower left, with her arm on the
back of her chair, turning toward the gentleman with the black
periwig and mustache, is believed to represent Barbara Villiers,
Countess of Castlemaine and Duchess of Cleveland, with her
famously sleepy "bedroom eyes," while the bright-eyed girl looking
up expectantly at the tipsy reveler who teeters on his chair is supposed to be Nell Gwyn. To Gwyn's left, and partially obscured, is
the face of the "famously chubby" Louise de Kéroualle, Duchess of
Portsmouth, rounding out the carnal medley.[33]

Victorian art critics, for whom the moral tone of the Restoration

Fig.10. Augustus Egg, *The Death of Buckingham*, 1853–55.
Yale Center for British Art, Paul Mellon Collection.

was an important touchstone, questioned the nature of the pleasure such images could induce in them. John Ruskin snobbishly
expressed intellectual disappointment: "The figures which sur-
round Buckingham in his riot are not of the class which could have
entertained a man either of wit or breeding."[34] Conceding the
effectiveness of the rendering, the reviewer for *The Spectator* was
nonetheless appalled by the content: "The ghastly dead wretch in
the second compartment of the painting is really almost a relief
rather than otherwise from the leering hardened women of the
first, and the blasé men to whom the orgie has lost every excitement but that of its wickedness."[35] Was Egg staging a morality play
about the wages of sin owed to the exceptionally debauched, crit-

ics wondered, or did he mean for his diptych to reflect more generally on human mortality? "The mind of the painter was too fastidious—too respectable to do justice to the depravity of the orgie," an 1864 reviewer for *The Reader* concluded anticlimactically, while contemplating the more dramatic alternative: "The moral implied, therefore, was on the mutability of human fortunes, rather than the unerring exercise of God's punishment to sinners."[36]

Egg was not too fastidious to have chosen this subject in the first place, however, and the single frame that originally held both paintings featured a border of skulls peering out from underneath bunches of grapes, an iconography that would seem to support the censorious, fire-and-brimstone interpretation of an individually tailored Last Judgment. But for beholders today, who view the pictures without their original frame, literally and figuratively out of context, the lesson of *The Life and Death of Buckingham* seems unequivocal: celebrity sooner or later extracts in abjection what it bestows in glamour. In contrast to the earnest moral vision of mid-Victorians, the postmodern reception aesthetic cannot disavow sartorial schadenfreude: before, the bigwig is on the best-dressed A-list; after, he's history.

Not that such an unbecoming but beguiling sentiment is wholly alien to the past. Alexander Pope, in *The Epistle to Bathhurst*, "On the Uses of Riches" (1733), which was contemporary with *A Rake's Progress*, penned the quotable but historically inaccurate lines that inspired Egg's riches-to-rags mise-en-scène. Augustan poet and Victorian painter alike misrepresented the actual details of Buckingham's death by turning the mundane coincidence that the duke took convenient refuge in a local farmhouse after falling ill while foxhunting on a distant portion of his estate into a denouement of catastrophic prodigality à la Hogarth or Greuze. In Pope's representation of the humble scene of Buckingham's final summons, a fate worse than death awaits the reprobate in the color scheme and fabric treatments:

> In the worst inn's worst room, with mat half-hung,
> The floors of plaister, and the walls of dung,

On once a flock-bed, but repair'd with straw,
With tape-ty'd curtains, never meant to draw,
The George and Garter dangling from that bed
Where tawdry yellow strove with dirty red,
Great Villers lies—alas! how chang'd from him,
That life of pleasure, and that soul of whim![37]

Bringing to mind the probably apocryphal but justly famous last words of Oscar Wilde—"Either this wallpaper goes or I do"— Pope's critique looks backward to the life of Buckingham through the tasteless décor of his death chamber to the indecorous hours he spent sporting in the bedroom at Cliveden with the Countess of Shrewsbury, in the privy chamber conducting no less unsanctioned affairs of state as a member of the "Cabal" of Charles II's ministers, or in the playhouse as the wickedly insouciant topical satirist who wrote part of *The Country Gentleman* and most of *The Rehearsal:*

Gallant and gay, in Cliveden's proud alcove,
The bow'r of wanton Shrewsbury and love;
Or just as gay, at Council, in a ring
Of mimick'd Statesmen, and their Merry King.
No Wit to flatter, left of all his store!
No Fool to laugh at, which he valu'd more.
There, Victor of his health, of fortune, friends,
And fame; this lord of useless thousands ends.[38]

Pope thus conjures the image that Egg dutifully illustrates from a mixture of lurid gossip and unvarnished truth: Buckingham *was* improvident in his dealings with money, women, and politics— failings that he can hardly be said to have monopolized but that his high station and attractive personality rendered peculiarly interesting. The poet's attribution of mimicry, licentiousness, and moral whimsy to the dead celebrity colored an already exaggerated portrait of the kind that rectitude likes to paint of glamour, especially when a dollop of envy tints the palette green.

In his project, the blackening of the afterimage of a complex public man of magnetic attractiveness to his contemporaries, Pope stood on the shoulders of a giant. John Dryden so successfully skewered Buckingham as "Zimri" in *Absalom and Achitophel* (1681) that virtually every subsequent account of the duke's life quotes the damning lines. The satirical indictment covered not only Buckingham's subversive role in fomenting the anarchy of the Exclusion Crisis, but also his across-the-board fecklessness and concupiscence. Well-versed contemporaries knew that the biblical Zimri threatened to bring down the wrath of God on the Israelites by his sexually deviant act of open cohabitation with a "Midianitish woman in the sight of Moses" (Num. 25:6–8). In a culture steeped in tendentious allusion, the evocation of these transgressions hit close enough to Buckingham's flagrant adultery with Lady Shrewsbury that even the victims of the satire could not pretend they didn't know who they were, especially when the inclusion of other identifying traits—Buckingham's mercurial temperament and his enthusiasms for chemistry, fiddle-playing, and faction—cemented the allegory. The biblical and yet Homeric detail that an assassin won the gratitude of the Israelites and the blessings of God by impaling both Zimri and his pregnant mistress with one spear-thrust through their coupled bodies cannot have contributed to the serenity of the erring countess and her politically embattled lover.

Dryden's reference jests at scars that once had felt a real wound. Buckingham's father, in his own time a royal favorite, had been stabbed to death by a religious zealot. Buckingham himself had already survived an assassination attempt in his own household as well as several duels, in which the motives of the challengers combined realpolitik with personal grievances, legitimate and otherwise. Knowing all that, Dryden chose his text with the special intimacy that only learned malice can perfectly inspire:

> Some of their Chiefs were Princes of the Land:
> In the first Rank of these did *Zimri* stand:
> A man so various, that he seemed to be
> Not one, but all Mankind's Epitome.
> Stiff in Opinions, always in the wrong;
> Was everything by starts, and nothing long:

But, in the course of one revolving Moon,
Was Chymist, Fidler, States-Man, and Buffoon:
Then all for Women, Painting, Rhiming, Drinking;
Besides ten thousand freaks that dy'd in thinking.[39]

Unlike Pope, Dryden makes no specific mention of the sexual scandal. He does not even need to name names in order for his readers to catch his drift. The imputation of inconstancy in all matters, large and small, "Not one, but all Mankind's Epitome," adds its insinuating testimony to the solemnity of citing scripture, as if the malediction was somehow sworn on the Bible.

Satire was long believed to have originated in the curse.[40] Cursing is the performance of imprecation, a prayer or invocation expressing the wish that harm will befall someone. A curse succeeds as performance to the extent that it actually does harm someone. Such a threat ought to strike fear not only in those who believe the curse to be magical, rendering it psychically if not otherwise self-fulfilling, but also in those who, however agnostic themselves, know that belief in the magical power of curses is widely shared by others. When sufficient numbers of believers congregate around an imprecation and are joined by those who fear the power of belief, a quorum forms. The damage then arises from the consensus of informed public opinion that damage must have been done, and that if damage has been done, it must somehow have been deserved. That this magic is of a social, not metaphysical variety makes it no less fearsome, for the court of public opinion enforces no rules of evidence and rarely hears appeals.

Satire might thus be imagined as powerfully enchanted, notwithstanding the apparent rationality of its vaunted intention to scourge vice and folly by subjecting them to ridicule. How does the victim protest his or her innocence in the face of derision, especially when an allegorical double stands in for the original under another name or with no name? In this sense, satire might be said to resemble the more sensationalized aspects of the practice of *envoûtement,* in which a charm representing an individual is tortured in his or her stead with malign consequences for the original. Satire similarly creates an effigy of the victim in the form of a

caricature. Traditionally, the immolation of the effigy also consumes the victim corporeally, but in modernized practices another
kind of witchcraft prevails: the harm occurs when the caricature
substitutes itself for the public image of the original. The victim's
character—as malleable as wax, as combustible as straw—is consumed by being tortured into grotesque shapes in the minds of
contemporaries and in the memories of generations yet unborn.

To understand the role of clothes in this occult process, let the
image of the designated victim be thought of as a doll. Distinctive
clothing or an individualized accessory item is one handy element
that can charm an effigy, identifying the caricature with its
intended object, in the same way that the proper construction of a
"voodoo doll" requires an article of clothing or similar token
belonging to the victim. In the ridiculous character of "Bayes" in
Buckingham's *The Rehearsal,* for instance, many contemporaries
thought that they saw the epitome of John Dryden, the poet laureate (hence "Bayes," after the distinctive laurels of the duly
crowned). Although it is true that the heroic plays of Dryden are
more frequently parodied in *The Rehearsal* than those by any other
dramatist, Buckingham and his collaborators seem to have been
aiming at a more generally composite portrait of dramatic excess,
and a number of features of the stage character's personality, such
as his fawning loquaciousness, fail to match up with the supposed
victim's attributes. Like the burning shirt of Nessus, however, the
satire stuck to Dryden throughout his lifetime and to his memory
during the eighteenth century, while the play long remained in
the repertoire, down to the present day as a truism among scholars.

One of the most popularly persuasive pieces of evidence linking
Dryden and Bayes exclusively, apart from their shared symbolic
headgear, is anecdotal testimony that the actor John Lacy, who
created the role in 1671, dressed the part in clothing that obviously resembled Dryden's. Oft repeated as fact, this story better
illustrates how the black magic of satire fictionalizes an image in
the public mind, wherein spurious details accumulate willy-nilly
around an attractive lampoon. Once unleashed on the world, the
afterimage takes on a gaudy life of its own, and finding a place of

origin for every ornament that adorns it is often impossible. The source of the story about Bayes's costume is the theatrical anecdotist Thomas Davies, writing a century after the premiere of *The Rehearsal*. In his account of how various actors dressed Bayes, Davies merely speculates on the likely effect of Lacy's "infinite comic humour" in preparing the role: "How the character was dressed by Lacy it is not now to be known. Dryden, it was said, was fond of wearing black velvet; and we may suppose the player endeavored to resemble him, as near as possible, in dress and deportment."[41] The import of the story resides not in its veracity or lack thereof, but in the way it seizes upon clothing to enhance the efficacy of the afterimage of Dryden as Bayes.

Davies goes on to repeat the gossip that Buckingham and the Earl of Dorset maliciously invited Dryden to the opening of *The Rehearsal* "and placed the poet between them to enjoy the feelings of his mind during the exhibition of his own picture."[42] However convincing the psychology of this story may or may not be, it is highly implausible in its social casting of the principals. Davies moves to firmer ground, however, when he traces the course of Dryden's revenge on Buckingham, after the identification of the laureate with the ludicrous poetaster had firmly taken root in the public mind: "Dryden put the best face on the matter, and endeavored to laugh at the grotesque picture drawn of him; but, though he was wise enough to conceal his wound, he felt the smart of it. The revenge he took in the character of Zimri, in his Absalom and Achitophel, which he drew for author of the Rehearsal, is proof that he was thoroughly angry."[43] Proof of the caricatured poet's rage the portrait of "Zimri" may well have been; it was certainly evidence of his deadly skill:

> Thus, wicked but in will, of means bereft,
> He left not Faction, but of that was left.[44]

Conflating the ruin of Buckingham's finances with his political isolation in the bitter denouement of the Exclusion Crisis, Dryden reverses the force field of the satirical curse and makes it rebound with double effect on the principal perpetrator of "Bayes": Evil to him who evil thinks.

The reverse malediction worked its poisonous magic. Buckingham left behind in his Commonplace Book clear evidence that he knew the extent of the damage, and in the unpublished epigram "To Dryden," he painfully tented the depths of his wounds. Even as he rejects the accuracy of the "resemblance," the speaker of the poem ruefully acknowledges the hurt done to his "Name." Explicitly comparing the public image fashioned of him by his tormentor to the kind of wax doll favored by witches in casting evil spells, he offers first-person testimony to the efficacy of the hex:

> As witches images of wax invent
> To torture those they're bid to represent,
> And as the true live substance does decay
> Whilst that slight idol melts in flames away,
> Such, and no lesser, witchcraft wounds my name;
> So thy ill-made resemblance wastes my fame;
> So as the charmed brand consumed i' th' fire,
> So did Meleager's vital heat expire.
> Poor Name! What medicine for that can I find,
> But thus with stronger charms thy charm t' unbind?[45]

In Greek mythology, Meleager, like Oedipus, brought upon himself the very catastrophe to which he had been foredoomed. Cursed at birth by the Fates, he would live only as long as the brand then burning on the hearth was not consumed. His quick-thinking mother pulled the brand out of the flames and preserved it, prolonging her son's life until, coming of age, he murdered her two brothers, whereupon she cast the brand into the flames to avenge them. Meleager, perforce, perished along with the charmed totem.

Buckingham, mining the mythical substrate of sympathetic magic, makes telling poetic use of the interlocking figures of the witches' "idol" and Meleager's "charmed brand." The former mimics the victim's vulnerability; the latter, his terrible fate. Buckingham may have recalled, as a bit of family lore, that a wax effigy of his father had been discovered during the proliferation of political scandals that led ultimately to his assassination and that "witchcraft" was alleged as its source.[46] Seeing himself burned in effigy, Buckingham suggests that the laureate's black magic binds Zimri's character fatefully to his as an indelible after-image. What he weakly hopes for at the end of the poem—and what accounts for the eerie contemporaneity of his vain longing for redress—is a way to "unbind" the cursed image from his name. Just such a "medicine" eluded him in life and in death, as it continues to elude us, the supposedly disenchanted moderns. In this emergent structure of relations, where fantasy continues under many names to determine fates, society is held together by no force of attraction stronger than its curses. Then and now, the idol may appear "slight," but the only proven antidote to its insidious magic, apart from increasingly large doses of the even more fragile imagery of virtue, is to embrace notoriety as a substitute for celebrity.

Buckingham's contemporaries seemed to imagine him in superlatives only. The astonishing celerity with which he thought and moved and spoke qualified him as a "wit" in Hobbesian terms and identifies him today as an historic exemplar of the It-Effect, marked by an aura, the effortlessly manifest balance of contraries. "When he came into the presence chamber," Dean Lockier recalled, "it was impossible for you not to follow him with your eyes." To Brian Fairfax, he was "of so graceful a body as gave luster to the ornaments of his mind, and made him the glory of the English court at home and abroad." Louis XIV called Buckingham "the only English *gentleman* he had ever seen." To Bishop Burnet, who deplored his character, he was a man of "great liveliness of wit," and to Clarendon, his political adversary, "[his] quality and condescensions, the pleasantness of his humour and conversation, the extravagance and sharpness of his wit, . . . drew persons of all affections and inclinations to like his person." Horace Walpole later remembered with wonder the man who "could equally charm the Presbyterian Fairfax and the Dissolute Charles," and a popular ballad of the duke's own time rhymed his charismatic presence with breathless enjambment:

No gallant peer by nature framed to warm
    The lovely Fair could boast a nobler form.[47]

What is a rake? A superb dancer and musician, Buckingham was also an effective, if unorthodox orator and advocate, especially in the cause of freedom of religious conscience. Andrew Marvell cheered him on when he routed the learned ecclesiastical bigots in Parliament by the timely application of his mimicry. The poet made Buckingham a kind of hero in *An Account of the Growth of Popery* (1677) and adapted his methods of staged burlesque satire to polemical tracts, first in *The Rehearsal Transpros'd* and then, quite hilariously, in *Mr. Smirke; or, the Divine in Mode* (1676), an answer, via Etherege's recent hit play, to the bishop of Hereford's orthodox *The Naked Truth*. Marvell makes *The Naked Truth* all about clothes, the author's "Wit consisting wholly in his Dress": "So that there was more to do in equipping Mr. Smirke [the Bishop] then there is about Dorimant; and the Divine in Mode might have vyed with Sir Fopling Flutter."[48] The use of clothes to charm an idol retains its magical efficacy, even in an argument where the motive of the author is to contain religious doctrine. The sensational story of Anna Maria's role in the duel between Shrewsbury and Buckingham collapses when historians point out the she had already fled to a convent in France before the fatal events took place, but it nevertheless continually reappears, like stigmata, defying all attempts at debunking, believed because it needs to be believed to charm the role-icon of "rake." After the premature end of his political career, Buckingham could savor at leisure the bitter distinction that he, unlike most high officeholders in his time or others, did not make a fortune while in public service but lost one, an abnegation for which the satirists ridiculed him.

As the example of the "beauty" Lillie Langtry shows, radiant in her white dress and with the red rose beside her ear, the word *charm* cuts two ways at least. For all Marvell's admiration for Buckingham's prescient invocation of ideas that later defined the Enlightenment or for the charismatic gifts of mind and body that gave those ideas such an eloquent voice from such an unexpected quarter, in the end nothing his eulogist said, no matter how impeccably and persuasively reasoned, could clothe the duke, "Not one, but all Mankind's Epitome," in anything but a bloody shirt.

# 3.

# hair

In the experience of the It-Effect, which "gives us back the Image of our Mind," hair can exert a magical power even greater than that of accessories and clothes, in part because it functions as both simultaneously. Since hair belongs (or at least appears to belong) to the body of the person who wears it, an anomaly such as an obvious wig or implausible bouffant provides a locally crowning self-assertion of the wearer and from time to time a crux in fashion history. In 1729, when the caretakers of Westminster Abbey first refreshed the funeral effigy of Charles II, they replaced the king's full-bottomed periwig with a new one in the same style.[1] They could not have kept faith with the afterimage of the king by abandoning his wig to the hungry moths or by redressing his effigy with a lesser substitute because the Carolean periwig so memorably characterized his person and his reign. It also, not coincidentally, characterized his theater.

At the dramaturgical high-water mark of the Restoration stage in 1676, the title character of Etherege's *Sir Fopling Flutter* makes a personal inventory, inscribing his periwig at the pinnacle of an array of luxury items imported from France. Disappointed but not discouraged by the lack of a looking glass in the room of an earlier scene, Sir Fopling ritually brands his wardrobe and accessories for

117

the edification of wondering witnesses, basking in their attention
to his image as if standing before a fun-house mirror (3.2). The
mirrorless room belongs to Dorimant, the rake-hero, who as we
have seen, unquestionably has It. As astutely mimicked by the doctrinally overdressed cleric "Mr. Smirke" in Marvell's appropriation
of *The Man of Mode* as *The Divine in Mode,* Sir Fopling purports to
have It, but on account of his exaggerations and pretenses he inadvertently clarifies by contrast It's true nature—the spark of the
divine original in the perfection of a fleshly type. Dressing well is a
means to Dorimant's ends, an erotically empowered control over
himself and others, not an end in itself, as it is for his foil.

Egged on by the other characters, who have lots of fun at his
expense even though they themselves participate in the same fashion system, Sir Fopling answers a mock catechism of questions on
contemporary name brands, gesturing back to sacred liturgy and
forward to modern advertising, including Hollywood's convention
of "product placement." Preening himself after the nubile Emilia
puffs him up by announcing, as if in admiration but also with
imperfect irony, "He wears nothing but what are originals of the
most famous brands in Paris," Sir Fopling spreads his feathers
majestically one by one; and since the god of fashion is in the
details, he and his chorus of interrogators run the gamut of desir-
able brand-names from trim and accents ("garniture") to scented
gloves, not forgetting, of course, the synecdochical periwig:

> LADY TOWNLEY.    The suit?
> SIR FOPLING.    Barroy.
> EMILIA.    The garniture?
> SIR FOPLING.    Le Gras—
> MEDLEY.    The shoes?
> SIR FOPLING.    Piccar!
> DORIMANT.    The periwig?
> SIR FOPLING.    Chedreux.
> LADY TOWNLEY [and] EMILIA.    The gloves?
> SIR FOPLING.    Orangerie! You know the smell, ladies—
> $$\text{(3.2.228–40; } BA \text{ 553–54)}$$

Sir Fopling's garments and accessories at once contain and
exhaust his image: as Medley sums him up, "He was yesterday at

the play, with a pair of gloves up to his elbows and a periwig more exactly curled than a lady's head newly dressed for a ball" (1.1.283–84; *BA* 534). Like the fashion house "Lucile," which in its time partially reversed the balance of trade from two centuries of dominant Parisian exports, the French names that he chants signal the modernity of the shopping destinations that flourish under the aura of fashionable logos, and they narrate the progress of his visits to them as shrines. In the magical precincts of synthetic experience, repeating their names enchants them anew; as it was in the beginning, is now, and ever shall be: Gucci, Pucci, Prada, and Dior. It also implicates the catechists themselves in the antiphonal chorus, culminating when the voices of Lady Townley and Emilia, cued in by the crowning citation of the wig, join in unison on "The gloves?" But in the end it is the truly modish Dorimant who asks Sir Fopling where he gets his hair.

Dorimant poses his question presciently. In its extremity, the periwig sported by the Restoration fop epitomized a larger movement toward bigger hair, which migrated, over the century between 1676 and 1776, from men to women, and from women to Macaronis.[2] This trend began, as did so many others in English dress and grooming, with the importation of a conventional look from France, in this case with Charles II's adoption of the hairstyles of the court of Louis XIV, but it reemerged, variously and periodically, in both men's and women's hairstyles later in the eighteenth century and beyond. At work and at play, what today we call "big hair" became the most immediately visible way of marking different social roles, occupations, aspirations, and conditions. Those assignments included a number of charismatic, stigmatized role-icons—first the "fop," later the socially commanding woman with a "head," and in between the "tragedy king," whose statuesque dignity required the management of a full-bottomed periwig as a badge of office.

Following the tonsorial progress of the English stage from the Restoration into the first half of the eighteenth century, this chapter will foreground the enchanted uses of hair in the careers of four actors whose claims to the possession of It remain unassailable and whose afterimages retain their vivacity: strong and vulnerable Thomas Betterton, whose portrait by Kneller shows him heavily bewigged; Colley Cibber (1671–1757), whose most famous prop helped to enrich the English language with the word *bigwig;* James Quin (1693–1766), whose unjust but informative fate is to be remembered by theater historians as a bigwig; and David Garrick (1717–1779), whose little-studied renovation of theatrical hairstyles complemented his famous revolution in acting. Hair, like justice, is something that in order to be credited must be done. Under the publicly intimate sway of that imperative, the changing shape and length of hair (and with that, potential activation of the taboos associated with haircutting) especially enchant the heads of celebrities, whether their style is big or bobbed. Developing the premise that the careful management of hair stands in for other kinds of control, this chapter will conclude with a brief reflection on the bouffant craze of 1950s and 1960s, culminating in the "Imperial Hair" of Margaret Thatcher at the denouement of the Cold War.[3] As Tory heirs to the three-dimensional eighteenth century, the flaks of her media-savvy regime accelerated an ongoing project that as of this writing remains unfinished: the de facto amendment of the unwritten English constitution by merging the visible branch of government with the efficient. Looking very much like a queen, she performed the end of her term in office in the tradition of the role-icon of the superannuated "tragedy king," and no detail of that doleful afterimage makes for a more expressive synecdoche than her helmet head—at once the shield of Achilles and his heel.

Part of the enduring magic of big hair from the deep eighteenth century may be traced to its traditional point of origin on the heads of others, potentially making the role that hair plays in the possession of It one of social entitlement and subordination. Of the array of statistics that might be adduced to document this ongoing imposition, which continues today in certain regions, ethnic and class enclaves, and camp revivals, let two suffice: in addition to the labor-intensive enlargement of "natural hair," which is teased, stacked, and sprayed into Marge Simpson–like helmets, wig sales from 1959 to 1967 rose 1,000 percent; and in just one six-month period of 1964, Indian entrepreneurs alone, scavenging temple altars for hair sacrificed to Lord Venkateswara, produced forty-eight thousand wigs for consumers in Europe and North America.[4] Reflecting, as in a not-so-distant mirror, this more recent style of resource-consuming self-decoration, a double-peaked, full-bottomed periwig of the type favored by tragedy kings and exaggerated by fops (and still worn by British judges and the Speaker of the House of Commons today) required about ten heads of natural hair to be sacrificed for its construction.[5] Such a fascinating emblem at once symbolizes and embodies the privileged command of the one over the lives and resources of the many.

Samuel Pepys, pioneering explorer of early modern synthetic experience, knew this about hair: that he could be well done or undone by his do. Many others before and since have known it too, but the *Diary* entries for the autumn of 1663 allow readers to eavesdrop on the naval clerk's uneasily evolving resolution to cut off his hair and replace it with a periwig. Like the accessory sword, the wig promises to improve his self-fashioning performance as a person of substance. Not coincidentally, it seems likely to improve his personal hygiene as well, because he has sadly found his own shoulder-length hair hard to keep clean and free of head-lice. Reluctant to part with his flowing locks (2:97), however, he begins tentatively in late August by borrowing a tryout wig from his barber Jervas, but making no further commitment for two months (4:290). On October 21, he and Elizabeth Pepys talk over his shabby wardrobe and decide the time has come to upgrade his overall look: "We did resolve of putting me into a better garbe; and among other things, to have a good velvet cloak, that is, a cloth lined with velvet, and other things modish, and a perruque" (4:343). On October 26, he goes wig shopping with his associate Creed, rejecting outright the "head of greazy old woman's haire" offered him from stock, but deciding that day to commission a wig maker named Chapman to fit him with two wigs, one made from hair freshly acquired from someone suitable, the other from his own hair, which he persuades himself to sacrifice for the tonsorial cause (4:350). Four days later he takes Elizabeth to Chapman's atelier to see the first wig under construction. She likes it (4:357). On November 3, the big day starts with a special delivery to the Pepys household:

By and by comes Chapman the periwig-maker, and [upon] my
liking it, without more ado I went up and there he cut off my
haire; which went a little to my heart at present to part with it,
but it being over and my periwig on, I paid him 3£ for it; and
away went he with my own hair to make up another of; and I by
and by, after I had caused all my maids to look upon it and they
conclude it to become me, though Jane was mightily troubled
for my parting with my own hair and so was Besse. (4:362)

Undiscouraged by his skeptical servants or at least resigned to
make the best of it, Pepys goes out the next day and buys a special
case to house whichever of the two wigs he's not wearing (4:364).
Two days after that he shows off his new wig to good effect at the
navy office, and the following Sunday he wears it proudly to
church (4:365, 369).

The results ultimately pleased Pepys, and rightly so, even
though he narrowly escaped serious injury when he carelessly set
his wig on fire by backing his head into a candle flame while gossiping with Lady Hinchinbrooke (9:322). An ambitious servant to
his stylish king, he had acted just in the nick of time to catch the
wave of fashion as novelty crested into convention. Meeting and
being recognized by Charles II and the Duke of York at Whitehall
on November 1, 1663, only three days before Chapman's eventful
house-call, Pepys confirms the gossip that both royal brothers
intend to adopt periwigs (4:360). Wigs will quickly become de
rigueur on the head of any man who aspires to come within the
orbit of the It-Effect under the restored king, including the actors
in the royal playhouses. In different shapes and sizes, wigs will
become increasingly necessary to nominate role-icons across a
variety of callings and professions. Later Pepys will further
upgrade his outfit by buying two "mighty fine" periwigs from a
French wig-maker (8:136), but he will also set aside a prized wig in
fear that it might have come from the hair of plague victims
(6:210). The threat of contagion quite reasonably accounts for
this phobic demurral, and that is in fact the reason he gives, but he
might possibly have had another, less obvious motive as well, one
related to his earlier rejection of "old woman's haire" as unsuitable

for his head. In the performance of his everyday life, perhaps he wanted to enjoy shopping as the synthetic experience of hunting, not scavenging, by seeking hair shorn from the heads of worthy donors—not carrion, but fair game.

Even in far smaller quantities, hair's magical symbolic power comes into play with special urgency when its ownership changes hands. Of the ugly feud that broke out when Robert Lord Petre snipped a lovelock from the head of Arabella Fermor without permission, Alexander Pope made a poem in which the speaker exclaims by way of preface: "What mighty Contests rise from trivial Things" (*The Rape of the Lock*, 1.2).[6] But the speaker does not (because in his mock-heroic voice he cannot) underplay the importance of hair to the perpetrator, the victim, or their friends and kinfolk, even if he finds their emphasis risible. Nor for that matter did the members of the rising professional class of eighteenth-century hairdressers, though frequently themselves the objects of ridicule, remain unassertive about the power attached to their medium and the corresponding importance of their art. With pomades as potions and curling irons as wands, they magically summoned the look and feel of It on demand. As conjurers, however, they needed a conceptual strategy as well as the technical means of teasing it out and coifing it with fashion's invisible hand. As *The New London Toilet* (1778) put it: "Hair dressing is not altogether a practical part of science, for unless theory is joined to it, the hair dresser will never make any proficiency in his business."[7] By contrast, today's historians and literary scholars have generally begged the theoretical question that has been known to vex them in practical terms of personal grooming: Hair—what to do with it?

Hair theory, such as it is, belongs mainly to anthropologists and psychoanalysts. In *Taboo and the Perils of the Soul*, the second part of *The Golden Bough*, Frazer takes up the question of hair. Obsolescent among ethnographers as Frazer's method may be, his observations nevertheless remain plausibly suggestive on the subjects of big hair, bad hair, and cut hair. The section called "The Hair Tabooed" closely follows "The Head Tabooed": "Among many peoples the head is peculiarly sacred," he reports; moreover, the "special sanctity attributed to it is sometimes explained by a belief that it is the seat of the spirit which is very sensitive to injury or dis-respect." For that substantial reason, cutting the hair on the head, in the opinion of many, is a procedure fraught with peril: "There is first the danger of disturbing the spirit of the head, which may be injured in the process and may revenge itself upon the person who molests him." In many societies, the "kings, priests, and wiz-ards" in order to remain unpolluted must remain unshorn, unless perhaps the cuttings from their heads and nails are offered up sacrificially.[8] And thus, reverent preservation of the severed hair, if it is to be cut at all, is a custom widely practiced with variations around the world, while wearing the hair cut from the heads of others potentially represents the acquisition of a particular power over them (hence, "scalping"), as well as a possible danger to the wearer on the rebound. In *The Rape of the Lock*, for instance, Pope's baron, uttering a public oath in the presence of the humiliated vic-tim, gloats over his talismanic prize, Belinda's severed lovelock:

> But by this Lock, this sacred Lock I swear,
> (Which never more shall join its parted Hair,
> Which never more its Honours shall renew,
> Clipt from the lovely Head where late it grew)
> That while my Nostrils draw the vital Air,
> This Hand, which won it, shall forever wear.
> He spoke, and speaking, in proud Triumph spread
> The long-contended Honours of her Head.
>
> (4.133–40)

The proud ravisher, however, has reason to dread the deed per-formed with "sacrilegious Hands" (4.174). Protected by Rosicru-cian spirits ("Swift to the Lock a thousand Sprights repair" [3.135]), Belinda's tresses unleash a legion of sylphs and gnomes to avenge their ruin. Drawing ironically on the mythopoetic sub-strate, Pope mocks, even as he mines, what Frazer earnestly reports: the widespread belief that daemons as well as gods inhabit the hair, a presence that makes it magical—the outward display of invisible powers. Despite the poet's ridicule of the trivial causes that set rival tribes to feuding, the power of the residual symbolism he invokes was essential to both the occasion of his poem and its cultural legibility. Since Medusa and Samson, hair has, in this sense, always been big, whatever its length.

Under provocative titles like "Magical Hair" and "Social Hair," anthropologists have updated Frazer's theories based on data from on-the-ground ethnographies, eschewing Frazer's armchair method, but not necessarily the general drift of his insights. Their paradigms have also been informed, but not wholly deflected, by psychoanalysis, which, following Sigmund Freud's generative note on "Medusa's Head," develops the symbolic meaning of hair in unconscious sexuality.[9] For Charles Berg, hair is a phallic symbol, an assertion that, if true, relocates the anthropological account of phobic responses to haircutting in a personal psychic anxiety too tedious to rehearse.[10] For Edmund Leach and Christopher Hallpike, hair has the symbolic power attributed to it by psycho-analysis, but they differ about the degree to which its private meanings can or ought to figure in its public ones.[11] Gananath Obeyesekere reconciles the opposing views of anthropology and psychoanalysis in his account of hair as a "personal symbol," on the cusp of the psychological and the social self, which may originate in the unconscious urges of individual subjects, but which operates in the publicly symbolic practices of a culture.[12] Suffused with the erotic ambience of its time and place, *The Rape of the Lock*, an on-the-ground ethnography in its own right, thus yields up a vivid synecdoche for the overall experience of It:

Fair Tresses Man's Imperial Race insnare,
And Beauty draws us with a single Hair.
(2.27–28)

In the actions and attitudes condensed by Pope, poetry presages the consensus of the human sciences in the deep eighteenth century: social hair is no less unnervingly charismatic than magical hair, never more so than when it has been in any way "done."

The word *bob*, which most people associate with the mass-cultural craze of haircutting in the 1920s, actually entered the English language as the *bob wigg* (a shorter type of periwig with its ends curled up) as early as the 1680s *(OED)*. As women's haircuts reemerged as an issue of sexual politics, no less fraught for F. Scott

Fitzgerald's Bernice than they were for Pope's Belinda, the old superstitions also reappeared, wreathed in a familiar haze of smoke and mirrors, totems and taboos, even as other long-standing norms evaporated. The fashionably bobbed sex-bomb Lillian Lorraine, for example, who became Florenz Ziegfeld's starring showgirl and "most influential mistress" a few years before Lady Duff-Gordon started designing for the *Follies*,[13] communicated an anecdote to actress Ruth Gordon that sheds light on the reenchantment of hair in the age of instrumental reason. Recounting "what Lillian Lorraine said was wrong with her life when the lady reporter came to interview her," Gordon's transcription of the "beauty's" mock-epic autobiography merits extensive quotation:

> Lillian Lorraine was old and broke and living up on Broadway at 96th. Some paper sent the lady interviewer up to do a piece: "What do you think happened, Miss Lorraine? Ziegfeld said you were the greatest beauty he ever had in the Follies. What went wrong?"
>
> "He was *right*. And he was crazy about me. He had me in a tower suite at the Hotel Ansonia and he and his wife lived in the tower suite above. And I cheated on him, like he cheated on Billie Burke. I had a whirl! I blew a lot of everybody's money, I got loaded, I was on the stuff, I got the syphilis, I tore around, stopped at nothing, if I wanted to do it I did it and didn't give a damn. I got knocked up, I had abortions, I broke up homes, I gave fellers the clap. So that's what happened."
>
> "Well, Miss Lorraine," gasped the lady reporter, "if you had it to do over would you do anything different?"
>
> "Yes," said Lillian Lorraine. "I never shoulda cut my hair."[14]

Hair can carry such a volatile, life-defining emotional charge for several reasons. First, because it grows, but not as living flesh does, hair falls between the categories of life and death. Second, because it may be cut and shaped, but in ways that flesh can't be (or at least not as easily), hair falls between nature and culture. Third, because its changing characteristics mark the passages of the body through different stages of life, but not with the same degree of challenge to prosthetic manipulation or replacement that other organs present, hair falls somewhere between no-maintenance and high-maintenance. Because hair often resists efforts to control it, apparently effortless grace in its management—the pseudo-unconscious gesture of the flirtatious hair-flip, for instance—can bestow the aura of It in an instant, and often only for an instant. Hair's (sub)liminal status, however, contradicts the implications of the prominent location of its most prolific growth: surveying any terrain, the eye of the beholder seeks out the highest feature as focal point for its gaze, marking all the head as a stage, and the features on it only players. More intimate than clothing and yet more reliably prearranged than countenance, hair represents a primary means of staking a claim to social space on the occasion of first impressions.

In other words, social hair is performance, with all its magic and its risks: hence the easy tactical success of Tony Lumpkin's prank at the expense of the superannuated Old Hardcastle in *She Stoops to Conquer; or, the Mistakes of a Night* (1773): "It was but yesterday he fastened my wig to the back of my chair, and when I went to make a bow, I popped my bald head in Mrs. Frizzle's face" (1.1.50–54; *BA* 1876). As an aggregation of arts and crafts that consume extra time and extra space beyond those required to meet basic human needs, performance encompasses conscious repetition and occasional revision of previous public behaviors, as in formal or informal social encounters, and precise enactments of scripted scenarios, as in theatrical representation or obligatory ritual. Performance implies a certain level of shared expectation about the way in which the participants will behave, predisposing them to special efforts in the ways in which they will make mutual use of the time and place of the event. This prior disposition rests on fundamental assumptions about the assignment of roles and the conduct appropriate to their execution. Exemplary embodiment activates the It-Effect, and performers frequently use hairstyle as a marker of their mastery of their preassigned or coveted roles, but supreme accomplishment introduces novelty into the conventional expectations. The dressing-room scene in *The Man of Mode* between Harriet and her maid, for instance, bookends the earlier one between Dorimant and Handy:

BUSY. Dear madam, let me set that curl in order!

HARRIET. Let me alone! I will shake 'em all out of order!

BUSY. Will you never leave this wildness?

HARRIET. Torment me not!

BUSY. Look, there's a knot falling off.

HARRIET. Let it drop!

(3.1.1–6; *BA* 545–46)

Here Harriet demonstrates yet another dimension of the paradoxical fascination exerted by abnormally interesting people: fashion enforces its conventions rigorously, and yet genius knows no rules.

Hairdressers and cosmetic merchants of the long eighteenth century well understood their roles as acolytes in such performances. In his compendious *Plocacosmos: or the Whole Art of Hair Dressing* (1782), James Stewart, hairdresser and hair historian, used leading actors and actresses as models and organized the chapters of his book around "The Seven Ages of Man" speech from Shakespeare's *As You Like It.* He begins by writing the general history of hair from antiquity to 1745, adding a technical treatise on his own practice of hairdressing to bring his volume up to the date of its publication. His data range from prescientific lore ("The ancients held the hair to be a sort of excrement, fed only with excrementitious matter") to microscopic examination of damaged hairs investigating the vexing problem of split ends.[15] He charts the progress of long versus short hair from Caesar's shaving of the Gauls to the Cavaliers sporting their curls shoulder length in stylized opposition to the Roundheads, but he clearly comes into his own element when recounting the development of the English peruke from the reign of Charles II to that of George II. He tells the story of increasingly specialized wig types deployed as costume accessories in the performance of social and professional roles. These are proper role-icons, in which the wig works as synecdoche to cue the beholder as to the identity and purposes of the wearer:

As the perukes became more common, their shape and forms altered. Hence we hear of the clerical, the physical, and the huge tie peruke for the man of the law, the brigadier, or the major for the army and navy, as also the tremendous fox ear, or cluster of temple curls, with a pig-tail behind. The merchant, the man of business and of letters, were distinguished by the grave full bottom, or more moderate tie, neatly curled; the tradesman by the snug bob, or the natty scratch; the country gentleman, by the natural fly and hunting peruke. All conditions of men were distinguished by the cut of the wig, and none more so than the coachman, who wore his, as there does some to this day, in imitation of the curled hair of a waterdog.[16]

The fashion that Stewart describes, the carefully calibrated use of wigs to define types of work and social position, provided William Hogarth with at least part of the impetus for his famous etching *The Five Orders of Perriwigs* of 1761.[17] A satire on the projectors of a volume on the proportional measurement of classical architecture, the print details five types or "orders" of headdress, each appropriate to a different station or profession represented at the coronation of King George III and Queen Charlotte: "Episcopal or Parsonic," "Old Peerian or Aldermanic," "Lexonic," "Composite, or Half Natural" and "Queerinthian" (fashionable beaux), and, finally, the profiles of the queen and her ladies. Hogarth illustrates Stewart's assertion that all conditions of men are to be distinguished by the cut of their wigs. Although recognizable portraits of individuals add interest to the faces in Hogarth's print, the wigs actually catalog a succession of stock types, as in the Italian commedia dell'arte or in any theatrical endeavor for that matter, including the London and provincial companies, with their set "lines of business," which defined the conventional type of character in which each player specialized, a rational division of labor worthy of Adam Smith.

At the apex of prestige in the division of theatrical labor stood the actor who made his name by taking the leading roles in tragedy, especially Shakespearean tragedy. Each succeeding era of

English theater history has had such a figure notionally inscribed under the role-icon of the tragedy king, for whom It presumes a certain gravitas: Betterton, Quin, and Garrick, for example, inspired the most commentary on their tragic acting, though all three also excelled in comedy over long and full careers, and Garrick made his principal innovation the incorporation of the less austere, more energetic business of comic and even pantomimic acting into his overall style.[18] Cibber, who aspired painfully to be a tragedian, succeeded mainly in acting comedies, but he left behind in his *Apology for the Life of Mr. Colley Cibber* (1740) the most prolific eyewitness account of the period, including an extensive eulogy of Betterton as a tragedian. To a degree not heretofore sufficiently appreciated, the record of all four actors in both genres contains important references to what they did with their hair. Generally speaking, they took advantage of its expressive power in assaying their role-icons even more ambitiously than Pepys did in his social performance as man-about-town and civil servant. Before Garrick, a fairly standardized arrangement of costume and headwear assisted in turning out the conventionally recognizable effigy of the tragedy king. As Joseph Addison remarks sardonically on the ubiquity of the full-bottomed periwigs topped with feathered helmets among English tragedians, "These superfluous Ornaments on the Head make a great Man."[19] In a repertoire consisting substantially of revivals of earlier plays and new works written to exploit successful formulas, however, the key to the actor's continuing appeal, like that of the social climber, resides in mastering a fundamental contradiction in the performance of existing role-icons: satisfying the audience members by embodying their expectations while exciting them by transforming their preconceptions.

Appearing as he did in a full-bottomed periwig in Sir Godfrey Kneller's portrait, Betterton epitomized the role-icon of the great English tragedian (fig. 11). He could not have sustained the It-Effect simply by donning a wig, however—he had to wear it in a special way. In that regard as in others, Hamlet became Betterton's signature role in his own time and for all time. As a "living role," one that thrived in popular imagination as long as its creator drew breath (and even longer through anecdotal lore), Ham-

Fig. 11. Robert Williams after Sir Godfrey Kneller's portrait of
Thomas Betterton, ca. 1690. National Portrait Gallery, London.

let stayed in the actor's repertoire for nearly fifty years, from the
time that Pepys first saw him act the part in 1661 until the death
of "the English Roscius" in 1710. Pepys spoke of Betterton's Hamlet as something that was "done," in the sense of bringing a work
to completion or perfection: "saw *Hamlet Prince of Denmarke,* done
with Scenes very well. But above all Batterton did the Prince's part
beyond imagination"; and then again, two years later: "saw *Hamlett*
done, giving us fresh reason never to think of enough of Bater-
ton" (2:161; 4:162). The diarist later discloses how the "To or not
to be" soliloquy entered even his most intimate dreams (6:191).
When he dreamed of the role he saw performed, the afterimage
he conjured with awe presaged the one that eventually passed

into theatrical history in the more extended descriptions of later critics.

Except for Pepys, all those who claim to have been eyewitnesses to Betterton's Hamlet saw him act late in his career. In earlier years the charismatic actor played many youthful leading men, including Dorimant in *The Man of Mode*. In later years he played fewer, but, following the custom of the theater of that time, he kept his hold on others, including Hamlet, as part of his "line." In assessing Betterton's performance, the eyewitnesses consistently remark on the actor's decorousness, the imposing restraint with which he controlled his movements regardless of the vicissitudes of the role. These anecdotes capture and sustain an aura that surrounds the memory of the great tragedian, making his vulnerabilities glow no less warmly than his strengths. Many historians believe that the illustration of the closet scene published in Nicholas Rowe's *Shakespear* of 1709 depicts Betterton's Hamlet, which the public still insisted that he keep on playing, even though he was by this time over seventy and hobbled by gout. The engraving shows Hamlet, periwig firmly in place, reacting to the appearance of the Ghost in the closet scene, where the son but not the mother sees him: his feet are planted firmly and not a hair is out of place, even though his arms are raised above his head. Like the rest of the role, hair must be performed under its own regime of decorum, the fittingness and propriety of action and appearance to character. For better or worse, it must be "done."

Cibber notes that the appalling sight of the Ghost tempted lesser actors to vociferate, whereas Betterton's "expostulation was still govern'd by Decency, manly, but not braving; his Voice never rising into that seeming Outrage or wild Defiance of what he naturally rever'd." Sir Richard Steele remembers "the prevalent Power of proper Manner, Gesture, and Voice" with which he acted Hamlet's "noble Ardor after seeing his Father's Ghost." The scenes struck no one as *under*played, but in acting them Betterton eschewed broad gesture and agitated movement and relied instead on his expressive face, his arresting voice, and his auratic presence. *The Laureat* marvels that the actor's countenance turned as pale as his jabot before the specter; the actor Barton Booth recalls the quasi-religious experience of playing Old Hamlet to Betterton's Prince: "When I acted the Ghost with Betterton, instead of my awing him, he terrified me. But divinity hung round that man!" While Steele suspended his disbelief in the gouty septuagenarian representing the glass of fashion and the mold of form, Anthony Aston, though admitting that no one else could hope to rival Betterton in *acting* the role while he lived, still remained unconvinced by his *impersonation,* "for, when he threw himself at Ophelia's Feet, he appear'd a little too grave for a young Student, lately come from the University of Wirtenberg; and his Repartees seem'd rather the Apothegms from a sage Philosopher, than the sporting flashes of a Young Hamlet."[20] Such contradictions plumb to the very depths George Meredith's description of It as "poignant antiphony," the recursive copresence of incommensurate imperatives.

The miscasting struck contemporaries, even Aston, as acceptable, however, because litheness counted for less than gravity in representing the role in the most beloved tragedy by the country's most revered poet. Their identification of Betterton as Shakespeare's proper heir and interpreter took its most hagiographic form in Nicholas Rowe's verses on the occasion of a benefit for the aging and impecunious star. Rowe makes use of the conjecture that Shakespeare had played the part of the Ghost in the original production of *Hamlet:*

> Had you with-held your Favours on this Night,
> Old SHAKESPEARE's Ghost had ris'n to do him Right.
> With Indignation had you seen him frown
> Upon a worthless, witless, tasteless Town;
> Griev'd and Repining you had heard him say,
> Why are the *Muses* Labours cast away?
> Why did I only Write what only he could Play?[21]

When Betterton came on stage as Hamlet, in other words, he never ceased playing the role of the great English Shakespearean, the tragedy king, a magnetically attractive part, undimmed by age or infirmity (or rather, intensified by them) pointing to an offstage life of its own steeped in history and aglow with patina, the It-Effect of hallowed memory. As an embodiment of a role-icon, it was as It was meant to be: "Betterton was an Actor," Cibber enthused, "as Shakespear was an Author, both without Competitors! form'd for the mutual Assistance and Illustration of each others Genius!"[22] The prompter John Downes believed that Hamlet's original stage business passed to Betterton like the crown jewels descending along the line of legitimate dynastic succession: Betterton, he reports, learned the particulars of the part from Sir William Davenant, who in turn had learned them from the actor Joseph Taylor, who had been instructed by Shakespeare himself.[23] Small wonder "divinity hung round that man," as Booth put it, or that when Betterton died, his bereaved admirers buried him in Westminster Abbey to join the eternal company of the other kings, once and future officeholders in the "visible government" under the unwritten English constitution.

Each of these oft-quoted accounts emphasizes in its own way the sovereign dignity of Bettertonian deportment. And well they all might, for while the stage fop could, if he liked, produce a richly comic effect with his periwig by shaking his head like a spaniel and sending his pendant curls into crisscrossing undulations around his head and about his face, the great tragedian dared not compromise his decorum in this way. Betterton's biographers explicitly quoted him as saying that the head "must turn gently on the Neck [and] ought always to be turned on the same side, to which the *actions* of the rest of the body are directed."[24] And so the tragedy king must moderate his motions, for to avoid a cascading pendulum effect in his full-bottomed peruke, he would have been obliged to maintain control over his head and upper body as well as his gait. Common sense supported by the best evidence suggests that Betterton did exactly that: "His Actions were few," Aston said, "but just." Most of the detailed instructions left behind by the revered actor or in his name underscore the importance of measured limitation of gesture and action. He was quoted as urging the actor to leave his head "in its just natural State and Upright Position," and while it should not be kept as still as a statue, neither "must it be on the contrary moving perpetually, and always throwing itself about on every different Expression."[25] In a contradiction that underscores the "poignant antiphony" animating modern enchantments generally, the performance of the tragic periwig is not a matter of flamboyant size and magnificence alone, but also of physical constraint, control, and economy of force.

The pretension to these very qualities animates the foppish exaggeration of the wig, which succeeds in attracting spectators to the magic of hair in a comic way, inverting the principles of tragic decorum. Cibber self-consciously knew this secret about his own triumph as a comic actor. In his *Apology,* he recalls his first meeting with the handsome and fashion-conscious Colonel Henry Brett. Seized with a sudden impulse while watching Cibber perform, Brett rushed backstage and offered to buy his wig right off his head. This encounter turned on the allure of charismatic hair, which took the form of the most famously enlarged periwig of the Augustan age, the one that the actor-playwright wore to create the role of Sir Novelty Fashion. Possessing what Cibber calls "an uncommon Share of Social Wit," Brett came down from Oxford on a beeline to the playhouse, pausing only briefly at "the Temple" under the pretext of preparing for the bar. Brett's "First View," Cibber assures us, as it was with many of his age and station who had "just broke loose, from Business," was "to cut a Figure (as they call it) in the Side-box, at the Play, from whence their next Step is, to the *Green Room.*" On this backstage errand, he was irresistibly drawn by a "sincere Passion he had conceiv'd for a fair full-bottomed Perriwig, which I then wore in my first Play of the *Fool in Fashion.*"[26] The in-joke behind Hamlet's pointed censure of "a periwig-pated fellow" who tore "a passion to tatters" hints that some Elizabethan actors (or at least one of them) wore false hair, but at the seventeenth century's end, Cibber's expansive self-advertisement shows that hair, like experience, had become something that any stagestruck beau, moved by the invisible hand, might expect to be able to buy or buy into.

Brett's acquisitive impulse, a tonsorial variety of mimetic desire, could not have found a more celebrated accessory object. Taking on an enchanted life of its own, this was the wig that entered the stage on its own sedan chair, borne by two lackeys, following in Sir Novelty's train, like plunder in a Triumph. This was the wig that

Alexander Pope immortalized in verse, as he enthroned Cibber as
the Dunce of all Dunces.[27] This was the wig that, like the character
of Sir Novelty himself, carried over into a sequel, *The Relapse; or,
Virtue in Danger* (1696) by Sir John Vanbrugh, in which both wig
and wearer were further enlarged—Sir Novelty into Lord Foppington, his flourishing accessory into an all-engulfing, hairy
cloak, and his "O" sounds into an affected "A": "Far a periwig to a
man should be like a mask to a woman," Foppington insists to
Foretop, his wig maker, "nothing should be seen but his eyes" (*The
Relapse*, 1.3.156–57; *BA* 1488).[28] And this was the wig that
remained so vividly behind as an afterimage in popular memory
that Horace Walpole, writing three-quarters of a century later,
seized on it to convey the size and scope of the sculpted hair he
found on the medieval sarcophagus of Lady Berkeley (d. 1385):
"It is like a long horseshoe quilted in quatrefoils, and like Lord
Foppington's wig, allows no more than the breadth of a half crown
to be discovered of the face."[29] That Lord Foppington's extravagant headgear remained a point of reference to Walpole suggests
the continuing importance of hairstyles from the later Stuart
period, when men of importance wore big wigs, to those under the
Hanoverians, when "a tête" was something that fashionable
women made even larger than men.

In the animating expansion of effigies from medieval tombs to
eighteenth-century stage personalities, stage fops might not at first
glance seem to provide the most obvious of fashion plates to anyone in full possession of his "Social Wit"; but clearly young Henry
Brett, if the *Apology* is to be credited, found himself impulsively
drawn to the crowning item in the wardrobe of the greatest fop of
the age. Cibber gave his most memorable character a revealing
name: Sir Novelty Fashion. Fashion, like the theater, replenishes
itself in the dynamic contest of novelty and convention, the push
and pull of the It-Effect. Fops turn convention into novelty by
pushing a certain look to extremes. This look might or might not
then attain the height of fashion, catching some of the concentrated magic before it diffuses into convention again, during the
enchanted interval between the time that everyone wants one and
everyone has one.

Hair thus not only provided material for the stage, but also mimicked it in return. Hairdresser William Barker, in *A Treatise on the Principles of Hair-Dressing* (1782), commends to his customers as fashion plates the hairstyles worn by Mrs. Yates as Medea, Mrs. Abington as Lady Betty Modish, and Mrs. Siddons as Belvidera.[30] In this way, the tonsorial opportunities to participate in the It-Effect received glamorous theatrical publicity. Each actress, widely followed by her own fans, served the role of what a pop analyst of today's fads calls a "connector" or "maven," a person whose wide social circulation resembles the role of a vector in spreading a communicable disease. The connector is crucial to "the tipping point," the moment when the progression of a contagion or craze leaps from the arithmetic to the geometric.[31] The late eighteenth century saw such a moment in the proliferation of very big hair: a satirical print titled *The Ridiculous Taste or the Ladies Absurdity* of 1771 shows a hairdresser on a ladder, hard at work concocting the hair his client has imagined for herself, which is not for the most part, of course, the hair she has (fig. 12).

In the movement of gigantism from men's periwigs to women's "heads," there is some evidence that Lord Foppington and his successors played the role of connectors. The afterlife of Cibber's prop wig carried over into the memoirs of his cross-dressing daughter, Charlotte Charke, who reports that at age four she stole into her father's wardrobe and put on his signature costume. She expressed her desire to do so, paraphrasing Cibber quoting Henry Brett, as "a passionate fondness for a periwig."[32] A contemporary print shows her completely engulfed by Cibber's hat and wig, much as in the style insisted on by Foppington to Foretop and described by Walpole on Lady Berkeley's effigy. The word *effigy*, meaning a substitute for an absent original, is cognate to *efficiency, efficacy, effervescence,* and *effeminacy* through their mutual connection to ideas of bringing forth, bringing out, and making. As Brett's backstage errand and Charke's transvestite mimicry show, fops could effectively perform as effigies in that sense, especially in a context marked by unstable and contested gender roles, which the theater has always been, especially so in the eighteenth century.[33]

Fig. 12. Mathew or Mary Darly, etching and engraving,
"The Ridiculous Taste or the Ladies Absurdity" (ca. 1771).
The Lewis Walpole Library, Yale University.

The feminization of big hair had serious consequences for the
tonsorial fate of the tragedy king. In the early years of the eighteenth century, Betterton's prestigious afterimage wrapped itself
around the tragic acting of James Quin, who made his debut in
1714, four years after his revered predecessor's death, but who
continued acting long enough into the century that his style came
to be perceived by some very quotable sources as superannuated
by the time of Garrick's ascendancy. Hairstyle accounts for at least
part of that perception (fig. 13). Remembered vividly as the "Bel-
lower" lampooned by Tobias Smollet, who compared his elocution
to the chanting of vespers and his gesture to the heaving of ballast

into the hold of a ship (*BD* 12:239), Quin makes an appearance in the memoirs of Richard Cumberland characterized as a kind of fossil relic cast up from an earlier cultural stratum. When Garrick played Lothario and Quin played Horatio side-by-side in *The Fair Penitent,* Cumberland recalls, in a passage oft-quoted by theater historians, the mimic world seemed to turn upside down, so marked was the contrast:

> Quin presented himself upon the rising of the curtain in a green velvet coat embroidered down the seams, an enormous full-bottomed periwig, rolled stockings and high-heeled, square-toed shoes. With very little variation in cadence, and in a deep full tone, accompanied by a sawing kind of action, which had more of the senate than the stage in it, he rolled out his heroics with an air of dignified indifference.

Suggesting to Cumberland a sea-change in theatrical style, the celerity and informal variety of comic acting seem to have insinuated themselves in tragic drama, renovating what counted as prestige in the role-icon of the great Shakespearean actor. When Garrick "came bounding" on stage, "young and light and alive in every muscle and in every feature,"

> Heavens, what a transition!—it seemed as if a whole century had been stept over in the transition of a single scene. Old things were done away, and a new order at once brought forward, bright and luminous and clearly destined to dispel the barbarisms and bigotry of a tasteless age, too long attached to the prejudices of custom and superstitiously devoted to the illusions of imposing declamation.[34]

With Garrick, Cumberland suggests, superstition gave way to a new kind of magic, one founded on the publicity owed to the abnormally interesting attraction of youthful indecorum superannuating the received protocols of the tragedy king. The contention was somewhat more nuanced than that, but the analogy of David versus Goliath still strikes scholars as apposite.[35]

Neglected by theater historians, however, is James Stewart's account in *Plocacosmos* of the role of hairstyles in the Garrick revo-

Fig. 13. William Hogarth, pencil drawing, "Facsimile of the
Proportions of Garrick and Quin," 1746. The Royal
Collection © 2006, Her Majesty Queen Elizabeth II.

lution. He details the care with which David Garrick introduced
appropriate wigs to assist his fellow actors in developing their characters and their lines of business. Setting aside the full-bottomed
periwig held over by Quin, Garrick installed his own version of
Hogarth's "five orders" in the Drury Lane wig room:

> We even find, and many now living have seen it, that Mr. Quin
> acted almost all his young characters, as Hamlet, Horatio,
> Pierre, etc. in a full-dress suit, and large peruke. But Mr. Gar-
> rick's active genius, soon determining on improvement in
> every department of the theatre, in order to realize the repre-

sentations, first attacked the mode of dress, and no part more than that of the head and hair. The consequence of this was, that a capital player's wardrobe, might be compared to a sale shop for all manner of dresses, and for nothing more than the various quantities of, what they call, natural heads of hair: there is the comedy head of hair, and the tragedy ditto; the silver locks, and the common gray; the carroty poll, and yellow caxon; the savage black, and the Italian brown, and Shylock's and Falstaff's very different heads of hair, and very different beards; with the Spanish fly, the foxes tail, &c. &c. &c.[36]

Anticipating the powers of delineation that later underscored George Alexander Stevens's monologue entertainment "Lecture Upon Heads," Garrick's reforms populated the midcentury stage with a new resource of expressive characterization. Hair could be worn at number of stylish lengths and in a number of shapes and colors, as appropriate to the particular role-icon they announced, promoted, and disseminated.

Though he does not, like Stewart, take up the question of the actor's hair per se, the philosophe Denis Diderot (1713–84) defined the paradigm shift in acting style embodied by Garrick as the calculated, even mechanical exertion of physical control over his body and its expression—less decorous, but more varied and expressive than that of Betterton or Quin. Allowing that the great actor's presence in England made a trip to London more aesthetically edifying than a trip to Italy to see the ruins of Rome, Diderot describes him demonstrating the passions to the salons during a visit to Paris in 1765:

> Garrick pushes his head out between the two halves of a double door and, in the space of five or six seconds, his expression goes successively from whild joy to moderate joy, from this joy to tranquillity, from tranquillity to surprise, from surprise to astonishment, from astonishment to sadness, from sadness to despondency, form despondency to fear, from fear to horror, from horror to despair, and then returns from this last level to the point from which it came.[37]

Such astonishing self-control has its pilatory counterpart in the custom-made fright-wig that Garrick developed for use in his production of *Hamlet,* which he sprang at the moment when the Prince first encounters his father's ghost. On the line "Look, my lord, it comes," the hairs of this innovative appliance rose up obligingly to simulate the horripilation of mortal dread (*BD* 6:72). This was the scene that prompted Dr. Johnson to express his concern for the effect of the shock on the ghost and set poor Partridge's knees to knocking in *Tom Jones.* In contrast to Betterton's more static enactment, Garrick's highly kinetic Hamlet flipped his wig.[38]

There is no doubt that Garrick, as much or more than any performer in history, had It—so absorbingly riddled with contradictions that he inspired *The Paradox of the Actor*—but Diderot does not exempt him from the social isolation of other self-exhibiting freaks, a fate their gifts cannot defer but might actually hasten. "Anyone in society who wants to please everyone, and has the unfortunate talent to be able to," Diderot wrote, in a desolating definition of It, "is nothing, possesses nothing which is proper to him or distinguishes him, nothing which might bring delight to some and tedium to others. He talks all the time, and always talks well; he is a professional sycophant, a great courtier, and a great actor." But the great actor's personal absence, a kind of affectively disabling autism, paradoxically enables his creation of the illusion of absolute presence: "It's because he's nothing that he's everything to perfection, since his particular form never stands in the way of the alien forms he has to assume." Diderot locates the paradox of the actor in the professionalization of the most fundamental of all human contradictions: "One is oneself by nature; one is another by imitation; the heart you imagine for yourself is not the heart you have." In a striking application of the theater to modern democratic politics, Diderot argues that the successful professional, having detached his or her heart from the emotions he or she represents, has fitted himself or herself for one function above all, even more consummately than for the stage: to become "a great king or a great minister."[39]

If style may be defined as social order inscribed upon and lived in the body, then the recurrence of big hair since the eighteenth century has raised style to a very ambitious scale, at no time more consequentially than in the Cold War bouffant craze. The resemblance between the style of Margaret Thatcher's stacked, lacquered hair and the principles of control, constraint, and economy of force noted in connection with English tragic acting by the bigwigs Betterton and Quin recalls the principle that time, measured in customs and practices, does not flow, but rather percolates. Without a hair out of place, The Lady, like Betterton's head, was not for turning (fig. 14). The former prime minister herself, like her collaborator Ronald Reagan, an innovator in the integration of the visible and efficient branches of government under the aegis of Hollywood mythmaking, whose hair was also mysteriously composed of some impermeable substance, forthrightly collapsed the distinction between accessories and implements. In her political testament *Statecraft*, deploring the idea of a combat role for women in modern warfare, Mrs. Thatcher wrote: "Women have plenty of roles in which they can serve with distinction: some of us even run countries. But generally we are better at wielding the handbag than the bayonet."[40] In parsing the English constitution in 1867, Bagehot, prescient as he was, could not have anticipated the utility of a weaponized accessory deployed to bludgeon adversaries into submission. If the efficacy of these principles is to be doubted, the skeptic should consult the unhappy memoirs of the Argentine junta. In a different register, the skeptic might ponder the fate of the millions affected by the British Nationality Act of 1981, which set aside nine hundred years of precedent to make "patriality" or race, not place of birth, the key to full subjecthood.[41] Governing in the reign of Elizabeth II, it was the prime minister who might have said, paraphrasing Elizabeth I: "I have the body of a frail woman, but the heart and stomach of a king—and a king of England too."

As a synecdoche infiltrating other political enchantments in a reactionary decade, Thatcherite coiffure sustained the deeply held intuition, fortified by anthropological fieldwork, that as hair goes, so goes power. Novelist Rhys Hughes remembers Mrs. Thatcher as "Le Bouffant Terrible." In the end, she seemed to him to have summarized all the formidable strength and poignant vulnerability of

Fig. 14. Lady Thatcher, in her Garter Robes, © Corbis.

her character in her hair—at once a burnished helmet and a brittle carapace. On the one hand, Hughes evokes her shadow stalking the halls of British politics in the 1970s and 1980s, intimidating allies and enemies alike, an irresistible force appearing to mortal constituents as a "silhouette crouched and leering with out-stretched talons, but half its height taken up by the penumbra of her hairdo." On the other hand, Hughes not unfeelingly senses her exhaustion and despondency at the end of her reign as she experi-enced the breath-stopping ingratitude of the erstwhile Tory pro-tégés who betrayed her. As she weakened politically as well as phys-ically, she became stronger as a dramatic role-icon of abnormally compelling interest: a hybrid of the tragedy queen and the tragedy king. When her cabinet ministers, men of her own party, did her in, they came to her one by one to tell her cravenly that while each and everyone of them supported her personally, she had insufficient support from the others to continue in office. She called it a farce, but at the denouement she broke down, like Marie Antoinette, and wept in front of them all. Rhys Hughes evokes the pathos of the latter scene: "Major occasionally went to 'Checkers' to visit Thatcher but these times became more and more infrequent. She had slumped into a deep armchair and deeper depression, her hairstyle now so tall and heavy it had to be supported from the ceiling by chains."[42] John Major, lithe as an acrobat, seemed then to bound onstage—a Garrick to Mrs. Thatcher's Quin: "heavens, what a transition!" As Lady Thatcher, wearing her Garter robes, her head looking much smaller than most will remember it, she releases the dark crescent of lacquered tresses like an accessory soul, completing her tragic metamorphosis from utensil to ornament. Samson, not Atlas, finally shrugged, and as the weight of the world fell from the PM's shoulders, she elicited an ancient gallantry to salve her shame: *Honi soi qui mal y pense.*

Social hair remains, as it was in the age of Pope and Garrick, where the balance we still keep today was struck, as beguiling as magical hair. It remains as vexing too. Under the sway of that ambivalence—split ends with roots stuck deep in the three-dimensional eighteenth century—"mighty Contests" still imperfectly conceal themselves behind "trivial Causes." For Lady Thatcher, as for many others whose Hogarthian afterimages flash like grotesque graphic satires through the ether of the It-Effect, the antiphony of charisma and stigma becomes as stark as the contention of white and black in the long-running performance of Britannia, who is herself the vauntedly patrial tragedy queen.

# 4.
# skin

Queen of the Coloured Hearts
Queen of the Devastated
Queen of the Unloved Ones
Queen of the Unknown
Love from the Unknown
　—Anonymous message left at
　　　　Kensington Palace
　(*Daily Mail,* September 4, 1997)

Sarah Siddons cared for her skin. According to her own account of her final sitting for Sir Joshua Reynolds, she intervened when he started to put the finishing touches on her portrait as *The Tragic Muse* and prevented him from applying a wash of color to her face and neck. Her purpose, like her complexion, was clear. As he daubed his brush contemplatively in the offending pigment, she warned him that heightening the color of her skin would sacrifice "that tone of complexion so accordant with the chilling and deeply concentrated musing of Pale Melancholy."[1] He put down his brush—and for good reason. Succeeding Garrick as the leading personality in tragic acting, Mrs. Siddons was by 1784 an unassailable authority on all that pertained to Melpomene, especially the representation of melancholy affect, the ancient tragic mask re-created in the modern female countenance. Affect depended on tint as well as hue. The lighter the skin, the more expressive the face, contemporaries reasoned. Some carried this peculiar idea to

146

the extent of denying the existence of the full range of emotional expression in the faces of dark-skinned peoples. But Siddons (and Reynolds, once he came around, if we are to believe the actress's account) had a more complicated investment in the meaning of her skin, a meaning that went beyond its vividly literal whiteness. Their shared investment in her skin—contrary to the shibboleth of feminine vanity about aging but consonant with the expectations of the cult of theatrical celebrity that William Hazlitt called "the Kemble Religion"—was in its apparent antiquity.

In the hierarchy of neoclassical dramatic genres, tragedy claimed pride of place. To be elevated to the ancient throne of the Muse of Tragedy, as Siddons was by Reynolds (supported by a number of other contemporary artists and rhapsodists), was to embody physically a cultural value that emulated traditional religious piety in the expressions of devotion it inspired. Judging from contemporary responses to her performances, strongly held generic preferences shaped the apotheosis of her late career: tragedy sacralized its objects and its agents; comedy, at which Mrs. Siddons did not excel, was its (and her) profane foil. The neoclassical opposition of tragedy and comedy served this dialectical purpose effectively because a sufficient number of bourgeois spectators were prepared to accept the replacement of the sacred by the antique. New sacraments required different but plausibly venerable icons, and beginning with Betterton (d. 1710) theatrical celebrities began to appear in the vacated niches at the altar of public devotion on the strength of their tragic performances, especially in Shakespeare, who was ever more obsequiously venerated by the Bardolators. From Betterton to John Henderson (d. 1785), thespians were buried in Westminster Abbey, with notable obsequies performed there for the actresses Anne Oldfield (d. 1730) and Anne Bracegirdle (d. 1748) and most spectacularly for David Garrick (d. 1779). Later, marble effigies of Siddons and her brother John Philip Kemble appeared in the same national shrine, a privilege once reserved to duly anointed sovereigns, saints, and benefactors. Their marmoreal whiteness supplanted the heavily pigmented wax that makes the clammy skin of Charles II's effigy seem so swarthily lifelike, but they continued through their own personal publicity campaigns to add to the historic proliferation of robust afterimages, creating resentment as well as adulation. Such effigies, whose pretensions disgusted Charles Lamb no less than they did Ruskin, marked with ambivalence the progress of synthetic experience, the migration of manna from conventionally religious icons to accessory ones. Lamb ridiculed the Abbey monument to David Garrick, in his view an excrescence and an imposition in Poet's Corner, as he worked himself up so far as to say that Shakespeare's plays ought to be read but not staged. Lamb came to this sad conclusion because he believed the vicarious experience of distinctively acted roles spuriously substituted for real communion with the characters created by the Bard: "We speak of Lady Macbeth," Lamb complained, "while in reality we are thinking of Mrs. S."[2] And no wonder: the actress had created such an unforgettable afterimage in this role that for decades memorabilia-collecting fans could buy a Wedgwood chess set designed by John Flaxman with her gesticulating Lady Macbeth used as the model for the figures of the queens, both white and black (*BD*, 14:67).

Exploring the network of imagery that depicts the tragedy queen's skin, this chapter juxtaposes Reynolds's *The Tragic Muse* and related eighteenth-century theatrical portraits with the earlier mezzotint, signed by J. Smith and W. Vincent (ca. 1690), showing Anne Bracegirdle as Semernia, the Indian Queen, in Aphra Behn's *The Widow Ranter* (1689). The similarities and differences between the careers of Bracegirdle, who retired from the stage in 1707, and Siddons, who retired in 1812, suggest the tentatively improving image of the actress in respectable society, but also the stubbornly lingering disapprobation of performers of any kind, especially successful women. What can't be doubted is that each of them possessed charismatic attraction in the highest degree, though not exactly of the same kind, and that each of them produced the most powerful version of the It-Effect for her own era of English history. Each tragedy queen was adored in her own time, and each was, like Diana, Princess of Wales in hers, despised and stalked as well as venerated. Each of them, in her own time, was represented in a way that emphasized her skin, her afterimage in each case supporting the broad claim of Richard Dyer: "Racial imagery is central to the organisation of the modern world."[3] Taking the long view, the time between their epochs did not merely pass, it percolated, plumbing the three-dimensional eighteenth century at one of its deepest points.

The celebrity of actors like Betterton and Garrick and actresses like Bracegirdle and Siddons sets the terms of the It-Effect, not only because their images began to circulate widely and hyperbolically in the absence of their persons (though that is no small matter), but also because their fame came at the price of an equally inflated notoriety. Opprobrium, the dark underside of modern adulation, especially eclipsed the moral reputations of actresses, whose profession, like the only other one that then welcomed women, entailed exhibiting themselves in public for pay. Today their heirs among movie stars and royals reign uneasily in the face of similarly intense contradictions between deification and denigration, but eighteenth-century performers were true pioneers in first unleashing, then suffering, and finally manipulating the hunger of their publics for the multifarious and contradictory charms of It.

Adopted by the Bettertons, Thomas and Mary, Anne Bracegirdle was raised within earshot of the playhouse. She debuted in children's roles, graduating into leading romantic heroine parts in comedy and tragedy, a number of which William Congreve and Nicholas Rowe wrote expressly to exploit her bewitching personality. Known as the "Romantick Virgin" because she kept her love life discreetly but tantalizingly veiled, she never married or suffered herself to be kept by a wealthy admirer; but she had many offers, some of them hard to refuse: one would-be keeper, Lord Mohun, attempted to abduct her and murdered the actor who tried to intervene (*BD* 2:269–81). Pursued by scurrilous gossip, which proved maddeningly impossible to verify, and mentioned romantically in connection with the many men who doted on her, all without apparent effect, she retired early as what Colley Cibber called "the *Cara,* the Darling of the Theatre." "For it will be no extravagant thing to say," Cibber continued, "Scarce an Audience saw her that were less than half of them Lovers, without a suspected Favorite among them." She excelled at high comedy, and

Congreve famously wrote for her the role of Millamant in *The Way of the World* (1700), but she also played the tragedy queen to good effect, eclipsed only by Elizabeth Barry in her time in that line of business; as Cibber recalls gratefully of Bracegirdle's contribution to the plausibility of motives in Nathaniel Lee's *The Rival Queens,* "If any thing could excuse that desperate Extravagance of Love, that almost frantick Passion of Lee's Alexander the Great, it must have been when Mrs. Bracegirdle was his Statira."[4] Numbered among the theatrical *Cara's* most memorable features was the paleness of her skin. Aston recalls that Bracegirdle boasted "a fresh blushy Complexion; and, whenever she exerted herself, had an involuntary Flushing in her Breast, Neck, and Face."[5]

Born Sarah Kemble in 1755 in the Shoulder of Mutton public house in Brecon, Wales where her strolling parents were playing, Siddons made her debut as Ariel in *The Tempest* at age eight, married the mediocrity William Siddons, bore seven children, and after a false start under David Garrick in 1770s, dominated tragic acting from her return to London in 1782 until her retirement in 1812—testimony to both her histrionic gifts and her considerable managerial acumen. Known to theatergoers as "The Siddons," she was recommended to tourists as one of the obligatory sights of London, like the Abbey or the Tower Lions. On days when she acted at Drury Lane, crushes occurred at the box office hours before it opened. When she toured the provincial cities, London pickpockets followed her to work the large (and presumably less street-wise) crowds that they knew she would draw there. When she played opposite John Wesley's sermons, she decimated his attendance. She sat for every major artist of the age and many minor ones, and her image circulated popularly through prints and book plates (*BD* 14:1–37). One extraordinary consequence of her success was her acquisition of the cultural authority that Reynolds both captured and exploited in *The Tragic Muse,* even while she continued to be deprecated for her profession and her financial success in advancing it. As part of the calculated construction of her *brand* in the modern corporate sense of the word, Siddons carefully protected her offstage image as wife and mother. Onstage she created a repertoire of roles that featured her contradictory capacity to project enormous, sometimes even frightening strengths—nobility, courage, and fortitude—while absorbing heartbreaking blows to her most delicately vulnerable feelings— filial duty, motherly tenderness, and spousal trust. Throughout her career, in other words, she traded on the uncanny durability of her thin skin, which was also an unusually white skin: Tom Davies spied her "paleness" even under the rouge she chose to wear to represent the title character of Calista in Rowe's *The Fair Penitent*.[6]

Reynolds's masterpiece of theatrical portraiture represents a crux in the history of It (fig. 15). He dramatizes the extent to which eighteenth-century tragic celebrity inherited the responsibilities of the time-honored but largely superannuated function of sacred kings. At the very least, *The Tragic Muse* helps to explain why Siddons's other hagiographic admirers—including painters, biographers, critics, and the political philosopher Edmund Burke— thought that it did. In a period marked by revolutionary change, tragic celebrities made claims on the prestige of antiquity in order to confer the appearance if not the substance of cultural legitimacy on their art. They were not alone in doing so. Burke numbered among the prominent intellectuals and politicians who devotedly attended Siddons's performances: according to her own account, Fox, Gibbon, Windham, Sheridan, and Reynolds sat together as a party in the orchestra seats and joined in congratulatory visits to her dressing room.[7]

What good is a tragedy queen to serious-minded men? In his famous excursus on the revolutionary outrages perpetrated against the person of the Queen of France, Burke put the case succinctly as he eulogized Mrs. Siddons and her precursor David Garrick. Remembering the sting of the manly tears that the great tragedians "extorted" from his eyes as he sat in front row seats at Drury Lane, he unburdened himself of the gallant outrage that he assumed his readers would share as he dramatized the indignities Marie Antoinette suffered at the hands of cockaded ruffians. He stages a terrific scene, inventing the details where he cannot embellish them. Rousted from her bed and terrorized by the bayonets of the revolutionary guards supposedly still dripping blood from the murder the faithful servant who sought to bar her door

Fig. 15. Sir Joshua Reynolds, *Sarah Siddons as the Tragic Muse,* 1784.
Courtesy of the Huntington Library, Art Collection and
Botanical Gardens, San Marino, California.

to their invasion, the queen still showed her presence of mind in hiding a dagger or perhaps poison on her "nearly naked" person as the ultimate "sharp antidote" to a fate worse than death.

Did the author of *Reflections on the Revolution in France* recall that Pity and Terror, the dark figures in the background of *The Tragic Muse,* proffer the choice of dagger or poisoned cup? He certainly knew that Siddons earned her salt by playing queens like these, her female vulnerability most movingly irradiated in pathetic distress by the strength of resolve she kept veiled. Given the press of current events, Burke could think of nothing more sublime than the stage she trod as a vicarious alternative to the superannuated

pulpit, at least for the duration of the emergency: "Indeed the theater is a better school of moral sentiments than churches, where
the feelings of humanity are thus outraged."[8] Tom Paine and Mary
Wollstonecraft appealed to the antitheatrical prejudice of their
readers in order to make Burke look pretty silly for having said
that, but in the unending state of emergency since then, his mod-
est proposal to turn churches into theaters has gained at least as
much political traction as their overreaching vindication of common sense and the universal rights of men and women.

On the occasion of the final sitting for *The Tragic Muse,* Reynolds
reportedly told the actress, as he affixed his signature in the most
reverent way in the most humble location, that he was content to
go down to posterity on the hem of her dress.[9] Such idolatry, which
characterizes a number of the most memorable reviews of Siddonian performances as well as the vast production of artworks featuring her as tragic icon, gestures grandly to generations yet unborn
even as it honors the forebears to which *The Tragic Muse* reverently
alludes. Such idolatry also represents a symbolic version of the
intergenerational social contract famously set forth by Burke,
"between those who are living, those who are dead, and those who
are to be born." In the neopagan deification of tragic celebrity, the
physical appearance of surfaces, their luster apparently burnished
as if by their passage through time, inspired in otherwise sober critics professions of mystical devotion. Reynolds wreathed the Muse's
skin in the halo of the saintly effigy or relic. Devotees attached to
her dramatically posed pallor a transhistorical power, one akin to
Burke's "eternal society, linking the lower with the higher natures,
connecting the visible and invisible world."[10] Adulating Sarah Siddons as Reynolds did (or as Burke did the Queen of France, "glit-
tering like the morning star, full of life, and splendor, and joy"),[11]
they also deferred to her as the conservator of whiteness, the visible
icon of its putative timelessness—not bone white, but the suffused
radiance of the golden penumbra, prompting her to powder her
hair orange to catch the aura-producing rays of the newly
intensified lighting of the Argand lamp.[12]

The evidence for this claim for the power of reenchantment
imputed to skin is both visual and textual.[13] Religious language is

a notable feature of several retrospective accounts of Sarah Siddons's life and work, and it is illuminated by the key concept of patina. The word *patina* connotes the appearance of an object grown beautiful and revered with age and use. It literally means a film or encrustation caused by the oxidization of the surface of bronze or, by extension, a similar alteration over time to the surface of marble. Horace Walpole has the first usage noted, when in 1748 he draws Conway's attention to squibs "bronzed over with a patina of gunpowder," but during the second half of the eighteenth century the word enlarges to suggest an appearance or aura that is derived from association, habit, or established character *(OED)*. It is a quality of an artificial surface that accretes its visible and invisible properties only over the passage of time; it cannot be painted on or appliquéd without falsification. But despite its tangible materiality, its value seems intangibly negotiable, like that of time itself. Patina's aura, which adds cultural and usually monetary value to the object, depends in part on its resistance to the artificial acceleration of its accumulation. In that way patina consoles the conservative as it vindicates the snob. To emphasize the secular iconicity of patina, it is important to reiterate that the term specifically derives from the medieval Latin word for the plate that holds the Eucharist: its roots in time thus strike deep into the genealogy of sacred practices, especially those performances that defined the migration of the holy from the ascetic to the aesthetic. Patina encourages beholders to feel an uncanny sense of belonging to history or of history belonging to them in the form of "heritage." As the synthetic experience of the past, patina converts apparently solid material objects and surfaces into vaporous nostalgia as mysteriously as bread and wine become body and blood in the minds of true believers. In sum, it percolates.

Layering on patina by the promiscuity of his allusions and the Rembrantian chastity of his palette, Reynolds's painterly exegesis of tragic celebrity paganized transubstantiation, turning a physical body into an immortal one through the powers of art. Specifically, he appropriated for modern portraiture the combined auras of religious painting and ancient sculpture. Early Siddons biographer James Boaden was among the first but not the last authority to have demonstrated the influence of Michelangelo's Sistine Chapel "Sibyls and Prophets" on the composition of Sarah Siddons as the Tragic Muse. Michelangelo's figures approach as close as painting dares to the sculptor's art, and Reynolds takes from them what Boaden calls "the descent of the Holy Spirit upon the Apostles" to compose his devotional scene.[14] In this regard, Siddons's official biographer Thomas Campbell narrates a particularly revealing story of his pilgrimage to the sculpture gallery of the Louvre in the company of the actress. A sculptor himself, he puts his anecdote into the form of a conversion experience before the god of light. Like the fifty-seven-year-old but ageless beauty Siddons, who reportedly attracted quiet murmurs of interest and even awe as she passed majestically through the galleries of the Louvre, the Apollo Belvedere seemed to Campbell to glow from within. No less important than the patina of the sculpture to his ecstasy as a beholder was the physical presence of the actress herself at his side as he approached the shrine:

> In the statuary hall of that place I had the honour of giving Mrs Siddons my arm the first time in both our lives that we saw the Apollo of Belvidere. From the farthest end of that spacious room, the god seemed to look down like a president on the chosen assembly of sculptured forms, and his glowing marble, unstained by time, appeared to my imagination as if he had stepped freshly from the sun. I had seen casts of the glorious statue with scarcely any admiration; and I must undoubtedly impute that circumstance in part to my inexperience in art, and to my taste having till then lain torpid. But still I prize the recollected impressions of that day too dearly to call them fanciful. They seemed to give my mind a new sense of the harmony of art—a new visual power of enjoying beauty. Nor is it mere fancy that makes the difference between the Apollo himself and his plaster casts. The dead whiteness of the stucco copies is glaringly monotonous, whilst the diaphanous surface of the original seems to soften the light which it reflects.[15]

Time measures the distance between "dead whiteness" and "glowing marble" by depositing on the surface of the latter an uncanny sense of depth. Quite beyond the aura of the original, which certainly gets its due here, Campbell, without naming it, speaks of "heritage," which mediates between the dead and those yet to be born. Here the museum itself, once a royal palace, takes on the function of a sacred temple or shrine—a modern place of devotion in which a cultural icon assumes the role of a religious one.

Campbell's devotional scene, juxtaposing the public persona of the actress and the patina of the ancient statue, had already been well rehearsed by such works as William Hamilton's portrait of Mrs. Siddons as Euphrasia in Arthur Murphy's tragedy *The Grecian Daughter*.[16] In its sculpturesque amplitude of scale, Hamilton's work intentionally blurs the boundary between history painting and portraiture. With the glowing aura of her flesh shining through her diaphanous white drapery, Mrs. Siddons, the stroller's daughter, is "antiqued." Campbell's account of the Louvre visit recapitulates the essential terms of Hamilton's stage illusion. "The dead whiteness of the stucco copies" cannot satisfy him. There is another property beyond its shape that elevates the Apollo into the transhistorical category of the dead, the living, and the unborn. That property is the sublime quality of its surface, which is produced by its capacity to glow. The essence of its patina is in its translucence, which suffuses an ambient white light that seems, as with the portraits of Siddons by Hamilton and Reynolds, "diaphanous," emanating as if from the skin itself, as if it *is* the skin itself.

Unless this revised history of theater as synthetic experience, which claims for one aspect of the eighteenth-century stage a partial usurpation of the social function of an established religion, was in fact anticipated by Siddons's contemporaries, it is difficult to account for the intensity and specificity of the language that Hazlitt used repeatedly to describe her position in the minds and hearts of her audiences. In *Table Talk* he recapitulated his idolatrous apostrophe of her in *The Examiner*, where he would have her be not only a queen but "no less than a goddess, or than a prophetess inspired by the gods," a veritable prodigy of pagan spirituality and vicarious royalty. The question before him as critical arbiter is whether the actress, now retired for good, should desist from seating herself in the stage boxes when she attends the theater, expanding the custom that players on the active list should not let themselves be seen in the front of the house. His decisive advice not to desist is especially useful because it highlights the degree to which the iconography of Reynolds's great portrait has influenced the afterimage of the star, as both painter and subject knew it would:

> Mrs. Siddons seldom if ever goes [to the boxes], and yet she is almost the only thing left worth seeing there. She need not stay away on account of any theory that I can form. She is out of the pale of all theories, and annihilates all rules. Wherever she sits there is grace and grandeur, there is tragedy personified. Her seat is the undivided throne of the Tragic Muse. She has no need of the robes, the sweeping train, the ornaments of the stage; in herself she is as great as any being she ever represented in the ripeness and plenitude of her power.[17]

Like Reynolds, Hazlitt as drama critic endowed Siddons with the patina of classical antiquity, placing her on the pedestal of the most prestigious genre in which she excels even her most illustrious male predecessors as tragic icon:

> We never saw Garrick; and Mrs. Siddons was the only person who ever embodied our idea of high tragedy. Her mind and person were both fitted for it. The effect of her acting was greater than could be conceived beforehand. It perfectly filled and overpowered the mind. The first time of seeing this great actress was an epoch in everyone's life, and left impressions which could never be forgotten. She appeared to belong to a superior order of beings, to be surrounded with a personal awe, like some prophetess of old, or Roman matron, the mother of Coriolanus or the Gracchi. Her voice answered her to her form, and her expression to both.[18]

Christian and pagan imagery share pride of place in Hazlitt's several encounters with her special brand of It, and he attributes to Siddons, in her office as tragedy queen by divine right, unwritten constitutional powers over the public imagination and will that in more recent times might have embarrassed even Evita.

It was a paganizing piety of this nature that brought Edward Gibbon with ritual punctuality to his pew in Covent Garden to worship when Siddons played, and it was this impulse that prompted Burke to name Siddons in connection with the sufferings of Marie Antoinette in *Reflections on the Revolution in France:* when one king is about to lose his head and another has already lost his mind, theatrical royals had better keep their wits about them. It was conclusively this kind of devotional public fantasy that nationalized Siddons's iconic status when she consented to appear in St. Paul's Cathedral costumed as "Britannia" to celebrate King George III's recovery from madness. Stepping easily into this nominated patriotic role-icon, she seated herself majestically, as Boaden reports, "in the exact attitude of Britannia as impressed upon our copper coin."[19] Her pose no doubt recalled that of the Reynolds's picture of the Tragic Muse, with the judicious addition of a spear borrowed from the property closet. But it also must have suggested to some the most desperate measure of Burke's cultural counterrevolution, his readiness, at least hypothetically, to replace the national church with a national stage: "because in events like these our passions instruct our reason; because when kings are hurl'd from their thrones by the Supreme Director of this great drama, and become the objects of insult to the base, and pity to the good, we behold such disasters in the moral, as we should behold a miracle in the physical order of things."[20] On the edge of this frightening abyss, Siddons made the word flesh and the flesh glow with the reassuring patina of tradition.

Percolating in the cultural brew best characterized by the portmanteau word *heritage,* this mystified legacy continued to bubble up in the counterrevolutionary (or the alternative-revolutionary) thinking of the prolifically opinionated Elinor Glyn. In *Romantic Adventure,* the Hollywood maven and Tory Radical reports that she began to develop her theory of "spiritual disguise" during her early childhood in Canada, listening to her grandmother's stories about the beauty of life under the ancien régime and their émigré family's flight from the Terror. To this recollected threat against her childhood innocence Glyn added her fear of what she called "race" as a menace to colonial empire and to her night thoughts, a revealing juxtaposition of terrors:

> At the age of about six I had been overcome with terror upon hearing of the murder of a neighbor, Mr. Neave, by a darkie who worked on his estate. About then I was also told about the execution of Marie Antoinette, and learned how my Grand-papa's family had taken refuge in Abbeville during the Revolution to escape the guillotine. My imagination after this had been full of fears, and I could not bear to break off the head of a flower without shuddering at the thought of the way Marie Antoinette had died.[21]

So into the breach against Jacobin and Bolshevik, Burke would rush the stroller's daughter and Glyn, the Nathan's counter girl because these actresses exerted a disarming power—It—over the hearts and minds of the masses, all the more miraculous because of the humbleness of its sources.

Britannia's effigy, Gibbon's devotion, Hazlitt's litany, and Burke's eulogy on Mrs. Siddons are important data in the history of the consolidation of the modern It-Effect in the figure of the performer. But they tell only one side of the story, the charismatic one. The nomination of a sacred effigy from the ranks of the socially marginal induces a need to demean the nominee, who acts as an anxiety-transmitting conduit between a mythologized past and an uncertain future. This was demonstrably the case in the career of "The Siddons," whose representation by artists includes cruel caricatures as well as idealized portraits. Boaden remarks: "Perhaps no actress was ever more persecuted by cabal than Mrs. Siddons."[22] Falsely attacked for her stinginess when she allegedly would not play in benefit performances for fellow actors or charity events, Siddons was forced to answer her critics in print and in person from the stage.[23] At this juncture, the dialectic of comedy and tragedy reemerges in the shape of a deep cultural confusion about Sarah Siddons's liminal position between the sacred and profane. As an actress who once appeared in comic "breeches" roles, she bore the taint that adhered to any woman who exhibited herself in

public for money: among the prostitutes of Covent Garden, "posture molls" were many of the most abject.

In this regard, contemporaries played Sarah Siddons off her
contemporary Frances Abington, née Barton (1737–1815), whose
flair for comedy was easily opposed to Siddons's reign as the unexcelled tragedienne. Reynolds painted Mrs. Abington as the "Muse
of Comedy" in what Shearer West perceptively describes as a companion piece and dialectical partner to *Mrs. Siddons as the Tragic
Muse.*[24] The beholder can readily imagine the model for the Muse
of Comedy entering the struggle with Tragedy for the soul of
David Garrick as in Reynolds famous picture of 1761, and emerging victorious, as Abington did in fact when she and Siddons were
rivals under Garrick's management of Drury Lane. In *Garrick
between the Muses of Comedy and Tragedy* (fig. 16), the struggle is one
of reversible polarities, but the ultimate outcome is not in doubt.[25]
The actor's body language—torso and pelvis surrendering to the
comic voluptuary even as his head turns back in embarrassed apology to the tragic scold—gives him away. Comedy, all sunshine and
diaphanous undress, smiles stupidly as his right thumb presses her
tummy; Tragedy, draped in sackcloth, hair braided up tightly
clings to his left arm. Or is she slapping his wrist? The connection
of Mrs. Siddon's famous pose to the figure of "Tragedy" in the earlier picture is a revealing one. If we could ask Tragedy to stop both-
ering Garrick for a moment and to make a one-quarter turn
toward us and to be seated, she would assume the posture that the
x-rays of *The Tragic Muse* reveal to be the one that Reynolds
confidently deployed as a steady point of reference around which
the rest of the composition fidgeted through redrawings and
changes of mind. The pose with which he began *Sarah Siddons as
the Tragic Muse,* quoting the figure of Tragedy in Garrick, is the
very one that we see in the finished painting: left arm bent at the
elbow, hand unfolding index finger first; right arm extended and
resting (on Garrick's arm or on the chair arm); lips slightly parted
as if in a solemn summons to a more noble destiny. As polarized
embodiments of the two ancient masks that stand for the theater
itself, tragedy and comedy are glossed by Aristotle as morally separated by the different kinds of people they take as objects of imita-

Fig. 16. Sir Joshua Reynolds, *David Garrick Between the Muses of Comedy and Tragedy*, 1760–61. Somerset Maugham Theatre Collection, London, UK. The Bridgeman Art Library.

tion—tragedy depicts men and women as better than they are; comedy as worse. By the strictures and deep ambivalence inherent in the binary scheme of these ancient genres—each with its own patina—tragedy coalesced as the genre of the high-culture virgin and comedy that of the popular whore.

Reynolds also painted Mrs. Abington as Miss Prue in a revival of William Congreve's *Love for Love* (fig. 17). In this mesmerizing performance of the stigmatized underside of a show-stopping personality, the It-Girl of her era, Reynolds has the Muse of Comedy violate herself with her own thumb; seated or rather indecorously draped over the back of the chair, legs carelessly flounced to one side, she assumes a posture that is the antitype and reversal of Sid-

Fig. 17. Sir Joshua Reynolds, *Mrs. Abington as Miss Prue in Congreve's* Love for Love, 1771. Yale Center for British Art, Paul Mellon Collection.

don's on the throne of Tragedy. For the accessory figures of Pity and Terror, backup band to the Siddonian threnody, Reynolds supplies Shock the lap dog instead to share the Muse's throne. The moment Reynolds depicts is the one in which Miss Prue, the putatively innocent country girl, gets her first lesson in love from the disreputable Tattle. The knowing expression on the face of the tutee suggests that she has already formulated some robust ideas of her own on the subject. The sexual atmosphere of *Mrs. Abington as Miss Prue in William Congreve's* Love for Love, which juxtaposes innocence and experience in the service of a dirty joke at the expense of the actress, recalls the ornate fantasy about Anne Bracegirdle concocted by journalist Tom Brown and printed in

*Amusements Serious and Comical, Calculated for the Meridian of London* (1700). Brown places himself (and implicitly his readers and Bracegirdle's audiences in the playhouse as well) in the position of the enamored but unrequited playwright, William Congreve, futilely pursuing the "Romantick Virgin." In the footsteps of the would-be lover, the narrator follows the actress backstage to her dressing room, pointing out the highlights of her lingerie on his guided tour:

> But 'tis the way of the World, to have an esteem for the fair Sex, and she looks to a Miracle when she acting a part in one of his own Plays. . . . Look upon him once more I say, if is She goes to her Shift, 'tis Ten to One but he follows her, not that I would say for never so much to take up her Smock; he Dines with her almost ev'ry day, yet she's a Maid, he rides out with her, and visits her in Publick and Private, yet She's a Maid; if I had not particular respect for her, I should go near to say he lies with her, yet She's a Maid.[26]

Activating well-established formulae of public intimacy and mimetic desire in making and marketing synthetic experience, Brown's leering joke presages a similar one made by Reynolds in his role-portrait of Miss Prue. The titillating byplay surrounding the picture trades on the well-known circumstances of Mrs. Abington's early life as a demimondaine in Covent Garden, which will come up again in connection with the Cinderella-Galatea myth in the next chapter. For present purposes the telling detail may be discerned in the lower right-hand portion of composition of *Mrs Abington as Miss Prue*. That is the anatomical fold, located where the sitter's thighs come together, thinly disguised as another contour in the fabric of Miss Prue's dress, a point of interest limned in black against the pink and gray to catch the shade of the velvet wrist bands and the darkly vivid eyes. With this indecency, Sir Joshua teaches his subject and her beholders another kind of lesson in love.

A woman bearing Abington's name appears in *Harris's List of Covent Garden Ladies* (4th ed., 1793), a flesh catalog listing the prostitutes of the theater district along with their prices and sexual specialties.[27] By that date such a flagrant brand-infringement must have seemed like an old joke around the It-Zone of the Garden, and Fanny Abington was not the only victim. Among the sixty or seventy sex workers who were advertised in *Harris's List for 1788*, at the height of the first decade of "Siddons-mania," there is another, more telling theatrical double. Reflecting the ambivalence generated by theatrical effigies—in a case where *charismata* and *stigmata* so clearly operate recursively in the production of It—this prostitute styled herself "Miss Sarah Siddons." Giving her address as Tavistock Row, Covent Garden, the catalog offers the following particulars for "this good-natured piece of luxury" who bears the famous name:

> She is about twenty-three, light hair and eyes, a good skin, and size compleatly adapted for this season, and which seems to please the greatest part of her friends and customers, who think two arms full of joy twice as good as one; she is remarkably good-natured and affable to those who favour her with a visit, and will take almost any sum rather than turn her visitor away; but if you absolutely bilk her, beware of the consequence; for she is so well convinced that she does not merit such treatment, that she will, if possible, revenge the injury.[28]

Like that of "The Siddons," the image of Miss Sarah Siddons, however tarnished by penuriousness, comes down to us in history as favored with "a good skin," which meant without exception in *Harris's List,* and not only there, a white skin.

The evidence for approaching Mrs. Siddons as a carrier of the burden of racialized whiteness in a world increasingly organized by skin is not entirely retrospective, though it is admittedly conjectural. Even in scenes of anger and passion, Mrs. Siddons kept the pallid complexion that prompted George III to chide her for using a white base makeup, which she professed not to need and denied having used. Associating her by proxy with prostitution, as *Harris's List* does, ironically intensifies her trading on that whiteness. But the *List* goes further. As with many of the whore biographies of that time and this, the advertisement for the charms of Miss Sarah Siddons in *Harris's List* includes a brief account of how she got into the life in the first place. Having insisted on her light complexion, the *List* continues:

> Going to partake of an innocent amusement, vulgarly called black hops, where twelve pence will gain admission, [Miss Sarah Siddons] beheld, oh dire misfortune! a lovely African, blooming with all the hue of the warm country that gave him birth, and fell at that instant a sacrifice to the charms of the well made sooty frizeur; for some time she ranked him amongst her own train, and charitably exerted herself for his support, but growing at length satiated with his dear company, and almost ruined in the bargain, she dismissed the gloomy object of her late desires, and parted mutual friends; since which time she has graced the purlieus of Covent-Garden with her presence, and is perfectly well known under the Piazza.[29]

In the history of whiteness as a performance practice, organizing the world on the basis of skin, miscegenation constitutes the primal scene, especially when the liaison is between a black man and white woman, as it was in popular and pointed tragedies like *Othello* and *Oroonoko*. When the woman is also a cultural effigy or even when she is merely the body double of the effigy (as Miss Sarah Siddons was), the stakes are higher still. What the narrative of the affair between Miss Sarah Siddons and the African intensifies is the phenomenon that might be called "deep skin," the attribution of enormously important (and not infrequently tragic) consequences to differences that are in fact only skin deep.

Deep skin appeared on the London stage as the synthetic experience of empire long before Siddons played Desdemona or created the role of Julia in *The Blackamoor Wash'd White*. The chiaroscuro of *Sarah Siddons as the Tragic Muse* illuminates and is illuminated by one of the most famous afterimages of a previous tragedy queen: the mezzotint, signed by J. Smith and W. Vincent, showing Anne Bracegirdle as Semernia, "the Indian Queen" in Aphra Behn's *The Widow Ranter* (1689). Like the effigy of King Charles II, the Indian Queen has turned *contraposto* in fourth position to align her body in an eye-catching way, making the most of her fabulous clothes and accessories (fig. 18). Nominally Native

American, Semernia has been blanched white, a trend in exotic
tragedy queens, conspicuously Imoinda in Thomas Southerne's
popular adaptation of Aphra Behn's *Oroonoko*. In the service of the
It-Effect, Bracegirdle holds lightness and darkness in a precarious
equilibrium (*BD* 2:270). The silhouette of her gown is European,
and she is tightly corseted, but her sandaled feet show skin
beneath the hem of her dress, an erotic provocation on the stage.
Like the Tragic Muse, she holds her arms daintily in opposition:
with her right hand she manages the salvage of her overskirt; with
her left she raises a fan made of feathers, which in turn draws
attention to her feathered headdress and to those of the children
attending her. As ominous clouds gather in the background, the
skin of the tragedy queen glows white enough to contrast with the
other signs and wonders of the scene.

Perhaps the most revealing connection between the two images
is that the dominant accessory object serves in each case to high-
light the whiteness of the principal subject's skin: the queen's
parasol by pretending to shade it, the Muse's strings of pearls by
contrasting with it. Weirdly descending from the Muse's neck to
her bosom without support on one side, the glinting strands coil
improbably on her bodice in a lazy figure eight. Onstage or at the
assembly of Muses, they couldn't even function as jewelry because
they wouldn't stay on, but in the still afterimage of the great actress
they plunge dynamically across her patinated skin like a proud
baldric, reflecting its fineness and luminosity. In "The Indian
Queen," as in many other contemporary images in which it
appears, the accessory parasol betokens the sovereignty of an alien
noble, registered by the high degree of deference shown to her as
one who deserves the labor-intensive perquisites of portable
shade. But that is not the only work the parasol does. Shading the
queen from the sun, it draws heightened attention to the delicacy
and radiance of her skin. Walking under the parasol, she should
logically be in shadow, not the brightest light, but the glow of
whiteness emanates from within her translucent skin, even her
Native American skin, a graphic representation of the miraculous
and contradictory experience of It. To have It, Elinor Glyn
believed, one must have "race," a quality generally evident in En-

Fig. 18. J. Smith and W. Vincent, mezzotint, Anne Bracegirdle
as Semernia, "The Indian Queen." Harvard Theatre Collection.

glishmen and women, in her view, but also immediately discern-
able in a different but no less meaningful way among the peoples
of the world that she casually refers to with an omnibus wave as
"darkies."[30]

Not all the accessories that emphasize Bracegirdle's pallor are
inanimate objects. A tragedienne in her time had to depend on a
boy whose job it was to mind the lengthy and heavy train of her
gown. He remained onstage as long as she did. Exits were particularly tricky because of the wide turning radius required by the
train, and if her departure was abrupt, as when the character was
in a rage or pout, the boy had to be everywhere at once—except in
the way. In his humorous complaints about overproduction in the

staging of English tragedy, Joseph Addison sets up against the superfluity of its train bearers, as he does against its literally feather-headed heroes: "As these superfluous Ornaments upon the Head make a great Man, a Princess generally receives her Grandeur from those additional Incumbrances that fall into her Tail: I mean the broad sweeping Train that follows her in all her Motions and finds constant Employment for a Boy who stands behind her to open and spread it to Advantage. I do not know how others are affected by this Sight, but, I must confess, my Eyes are wholly taken up with the Page's Part; and, as for the Queen, I am not so attentive to anything she speaks, as to the right adjustment of her Train."[31] The Indian Queen merits two accessory boys, the one for the train, the other for the parasol. Each of their tasks takes two hands, but the real work they do here is symbolic—like that of the train and parasol themselves. They work their magic by transforming apparently excrescent details into crucial signs, and the type-casting of the title role underscores their meaning: the one stands in for the many, and the many for the one. The x-rays of *Sarah Siddons as the Tragic Muse* show that Reynolds originally intended to place a boy or cherub at the foot of the Muse's throne. He was to have looked up to her adoringly from about the place where Reynolds later signed the canvas on the hem of her dress. Like the boys in *The Widow Ranter,* the erased attendant in the Reynolds portrait was to have been an animate accessory, but the painter replaced him by the pairing of Pity and Terror in the finished work. Their tortured, shadowy faces attend to the Muse like miserable adult versions of the jolly boys who follow the Indian Queen and whose smiles were accurately minstrelized by the exclamation of a pioneering theater historian writing in the 1920s: "How proud they are, and what fun they are having!"[32] The Indian Queen and the Muse of Tragedy thus rule over their darkly complexioned subalterns, who serve as the most loyal of subjects in their respective empires, producing by contrast the whiteness of the principals.

Here the play of surfaces, skin against skin, threatens to shatter the mystery of the patina of whiteness—its authenticity claimed in a genealogy of performance that stretches back to a moment of completely mystified origin and forward to pervasively identifiable icons of mass culture: like the Indian Queen, regally glowing in the darkness, the King of Pop appears radiant beneath his protective parasol; and like Sarah Siddons, he obviously cares for his skin (fig. 19). In the neopagan revival of the deep eighteenth century, which coincided historically with the ever-more ambitious classification the world by skin color, the prevailing myth of origin touted the importance of the Greeks as the primordial white folks, despite ample evidence to the contrary, for even their statues were colored, Campbell's excursus on the Apollo Belvedere notwithstanding. But profane Comedy as well as sacred Tragedy also descended from the Greeks, and the aura of purity begins to disintegrate even as the ancient Muses begin to assemble. This disintegration is most evident as it overtakes the very effigies that a culture creates under the aegis of the It-Effect, perhaps because modern anxiety is expressed in the longing for what most people fear, even as modern grief is expressed in the unconsummated mourning for what they never really had.

In the performance genealogy of It, the charismatic effigy can be rescued from stigmatization only by death—and sometimes not even then. In Westminster Abbey, Mrs. Siddons is remembered by an outsized marble statue "unstained by time," but her body rests elsewhere, as the practice of burying actors in the cathedral of national memory lapsed after its obscure purpose in the transitional eighteenth century had been served. Thanks to Reynolds, the Siddonian afterimage reappears most materially, eerily enough, in Los Angeles, where it has periodically commuted down the interstate from its home at the Huntington Library, Art Collections, and Botanical Gardens to be the centerpiece of a show at the Getty Museum (1999), to be recycled in the Laguna Beach Pageant of the Masters, with Bette Davis taking Siddons's place on the throne for the tableau of *Tragic Muse* (1957), and to pop up, Oscar-like, in the hands of Anne Baxter as Eve, recipient of the "Sarah Siddons Award for Distinguished Achievement" in Joseph L. Mankiewicz's *All about Eve* (1950).[33] A robust afterimage extends the life of the tragedy queen, who otherwise flickers like a

Fig. 19. Michael Jackson, the King of Pop, © Getty Images.

candle in the wind: Melpomene, the Tragic Muse, chooses between the dagger and the cup; Semernia, the Indian Queen, dies at the hands of her white lover; Marie Antoinette, lovely and despised, feels the puff of wind on her neck.

Diana, Princess of Wales, the adored and the castoff queen of hearts, made her final exit within the ambivalent conventions of this historic genre of tragic performance. Her singularity let her speak for many. Of the supposed Benjaminian "aura" surrounding the inescapably pervasive images of Diana, Adrian Kear has written: "The 'auratic' quality of these portraits was accentuated by the media's ceaseless circulation of them at the time of her death as 'effigies' directly designed to stand in for the dead Diana."[34] The response to her passing marks the mass-mediated extension of

Durkheimian "effervescence" from the tribal village to the global one. Eulogizing her at her funeral in Westminster Abbey, her grieving brother captured the peculiar and mesmerizing pathos of her memory, even as he faced up to the unwelcome but irrepressible forces generated by the negative energies of the It-Effect. Diana—strong and vulnerable, experienced and innocent, stigmatized and revered—surely had It. On walking into a room—whether she was visiting a prison, a hospice, or a leprosarium—she saw right away which ones needed her most, and they felt uniquely valued because she needed *them.* They gave her back the image of her mind—the unloved, the untouchable, and the unknown.

At the same time, as Charles Spencer, Viscount Althorp, pointedly acknowledged in his eulogy, there were others she didn't have much use for, but who nevertheless needed her. Recognizing the menace of that need, he glossed the classical derivation and savored the irony of her name: "A girl given the name of the ancient goddess of hunting was, in the end, the most hunted person of the modern age." The manuscript for his tribute shows that he cancelled a darker elaboration of his thought in which he spoke ominously of "those who inhabit the murky swamps of malevolence and who need to suck their victims dry of their souls."[35] His gallant defense of Diana's royal person recalls Elinor Glyn's remark about the men walking behind the casket at Victoria's funeral: "A sublime spirit of chivalry must be innate in a people whose highest response of loyalty and valor is always made to Queens."[36] But more pessimistic conservatives have long echoed the more somber resonances of the viscount's cancelled but clearly heartfelt line. Across the generations of the dead, the living, and the unborn, Burke described the process of celebrity desacralization: "On this scheme of things, a king is but a man; a queen is but a woman; a woman is but an animal; and an animal not of the highest order."[37]

Patina—the depth of surfaces—is a very tangible paradox in the contemporary world of hyperrepresentation and the runaway It-Effect. Diana, like the Latter Day Muse of Tragedy, bends her arm at the elbow and approaches her plastic throne (fig. 20). Her patina is à la mode—burnished by the sun, the golden tan a

Fig. 20. Diana, Princess of Wales, and Dodi Fayed, 1997,
© AP/Wide World Photos.

signifier of social importance among women as pallor once was, but not nearly so dark as the figure in the background, who takes the place of either Pity or Terror in Reynolds's composition. Speaking of the massive public mourning for Diana, which seemed to encompass all Britains as her multiracial subjects in a "modern rainbow nation," Mica Nava wistfully defined the sense of personal loss and lost social possibility felt by so many at the moment of her queenly passing: "The tragedy is that there was no opportunity to consolidate this racial reconfiguration. Maybe a child of Diana and Dodi, a mixed race half-sibling to the future king, would have done the trick."[38] Or maybe not, skeptics might feel obliged to add, for Diana still reigns as the queen of suddenly reversible polarities. Uncannily, her sculpted silhouette at her shrine on the grounds of Althorp, a landscape garden with mortuary architecture in the finest eighteenth-century tradition, eternalizes her profile, "in black marble on a white marble background."[39] Dynastic successor to Siddons as the "stateliest ornament of the public mind," Diana's persistent afterlife, as much as or more than her unfinished life, shows how the public for tragic celebrity continues to put its faith in skin.

# 5.
## flesh

I sold flowers—I didn't sell myself. Now you've made a lady of me I'm not fit to sell anything else.

—Eliza Doolittle, *Pygmalion*

$W$ax looks and even feels like flesh; but more creepily still, not exactly like flesh. Such an unnerving category crisis ("it's just like chicken") makes every wax museum fascinating and repulsive by degrees. So it was with the effigies in the Abbey. Once known face-tiously in their decaying oaken versions as the "Ragged Regiment" (a phrase coined by the wiseacres among the boys at the Westminster School), the royal funeral icons, wooden and waxen alike, served as a tourist attraction for centuries and as an embarrassment for almost that long. They competed over time with dozens of rival celebrity waxworks, from Mrs. Salmon's to Madame Tussaud's, which flourished amid the profusion of London's burgeoning catchpennies.[1] And yet these disintegrating mannequins occupied a place in the *sanctum sanctorum* of national memory near the hallowed bones of the sovereigns on whom they conferred a tawdry kind of immortality, ambivalently preserved and neglected as the sharpest possible afterimages by which a dozen or so kings and queens of England could best be known to posterity as they had appeared in the flesh. After World War II, they were lovingly refurbished—and put in the basement.

The modern archeologists charged with the restoration and display of the effigies pondered a contradiction in the quality of the

174

original materials, which ranged from the exalted to the mean, suggesting that a similar ambivalence had colored their construction in the first place. In order to simulate the look and feel of resilient flesh under the suit as well as in the waxen face and hands, the artisans who made the figure of Charles II seem "astonishingly lifelike" stuffed the canvas skin with hay and tow (hemp fibers).[2] These materials were scarcely more regal than the straw that fleshed out workaday effigies to make them suitable for immolation in the popular pope-burning pageants of the Restoration. That may well have been the point. Under all the finery of the royal effigy's Garter robes, the humble chaff recalls the general applicability of the biblical reminder: "All flesh is grass" (Isa. 40:6). The waxen mold of the visible features, however, captured the haughty vitality of the king's personality with a kind of warts-and-all fidelity unrivaled until the invention of photography and never surpassed. *Charismata* and *stigmata* still emanate from the icon as they once did from the man, exuding the most intense of the contradictory qualities that reliably excite the fascination of It: vulnerability in strength, profanity in sanctity, and intimacy in public.

The effigy's face is almost certainly the product of a life mask, very likely one similar to the cast that Samuel Pepys had made of his own face by the specialist artificer William Larson. The diarist's account of the sitting for Larson, like his description of his wife posing as St. Catherine for the painter John Hayls, imparts an uncanny sense of the truly synthetic experience of having oneself duplicated, of having a "conceit," in this case a self-image, brought to the fullest imaginable state of lifelikeness, but framed by the luxury of its production in the raiment of iconic glamour. Once the privilege of kings, reproducibility is now a service at the beck and call of the self-fashioning parvenu:

> I to my wife, and with her to the Plasterer's at Charing-Cross that casts heads and bodies in plaster, and there I had my whole face done; but I was vexed first to be forced to daub my face over with Pomatum, but it was pretty to feel how saft and easily it is done on the face, and by and by, by degrees, how hard it becomes, that you cannot break it, and sits so close that you can-

not pull it off, and yet so easy that it is soft as a pillow, so safe is everything where many parts of the body do bear like. Thus was the mold made; but when it came off, there was little pleasure in it as it looks in the mold, nor any resemblance whatever there will be in the figure when I come to see it cast off—which I am to call for a day or two hence; which I shall long to see. (9:442)

Unimpressed though Pepys was by the negative image of the cast, when he returned to Larsen's atelier to claim the finished work, the results delighted him: "and then to the Plasterers and there saw the figure of my face taken from the Mold; and it is most admirably like, and I will have another made before I take it away" (9:449). As he does with the engravings of the Lely portrait of Lady Castlemaine, Pepys requires multiple copies of his face. A truly modern iconophile, he prefers the images he consumes to be both infinitely replicable and "like." By the terms of that likeness, he expects a certain vitality as well as accuracy. Only then can he fall completely in love.

Pygmalionism, the affliction that makes creators fall in love with the images they themselves have forged, is intimately allied with narcissism, the affliction that makes them fall in love with images of themselves. Pepys's auto-Pygmalionism is one of the wormholes in the *Diary* that opens up uncannily in the 1660s and drops the reader off, as Elinor Glyn rightly intuited, at the movies in the 1920s. Such a Kodak Moment *avant la lettre,* currently described in business-managerial literature as the "Pygmalion effect" (of executives falling in love with their own preconceived expectations),[3] presages the modern technical expansion of personal imagery infused with iconic attraction and confused with it too. It does so by promising to reenchant lifeless replicas, even if they have been fashioned from materials as humble as plaster, straw, or celluloid, with the animating pulse of the twice-born. In that reproductive process, the key technique of celebrity advertisement, the image may gain sufficient strength to break its mold and become an idea.

"It" is the idea of him or her that resides in us—inspired by the "*Something*" in them, as Pope has it, "That gives us back the Image of our Mind." Although the perception of It must be excited by some extraordinary perturbation in the looks and personality of the adored, the aura that It broadcasts arises not merely from the singularity of an original, as Walter Benjamin supposed, but also from the fabulous success of its reproducibility in the imaginations of many others, charmed exponentially by the number of its copies. The one-of-kind item must become a type, a replicable role-icon of itself—from "a Charles Hart" or "a Nell Gwyn" to "a Mary Pickford" or "a Douglas Fairbanks"—in order to unleash the Pygmalion effect in the hearts and minds of the fans, making the idea of him or her *theirs*—as much or more than anything else they might call their own. Pepys found Hart's and Gwyn's acting in James Howard's *The Mad Couple* (1667) miraculous, "especially hers" (8:594), and he joined in the general distress over her temporary retirement from the King's Company to be kept by Lord Buckhurst (8:334, 337, 503), leaving her colleagues, the management, and her fans to their bereft fates, like the ship deserting the sinking rats. Aphra Behn, it will be recalled, in her dedication of *The Feigned Courtesans* (1679) "To Mrs Ellen Gwynn," which appeared well after the actress's next and final retirement from the stage, this time to be kept by none other than the king himself, pitied generations yet to come, whose mental image of the vivacious star would necessarily have to be derived not firsthand from life but from the pencils of artists and the pens of writers. In her adulation, Behn underestimated posterity's capacity for vivifying a beloved celebrity's afterimage by multiplying the number of times they copied it and passed it around.

Like the patentees and playwrights of the Restoration, Hollywood moguls quickly learned that they had to search out the aura of the uniquely oft-repeatable or lose their shirts. In *Breaking into the Movies* (1921), John Emerson and Anita Loos, self-described insiders writing a handbook of practical advice for aspiring stars and especially starlets, anecdotally illustrated the very phenomenon that Pepys's *Diary* inadvertently but vividly disclosed. When a friend naively speculated about the difficulty of finding willing candidates to audition as Mary Pickford's double, the authors had a ready answer. Their witty riposte offers cinematic celebrity's version of Adam's Smith's "great wheel of circulation," turned by the "invisible hand," whereby the initial loan of one sum to one borrower magically generates a cascading effect of other loans and purchases, enlarging the common stock of capital, in this case cultural capital, issued under one name, but circulated everywhere:

> We know a way to get them all together on twenty-four hours notice. Just insert a small advertisement in the local newspaper, reading: "Wanted for the movies—a girl who looks like Mary Pickford—apply at such-and-such a studio to-morrow morning." We guarantee that not only will every woman who looks like Mary Pickford be on the spot at sunrise, but that a large preponderance of the entire female population will drop in during the morning.[4]

Singling out one persona with the power to replicate itself in a procession of would-be doubles—the same power of transferring and hence creating value that money has—Emerson and Loos humorously but pointedly describe the all-enveloping caress of the starring attraction's invisible hand.

Mary Pickford certainly did possess the kind of looks and personality that drew almost everyone's attention, as both Elinor Glyn and her sister noted in their memoirs. Dropping by "Lucile's" for a fitting, the starlet made even the jaded Lady Duff-Gordon, who had surrounded herself with the most beautiful women her expert fashion-designer's eye could find, blink with wonder as the entire studio magically seemed to fill with light on the actress's entrance into it. Effortlessly harmonizing innocence and experience, vulnerability and strength, availability and unbiddability, "Her shinning golden hair fell in long curls around her face, her pink and white skin, which was innocent of all make-up, had the transparent bloom of a child's and her hazel eyes had the wide gaze one generally notices in children." Although in point of fact, "no business magnate had a keener judgment or sounder grasp of affairs" than she, Pickford, always "bubbling with animation" and ingenuous joie de vivre, also retained in adulthood an implacably childlike way of making sure that her dreams would come true; at her most radiant, Lucy recounts, the movie queen's jocund countenance was serrated with dimples of steel:

> She told me that if she ever wanted anything to happen she always made a mental picture of it and concentrated on it. No matter how many discouragements she met with, and how impossible her wish seemed, she always kept the picture steadily in mind. She believed that this system always brought about what she wanted.

As if in illustration of Alexander Pope's "*Something,*" Pickford volunteered the example of a recurring wish she had during her impoverished childhood. She and her little sister longed to have an automobile, and every day they would create an imaginary one out of the four kitchen chairs in order to play a "limousine game," wherein the sister played the chauffeur and Mary the elegant passenger in back. Pickford related this story to Lucy as the two of them rode together in the plush back seat of the starlet's chauffeured Rolls-Royce: "We made our mental picture," Pickford concluded, "and we got our wish."[5] That her fantasy involved an automobile is apposite: next to their celebrities, Americans find the image of themselves most often returned to them as cars. Pickford's visualization technique was professional, but she and her film-colony colleagues inspired legions of amateurs to try something like it at home, making her sovereign in the imaginations of the American public under Hollywood's franchise of Walter Bagehot's "visible government." When the star pitched war bonds during World War I, for example, she astonished officials at the Treasury Department by raising subscriptions of four or five million dollars at a single bid in every sizable city she visited, and she probably helped out considerably even in the ones she skipped. Banking speculatively on the It-Effect, the feds still underestimated the *idea* of "Mary Pickford," aka "America's Sweetheart," who was really something all right, the very thing, in the flesh and in fiction, "That gives us back the Image of our Mind."

Michael Quinn has called this phenomenon "the illusion of absolute presence." A good working definition of stardom, this illusion, which is as real in its effects as anything else in modern experience, emerges from a singular nexus of personal quirks, irreducible to type, yet paradoxically the epitome of a type or prototype that almost everyone wants to be, to be like, or at least to pay to see.[6] The authors of *Breaking into the Movies* note the miraculous birth of such stars out of the swirling nebulae of casting calls and crowd scenes—a second birth, so to speak, more immaculate than the first, which tends throughout the history of stage and screen to be authentically humble, as dross yields small quantities of gold, and the smaller the dearer: "Almost all the stars of to-day—Norma Talmadge, Constance Talmadge, Mary Pickford, and dozens of others—have risen from these mob scenes. Their faces, even when seen among hundreds of others, attracted instant attention."[7] Their inauspicious origins, often from among the humblest of working people, add a particular poignancy to their plucky ascent from supernumeraries to stardom, trailing the humanizing memory of their initial place among the plebes. Like the royal effigies, they glitter in diadem and velvet, but underneath the waxed skin, their flesh is grass, just like a beggar's—sacred icons fashioned from the detritus of the quotidian, the abject, and the profane.

There is a pyramid shape to the It-Effect—broad at the base, lonely at the top. As Ponzi schemes of a self-perpetuating irresistibility, these celebrity pyramids often involve a narrative of a particular kind: the rise of a working person from the shop or the streets into a position of glamorous ascendancy—a process, by now familiar, in which his or her utility falls away, only to be replaced by his or her attractiveness as an accessory. The drama of lowly birth and enchanted ascent plays itself out on the tangibly visible person of the celebrity, tapping a deep-seated ambivalence about ordinary human flesh—just like one of us after all—morphing into a container of auratic transcendence—not like one of us at all. Like the confused feelings about money that come out in common phrases like *filthy lucre, stinking rich,* or the apostrophe of a toilet as *the throne,* flesh, as a corruptible husk and as a sacred vessel, carries strongly contradictory associations of waste and redemption. The dream of finding the secret of such a metamorphosis or discovery, on which Emerson and Loos seek to capitalize in *Breaking into the*

*Movies* by tapping into the cluelessness of wannabes, reappears frequently in literature, from Ovid to George Bernard Shaw, under the previously noted rubric of Pygmalionism.[8] The thrilling performance of a statue or other inert body coming to sentient life dominates retellings of this diehard myth, the siren song of lonely sculptors and optimistic talent scouts. But the same performance acts out ambivalent feelings about the lowly origins of a body so transformed. Pygmalionism, as the following account will show, unites innocence and experience in poignant antiphony to nominate the role-icon "Galatea," the lovelorn artist's made-to-order It-Girl. Her scenario reappears frequently in the history of performance, but Shaw dramatized it most memorably in *Pygmalion* (1912; London premiere, 1914) followed by Alan Jay Lerner and Frederick Lowe in the hit musical comedy *My Fair Lady* (1956; film, 1964).

In his afterword to *Pygmalion*, Shaw specified the genealogical descent of the story he told of his Galatea, Eliza Doolittle, from that of her most famous prototype in the theater of Charles II: "Such transfigurations have been achieved by hundreds of resolutely ambitious young women since Nell Gwynne set them the example by playing queens and fascinating kings in the theater in which she began by selling oranges."[9] Shaw knew his theater history well enough, but he chose to cite the favorite Victorian version of the actress's humble start in show business rather than the grittier contemporary anecdote: Pepys reports that Gwyn by her own account "was brought up in a bawdy-house to fill strong water to the guest[s]" (8:503). Pepys, whose own social trajectory followed an upwardly mobile arc during the years of the *Diary*, took sympathetic note. Limning the very picture of public intimacy and rags-to-riches ascent, he rhapsodizes that he once encountered the actress at her lodgings in the theater-and-market district, framed in her doorway *en déshabillé*, as if rising, divalike, from a musical chorus of supernumerary dairy maids: "Thence to Westminster, in the way of meeting many milkmaids with their garlands upon their pails, dancing with their fiddler before them, and saw pretty Nelly standing at her lodgings door in Drury Lane in her smock-sleeves and bodice, looking upon one—she seemed a mighty pretty creature" (8:193). Pepys was in fact on his way to an assignation with Doll Lane, one of the working-class mistresses he acquired as a perquisite of office, when the social-climbing celebrity detained him, momentarily but stunningly, by fixing him with her gaze. At that instant of desire and identification, he made her his own in imagination and memory, a pastoral goddess leaving the bovine street-vendors behind her at the threshold of her life as English history's most sacred whore.

Pygmalionism not only preserves an ancient myth of metamorphosis; it also enacts a modern social scenario, situating Galatea's drama not in her being, but in her becoming. Protean and expansionist like all myths, Pygmalionism annexes to Galatea's scenario that of the Cinderella, wherein a highly efficient but largely invisible maid-of-all-work experiences a transformation into a high-profile princess, thanks in part to the timely reappearance of a custom-made accessory.[10] Her elevation from utensil to ornament activates the It-Effect, and the greater the distance she travels from where she began, the more electrifying her ascent in the eyes of her beholders—her flesh charmed by its miraculous rescue from usefulness. For either Galatea or Cinderella, the less auspicious her origin, the more enchanted her metamorphosis. Thus set apart and denominated by the miracle of her second birth, each newly crowned It-Girl, like the last of the sacred monarchs, has two bodies, one of common clay, the other of pure magic.

Probably on account of the taboo against male hypergamy (the double standard at the intersection of sexes and classes that discourages more men than women from marrying up), Galatea has no avowed mythically masculine counterpart, unless the special case of Frankenstein might qualify on the grounds that the doctor's monstrous creation also represents the effigy of a passionate idea brought to abnormally interesting life. Monsters aside, the closest male role-icons to the Galatea type are "parvenu" and "gigolo," each upwardly mobile in his own special way. But then of course there are also the special cases that the French call "Sacred Monsters." The salient fact that the theater has recruited largely— indeed, almost exclusively—from the ranks of the working or lower-middle classes to deck its stage with kings and queens confirms an underlying social contradiction in the production of It: earned charisma radiates from workers and especially from slaves as they ascend from utility to visibility. From Roscius (ca. 162–20 B.C.) to the "African Roscius," Ira Aldridge (1804–1867), and at many points in between and beyond, the possession of It has provided ambitious self-fashioners with a tool to sculpt their own effigies from the unpromising bedrock of a world that would otherwise enslave them, though the American expatriate Aldridge found the carving easier everywhere but in his homeland. Across class and eventually ethnic and racial lines, the driving motive of marginalized performers to attain celebrity mirrors that of the public to identify with and to desire the excluded, the secret sharers of their fears and dreams. As Galatea's responsiveness to her creator shows, charisma is an expression of shared needs. It is a libidinous category with both an aura of wonder and a frisson of transgression about it, a mutual attraction precariously balanced on the thin edge of resentment, neither always reducible to, nor ever separable from, the real or imaginary flesh of the prodigy. The theater of the deep eighteenth century pioneered this cruelly selective economy of celebrity authentication, and, in its emergence as the triumphant synthetic-experience industry, it is still expanding today with a ferocity that might astonish but probably not baffle its earlier executants.

Perusing the absorbingly anecdotal volumes of *The Biographical Dictionary of Actors, Actresses and other Stage Personnel in London, 1660–1800,* even the most sanguine reader cannot escape the fact that while many are called, few are chosen. For every long entry with a running title like "Siddons" or "Betterton," half a dozen squibs accumulate like "Mrs. Simon (fl. 1749), actress," which reads in its entirety, "Mrs. Simon played Pert in *The Adventures of Sir Lubberly Lackbrain and His Man Blunderbuss* at Cushing's booth at Bartholomew Fair on 23 August, 1749" or "Benson, Mr. (fl. 1735), actor": "The Mr. Benson who played Morelove in *The Careless Husband* on 19 June 1735 at Lincoln's Inn Fields may possibly be related to one of the later eighteenth-century Bensons" (*BD* 14:76; 2:43). The use of the abbreviation for *flourished* in these instances seems almost punitively ironic. Then as now, the public deems only exceptional performers worthy of a regular living, and among those, only the rarest few acquire sufficient materials in a lifetime of triumphs to compose a robust afterimage. Recent historical scholarship has drawn welcome attention to wider and deeper constituencies of performers and entertainers, particularly in "illegitimate theatres," in colonial and provincial touring circuits, and among working women, but such ambitious recuperative projects still struggle to exorcise the demon of the It-Effect, which tends to idolize the prima ballerina while neglecting the memory of the corps de ballet.[11]

It's not a question of talent. A shade or two closer to skill, *talent* betokens a capacity for making something difficult, such as smiling while juggling, look easy. Talent may draw a crowd, but it alone will not hold one for long unless the performer also has It. Talents abound. Far fewer have It, but those who do make charisma look easy, even if they require a lot of help in doing so. There must be social as well as individual chemistry here, a volatile mixture of common needs catalyzed by special opportunities. Historians rightly try to remind themselves that charmed careers function as nodal points in a network of exceptional, if underappreciated and historically underpaid supporting players. The double meaning of the word *gift* expresses a poignant disjunction between these two mutually dependent groups, the charismatic and the talented: the first meaning pertains to those endowed by God or nature with some preternatural capacity, as in "the gift of tongues" (1 Cor. 12:1–13); the second describes a thing or a service voluntarily transferred or given, as in the sacrificial expenditures studied by anthropologists of premonetary "gift economies."[12] The electricity generated by the interdependent efforts of these differently treated artists, the worshiped and the sacrificed, adds its power to the entire grid of attraction that makes the theater district and hence the entertainment industry itself possible. Their joint participation is necessary for the running of "It-Zones," where specialists manufacture and market experiences like sausages: the full title of the *Biographical Dictionary,* which encompasses *Actors, Actresses, Dancers, Musicians, Managers, and other Stage Personnel,* parses this theatrical division of labor, right down to the ticket-takers and candle-snuffers. Such enchanted places—say "Covent Garden" or "Hollywood"—take on a mythic life of their own as epicenters of squalor and glory, even if they seem somehow empty in the middle, despite the long list of names that flash by whenever the credits roll.[13] Any research into the experience industry that recovers and honors its secondary careers contributes innovatively to theatrical and cinematic history. The fact remains, however, that the preponderance of evidence follows the partiality of audiences, then and now, for the talented charismatic over the merely talented.

Covent Garden has long served Londoners and tourists as a landmark and theme park of synthetic experience: back then, puppet booths, coffeehouses, flower stalls, kiosks vending everything from parakeets to pornographic prints; mountebanks, beggars, rakes, and bawds running specialty brothels and molly-houses such as the "Elysium Flogging House"; and down the street, attractions such as the eye-popping ballet *Pygmalion* (1731), starring Marie Sallé at the Theatre Royal, Covent Garden;[14] in more recent years, popular concerts at afternoon tea, Diana memorabilia, Union Jacks on little sticks, the wonderful theater museum, and the eye-popping musical *My Fair Lady* (2001), starring Jonathan Pryce at the Theatre Royal, Drury Lane. As an exemplary It-Zone, Covent Garden provides a place to invent, revive, and play out the most compelling scenarios, which, like the Galatea-Cinderella action, promise surefire excitement in the promotion of an overall economy of reenchantment. In this charged space, with a church at one end and the patent theaters at the other, the varieties of religious experience underwent an effervescent alteration and enlargement.

Pepys relates this kind of transitional experience, predicated on the magic of animated icons, in his delighted response to Signor Bologna's puppets, which the diarist sought out in the Covent Garden Piazza in May 1662. Covent Garden, laid out by Inigo Jones in 1638 as a real-estate speculation for the Duke of Bedford, began as a high-end residential and shopping area convenient to the New Exchange and the Strand. Ancient custom, however, preserved its name from the "convent garden" that served the Abbey of West-

minster in medieval times. Gradually, during Pepys's lifetime and
beyond, Covent Garden developed into a flower-and-vegetable
market and later into the combined theater-and-brothel district
that accounted for the neighborhood's notoriety and cachet—
London's rough-and-tumble It-Zone for the ages. The Piazza, a
rare open space in the close-built tracery of medieval streets, obviously lent itself to open-air performances of many kinds, and
Bologna set up his puppet booth in front of St. Paul's, the austerely classical parish church added by Jones on the west end of
the Piazza. As Pepys recalls: "Thence to see an Italian puppet play
that is within the rayles there, which is very pretty, the best I ever
saw, and a great resort of gallants" (3:80). Over several generations, gallants resorting to the other kinds of entertainment that
Covent Garden increasingly offered made it a place where women
of good character would be ill-advised to tarry; but that lay in the
future when Pepys returned to the Piazza with Elizabeth at his side
to show her Bologna's puppets and to enjoy the music that accompanied their uncannily lifelike "motions": "My wife and I to the
puppet play in Covent garden, which I saw the other day, endeed
it is very pleasant. Here among the Fidlers I first saw a Dulcimore
played on, with sticks knocking of the strings, and very pretty"
(3:90). Pepys remarks on the guilty pleasure of puppet performance later when he takes in "the Puppet-show of Whittington" at
Southwark Fair and finds it "very pretty to see; and how that idle
thing doth work upon people that see it, and even myself too"
(9:313). Filled like a fairground with behaviors suited to a ludic
space, the daily life of Covent Garden remained charmed because
of the "low" diversions and spectacles it offered cheek by jowl with
the artistic prestige and glamour of the two great patent theaters
that finally settled there.

These mixed diversions intensified, among other things, the
ever-present possibility that patrons of Covent Garden entertain-
ments and services might encounter a Cinderella in their midst.
The prostitute Miss Sarah Siddons, as we have seen, setting herself
up in "Tavistock Row, Covent Garden," capitalized on this fantasy
by appropriating the name of the revered star who worked just
around the corner in Drury Lane. The beloved comedienne

Frances Abington, who rose to such heights as a fashion plate that a fad in headwear she initiated took her name like a brand (the "Abington cap"), began at age fourteen selling flowers and probably favors as "Nosegay Fan" in the Piazza of Covent Garden. Of all the historic Galateas of the English stage who flaunted It, none surpass and only Nell Gywn equals Fanny Abington, who created the role of Lady Teazle in *The School for Scandal* (1777), a part written for her by Sheridan. The daughter of a soldier turned cobbler, Frances Barton debuted by reciting comic speeches from tabletops in local taverns and singing ballads in the streets. In the confection of innuendo that passes for candor in actress biographies, Fanny allegedly went on to serve as an "assistant to a French milliner" and a "companion" in the "house" of one Mrs. Parker, who lived under the protection of the rich West Indian Mr. Byron. Taking an interest in Fanny's talents, Byron took the Pygamalion role vicariously and "engaged masters to instruct her" in subjects suited to her obvious aptitudes such as language and deportment. This all apparently went well until the simmering cauldron of Mrs. Parker's jealousy boiled over and swept the flower girl back into the streets (*BD* 1:12). Claiming her as kin after her meteoric rise to stardom and fashionableness, the bawdy *Covent Garden Jester; or the Rambler's Companion* (1775) was dedicated on its title page to "the celebrated Mrs. Abington, the Genius of the Comic Muse."[15] The playwriting General "Gentleman Johnny" Burgoyne capitalized ironically on the magic of her ascent when he wrote for her the part of Lady Bab Lardoon in *Maid of the Oaks* (1775) and gave her this show-stopping line: "You shall see what an excellent actress I should have made, if fortune had not unluckily brought me into the world an Earl's daughter" (qtd. *BD* 1:17). In Covent Garden, therefore, a chapter in the early history of the transformation of vernacular religion into popular culture, and of popular culture into mass culture, was written, but only after it had been performed first by humbly born comers with the gift of tongues.

Today a commemorative plaque marks the spot where Pepys stood to watch the Punch-and-Judy show. For any student of Pygmalionism, especially for any devotee of Shavian drama or stage and movie musicals, that very spot is sacred ground. There, beneath the severity of the Tuscan portico of Inigo Jones's St. Paul's Church, Rex Harrison as Professor Henry Higgins, arguing on behalf of classical order in building as well as in speaking, berates a copiously weeping Eliza Doolittle, hydraulically enacted by Audrey Hepburn: "You squashed cabbage leaf, you disgrace to the noble architecture of these columns, you incarnate insult to the English language."[16] No more worthy of consideration as a sentient being to Higgins than the puppets were to Pepys, this Galatea introduces herself to her future Pygmalion by performing her rawness as material, her reputation as disposable as vegetable waste, her tongue as vulgar as her dress. Jay Lerner's book for *My Fair Lady* follows the dialogue of George Bernard Shaw's *Pygmalion* closely, especially in the introduction of the flower girl as an example of human refuse. The flowers she has been selling from her basket are purported to be fresh. She is not. Only as "clean as she can afford to be," foul of odor and of speech, she is but one inmate among many, a "pris'ner of the gutters" serving time in the streets of Edwardian London (*My Fair Lady*, 20, 27). With his characteristically enthusiastic insensitivity, Shaw's Professor Higgins waxes eloquent on the vividness of her abjection: "Oh it's a fine life, the life of the gutter. It's real: it's warm: it's violent: you can feel it through the thickest skin: you can taste it and smell it without any training or any work" (*Pygmalion*, 278–79). However much Shaw may have believed that the difference between a flower girl and a duchess is not in how she behaves but in how she is treated (270), he sees to it that this flamboyantly successful Pygmalion treats his Galatea like garbage. Not only is Eliza, like Covent Garden market itself, dirty, noisy, and smelly, as Higgins tells her to her face; she leaks. She first enters St. Paul's portico out of chaos ("torrents of heavy summer rain"), spouting glossolalic ejaculations, "Aaaooowah" and "Garn." On the cusp of utterance and secretion, the *gestus* of her role is that of a bathtub overflowing. She is repeatedly reproved for "boohooing," which the Professor equates with nothing less than blasphemy, a taboo, a pollution worthy of expulsion from a sacred place: "Woman: cease this detestable boohooing instantly; or else seek the shelter of some other place of worship" (205–6). Higgins's counter-*gestus* is to staunch the flow of her excretions with rags and to cleanse her, offering her his silk handkerchief, "To wipe your eyes. To wipe any part of your face that feels moist. Remember: thats your handkerchief; and thats your sleeve" (214). This Pygmalion clearly despises her flesh, the transformed image of which his labors will lead him to idolize and adore as his idea.

Actually, Eliza plays her hand as gamely as she can against a stacked deck. As a merchant who sells to others the opportunity to condescend to her condition, her pitch to the toffs sheltering in the portico during a sudden shower after the opera has let out— "Buy a flower off a poor girl?"—while only a notch above begging, also shrewdly offers her potential patrons a choice between two kinds of value (*Pygmalion*, 200). Looked at as philanthropy, handing her a coin turns the flower into a token in an uneven gift-exchange, adding to the prestige and amour propre of the superior benefactor; looked at as business, the same action makes the flower a commodity. In the first scenario, value is regulated by religious traditions of charity; in the second, by Adam Smith's "invisible hand." The difference in value in the performance of each scenario depends on the spell cast by its charm, each as mysterious in its own way as the magic of It itself. What *is* the value of a flower?

On the precarious cusp of innocence and experience, Eliza shows an intense but fragile pride in her own value. A chaste working girl, she knows enough to fear, not without reason, that she will be (mis)taken for a prostitute: "Freddy," Shaw's name for the well-born twit who bumps into her, knocking a day's wages worth of unsold flowers into the muddy street, was a generic name for the young men who cruised Covent Garden in search of tarts; "Captain," the title by which she carelessly addresses the upright (and uptight) Colonel Pickering, harkens perhaps all the way back to the whoremaster Macheath, a sybaritic fixture in nearby Drury Lane, from John Gay's *The Beggar's Opera* of 1728. Her use of such a dubious honorific threatens to mark her more discreditably than it does the object of her salutation, and she knows it: "Oh, sir," she implores, "crying wildly" in fear that Higgins, who has been recording her speech stenographically, is a police informer, "dont let him charge me. You dunno what it means to me. Theyll take away my character and drive me on the streets for speaking to gentlemen" (201). She has taken Higgins for the law, someone who can make or mar her character in a stroke, and so he turns out to be, in his own realm and for his own purposes. Higgins can take her for what he will, for even the church front under which she shelters bears a stigma recognized early on by such prurient reformist tracts as *The Night Walker: or, Evening Rambles in Search of Lewd Women* (1696), which inveighs against the false piety on display in little St. Paul's, later known as "The Actors' Church" (because so many thespians worshiped and are buried there): "I Rambled to [Covent Garden] Church," the Night Walker writes, "Where I understood, that under the pretence of attending *Evening Prayers,* many loose Women made their *Assignations* with their Gallants."[17] Against the incriminating presuppositions leveled at her, unrebutted by her dirty face, Eliza's refrain is, "I'm a good girl I am" (203, 217, and 219). Chief among the circumstances that impugn her goodness is the locale—Shaw's pointed placement of the scene in the once and future It-Zone of Covent Garden Piazza with all its historic associations of unsavory characters and fleshy performances.

As in so many other instances of the transmission of ideas about the moral flavor of the Restoration and eighteenth-century theater, Victorian representations of Covent Garden, particularly those by Charles Dickens and John Ruskin, mark its place in memory, Shaw's included. Dickens invokes the Garden as a fallen world twice: in *Our Mutual Friend* (1864) as the last stop of homeless drunks, derelict women especially, an unrivaled stew in which "such a stale vapid rejected cabbage-leaf and cabbage-stalk dress, such damaged-orange countenance, such squashed pulp of humanity, are open to the day as nowhere else";[18] and earlier and even more elaborately in *Little Dorrit* (1857), when the eponymous heroine visits Arthur Clennam's lodgings there and is dazzled by the jumble of past and present images of the neighborhood "as a place where gentlemen wearing gold-lace coats and swords had quarreled and fought duels [but where now] the miserable children in rags among whom she had just now passed, like young rats, slunk and hid, fed on offal, huddled together for warmth, and were hunted about."[19] Shaw felt a kinship with Dickens as with no other author, living or dead, and part of the affinity he perceived resides in his predecessor's treatment of the effects of environment on character. Shaw may be paraphrasing *Our Mutual Friend* directly when he has Higgins call Eliza a "squashed cabbage-leaf." In any event, the act 1 stage direction of *Pygmalion*, "Covent Garden at 11:15 P.M.," after the opera has let out, boisterously initiates the action of play—the passing off of a "guttersnipe" as a duchess—in a setting strongly associated with metamorphoses, Dickensian and otherwise, of the raw materials of common flesh into either glamorous excrescences or trash.

Pursuant to the earlier development of locale-appropriate scenarios for previous Galateas of the It-Zone, the journalist Tom Brown, gossiping in *Amusements Serious and Comical, Calculated for the Meridian of London* (1700), began his promotion of the archipelago of the emerging theater district and what he called the "Inchanted Island" of the playhouse with this lurid come-on:

> The Play-house was the Land of Enchantment, the Country of Metamorphosis, and perform'd it with the greatest speed imaginable. Here, in the twinkling of an Eye, you shall see Men transform'd into Demi-gods, and Goddesses made as true Flesh and Blood as our Common Women. Here Fools by sleight of hand are converted into Wits, Honest Women into errant Whores, and which is most miraculous, Cowards into valiant Heroes, and rank Cocquets and Jilts into as Chast and Vertuous Mistresses as a Man would desire to put his Knife into.[20]

The emphasis of Brown's final image, which conflates the stage with the fantasy life of brothels, suggests that sexual tourism attracts visitors to the enchanted island, but as a chatty tour guide he knows that innocence and experience must be kept in suspense to maintain the mystery of the "Metamorphosis." Their values oscillate back and forth in poignant antiphony in the minds of the visitors, who seek the synthetic experience of their own prelapsarian world in the company of the merchants of flowers and flesh.

In her unreconstructed state, Eliza strikes Higgins as repulsive if latently intriguing raw material, little more sensate than the block of stone in the mythological original, but at the same time irresistibly malleable, like wax, as she quickens to his transformative and ultimately adoring touch. Her rite of passage into the Higgins household is celebrated by the burning of her clothes and the imposition of a scalding bath, overseen by the implacably postmenopausal Mrs. Pearce and her starchy housekeeping acolytes, who hold the screaming Eliza all the way under to make her as clean as she can be. The medium here is no longer sculpted marble exactly or wax for that matter, but its equivalent in English speech, performed as Higgins insists that it must be in the airy transhistorical community of Shakespeare and Milton. By turning untutored vitality into refined inutility before our very eyes, the action of *Pygmalion* recapitulates the transformative act of performance itself. As synthetic experience, performance furnishes forth the products that imagination wrests from the raw material of inchoate possibility. That is why the word *performance* has proven so powerfully descriptive of such a variety of practices, from dancing to cooking, any one of which will consist of a set of conscious adjustments called "art" in a preexisting structure of expectation to which experience gives the name of "life." The theater is central to the study of performance in this sense, but it does not by any means stand alone or even supreme in the capacious category of synthetic experience. Performance, like Galatea's animation or Cinderella's abracadabra quick-change for the ball, effects the most important change of all in the symbolic economy of It: the metamorphosis from implement to accessory. This includes the experience of innocence and the experience of losing it, a metamorphosis that the "Inchanted Island" was especially good at marketing and that one of the greatest hits of the Restoration stage, *The Tempest; or, The Enchanted Island* (1667; revised 1674), an operatic adaptation of Shakespeare's play, was created especially to exploit. Enlivened throughout by Prospero's Pygmalion-like magic acts, *The Tempest* became a special favorite of Samuel Pepys, who had trouble finding a seat among the glamorous throng on opening night: "close by my Lady Dorsett and a great many great ones: the house mighty full, the King and Court there." Trailing the stardust of proximate celebrity, Pepys's summary remark reveals a good deal about the nature of the vicarious experience he had purchased, which included the full range of smutty double entendres about the actresses: "the most innocent play that I ever saw" (8:521–22).

"Modern man," argues Dean MacCannell in *The Tourist,* "has been condemned to look elsewhere, everywhere, for his authenticity, to see if he can catch a glimpse of it reflected in the simplicity, poverty, chastity or purity of others."[21] Even those brought up in the hurly-burly of an active It-Zone, however, gain no guarantee of immunity from the tourist mentality—even when their exotic destination beckons to them from a location no further distant than around the corner. Confronted with the cacophonous inequalities of modern London, the Victorians understood this clearly. John Ruskin, reconstructing the boyhood of the artist J. M. W. Turner, who was born in 1775 adjacent to the Piazza in Maiden Lane and raised there, contrasts the painter's "Covent Garden training" with that of the Venetian Giorgione. Ruskin writes of the urban node and the living figures populating it as if their relationships of inequality offered a naturalized object to the artist's gaze, as in the misty landscapes or seascapes more readily associated with Turner's oeuvre:

> The second great result of this Covent Garden training was, understanding of and regard for the poor, whom the Venetians, we saw, despised; whom, contrarily, Turner loved, and more than loved—understood. He got no romantic sight of them, but an infallible one, as he prowled about the end of his lane, watching night effects in the wintry streets; nor of sight of the poor alone, but the poor in direct relations with the rich. He knew, in good and evil, what both classes thought of, and how they dealt with, each other.[22]

Or as Shaw puts it more fiercely in the Preface to *Pygmalion:* "It is impossible for an Englishman to open his mouth without making some other Englishman hate or despise him" (191). Professor Higgins, like Turner, has no romantic sight of the poor, but a technically "infallible" one. He can place Eliza's accent precisely to the London block, but his love at first goes no farther than her value (or lack thereof) to the great project of his grand ethnolinguistic tour; at least until she herself, in all her innocence, becomes his project and makes the conquest of her tongue a more daunting challenge to his aggression than her maidenhead would have been.

Not every Galatea, however, turns into a Cinderella. Eliza rightly apprehends and deeply fears for the precariousness of her fate. She could read one possible future in the neighborhood's past. As a market for flowers, produce, and flesh, Covent Garden witnessed daily metamorphoses not only from obscurity to celebrity, but also from wholesomeness to filth. Whereas the morning tide of market-fresh succulents rolled in on carts from the countryside, the afternoon leftovers were tossed in the gutters to rot. Sir Richard Steele, writing in a number of *The Spectator* devoted to London *flanerie,* describes a walk by "Mr Spectator" that begins at dawn on the Thames and takes in the market scenes, measuring the differences between the people in them by the fine calibration of the times of day at which they make their appearances on the stage. In so doing, he also distinguishes between a proper business address and an It-Zone: "It was very easy to observe by their Sailing, and the Countenances of the ruddy Virgins who were Supercargoes, the Parts of the Town to which they were bound. There was Air in the Purveyors for *Covent-Garden,* who frequently converse with Morning Rakes, very unlike the seemly Sobriety of those bound for *Stocks-Market.*"[23] Steele echoes an earlier *Spectator* number in which Mr. Spectator is accosted by a very young prostitute in the Piazza of Covent Garden. His intertwined descriptions elide the sale of fresh produce and the sale of human flesh. Read together with the allusion to the "Ruddy Virgins" who are arriving from the country with their fresh produce (and as fresh produce) to talk with "Morning Rakes," the earlier number marks a later stage in the transformation of morning into evening and wholesomeness into waste:

> The other Evening passing along near *Covent-Garden,* I was jogged on the Elbow as I turned into the Piazza, on the right Hand coming out of *James-Street,* by a slim young Girl of about

Seventeen, who with a pert Air asked me if I was for a Pint of
Wine. . . . We stood under one of the Arches by Twilight; and
there I could observe as exact Features as I had ever seen, the
most agreeable Shape, the finest Neck and Bosom, in a Word,
the whole Person of a Woman exquisitely beautiful. She
affected to allure me with a forced Wantonness in her Look and
Air; but I saw it checked with Hunger and Cold: Her Eyes were
wan and eager, her Dress thin and tawdry, her Mein genteel and
childish. This strange figure gave me much Anguish of Heart,
and to avoid being seen with her I went away, but could not for-
bear giving her a Crown. The poor thing sighed, curtisied, and
with a Blessing, expressed with utmost Vehemence, turned
from me.[24]

In Steele's own reckoning, Covent Garden Piazza functions not
only as a market but also as a kind of clock, measuring with its own
manner of precision the passage of time in the diurnal withering
of flower petals and the seasonal etiolation of flesh, as girls "newly
come upon the Town" sold themselves, infected themselves,
exhausted themselves, and finally beggared themselves, when pity
was at last the only desire they could engender in the hearts of
men. But in the economy of the gift, pity is no negligible desire.
Returning Mr. Spectator's offering in kind, the child's performance of gratitude, punctuated by her heartbreaking curtsy,
offers value for value received.

In 1738, a century after the construction of the Piazza and
nearly two before Shaw wrote the Covent Garden scene in *Pygmalion,* William Hogarth published four engravings done from
paintings representing *The Four Times of the Day.* The first of these,
titled "Morning," is set in the same spot where Freddy Aynsford-
Hill upsets Eliza Doolittle's basket and spoils her goods, fatefully
drawing Henry Higgins's attention to the overflowing Billingsgate
of her speech (fig. 21). Hogarth, quoting from his own moralizing
narrative in *The Harlot's Progress* (1732), reinforces in *Morning* the
connections Steele makes between Covent Garden produce and
Covent Garden flesh. Baskets of cabbages and bunches of mush-
rooms, winter fruits, dot the scene along with the refuse into which

they are being transformed. The hasty observer might conclude
that sex work begins early in the morning, but closer scrutiny
establishes the fact that it runs round the clock. In the geometric
grouping of the younger prostitutes and their demanding "Captains" on the right, the base of the compositional triangle culmi-
nates with a conspicuous figure at its lower left apex, which
extends to the center-line of the image: a blind beggar woman of
African or West Indian extraction, her hand extended and her
mouth opened in unanswered supplication.

A long way from home, we imagine, hunched in her threadbare
cloak against the London winter and apparently unwarmed by the
meager fire, she labors in the superannuated economy of the gift,
while everyone around her seems to have something or someone
to sell, something or someone to buy, or at the very least something (or someone) to do. Like unsold produce, she is a prisoner
of the gutter. What language, we wonder, is she speaking? Who is
listening? Unhearing and unseeing, an overdressed but under-
wrapped coquette, actually a notorious bawd, passes by the beggar
on her pretentious way to church, fan raised to her lips, while her
link boy carries her prayer book under his arm and reaches into
his pocket in apparent readiness to give alms at his mistress's med-
itatively pious request. The unmet needs of the blind beggar
woman, homeless and hungry in the cold, reappear like the
repressed in Eliza's musical wish list in *My Fair Lady:*

> All I want is a room somewhere,
> Far away from the cold night air;
> With one enormous chair . . .
> Oh, wouldn't it be loverly?
>
> Lots of choc'late for me to eat;
> Lots of coal makin' lots of heat;
> Warm face, warm hands, warm feet . . . !
> Oh, wouldn't it be loverly?

(33)

This resonance would be uncanny except for the fact that it
records an evolved but genealogically related system of social rela-

Fig. 21. William Hogarth, from *The Four Times of Day*, 1738, Plate I,
"Morning" (Covent Garden). Upton House, Oxfordshire, UK,
The Bridgman Art Library International.

tions founded on ambivalence about the value of human flesh in
the great wheel of circulation.

That Covent Garden represented a nodal point in this vast grid
of displacement is a theme in Ruskin's commentary on the boyhood of Turner and the way in which the painter of *The Slave Ship*
developed his "infallible" sense of the poor from the Covent Garden scene. This Ruskin calls "English death," and he notes that it
contains no "gentle processions to churchyards among the fields":

> But the life trampled out in the slime of the street, crushed to
> dust amidst the roaring of the wheel, tossed countlessly away
> into howling winter wind along five hundred leagues of rock-

fanged shore. Or, worst of all, rotted down to forgotten graves through years of ignorant patience, and vainly seeking for help from man, for hope in God—infirm, imperfect yearning, as of motherless infants starving at the dawn; oppressed royalties of captive thought, vague ague-fits of bleak, amazed despair.[25]

And for the all the important ways in which the experience of a Cockney flower girl who shines like Cinderella at the Embassy Ball can't be compared with Ruskin's dispossessed, her own sense of loss—her humiliation at being separated forever from her self-employed past—comes out in a most revealing turn of phrase, bitterly recognizing the transformed value of her flesh: "I'm a slave now, for all my fine clothes" (*Pygmalion*, 277).[26]

The audacious mobility of the two-faced and the twice-born has always struck some as a danger. A deep-seated prejudice against those who rise by pretense is a historic condition of the theater and the source of many moralistic attacks against it, from Solon's rebuke of Thespis to the censures of the Reverend Jeremy Collier, who understood very well that the theater competes effectively with religion because it is a variety of religion. In such a place as Covent Garden, the agon of attraction and abjection rarely exhausts its interest, recalling its deep roots in the religious interdependence of holy *charismata* ("This is my body") and *stigmata* ("All flesh is grass").

In the upper right-hand corner of Hogarth's "Morning," the portico of St. Paul's Church looms austerely, sending a galvanic current of emotional electricity arcing through the social space of the Piazza, anchored by the positively charged church on the one side and the negatively charged playhouses and brothels on the other. The church clock is pointedly surmounted by the figure of Time, bearing a scythe, and subscribed with the warning, *Sic Transit Gloria Mundi*. The chimes of this clock, in fact, striking ominously at the moment Henry Higgins turns to leave the Piazza, remind the Professor to be more charitable to Eliza Doolittle. He hears the chimes as *the voice of God* (207). Nowhere else in the play is Higgins's piety an issue. Like the antiquity of the Tuscan order that Jones selected for the portico of the church, God's voice moves Higgins to an anachronistic performance of spontaneous but self-interested philanthropy that belongs not to the economy of exchange but to the economy of the gift. Higgins leaves without a flower in return for his shower of coins, but in time, the measure of all things, Eliza's sacrifice will return his gift with interest. Repeating the scene enacted by Mr. Spectator and the girl, Shaw's stage directions for the performance of charity in *Pygmalion* read:

> *The church clock strikes the second quarter.*
> HIGGINS, *hearing in it the voice of God, rebuking him for his Pharisaic want of charity to the poor girl.* A reminder. *(He raises his hat solemnly; then throws a handful of money into the basket and follows Pickering.)*
> THE FLOWER GIRL, *picking up a half-crown.* Ah-ow-ooh! (*Picking up a couple of florins*) Aaah-ow-ooh! (*Picking up several coins*) Aaaaaah-ow-ooh! (*Picking up a half-sovereign*) Aaaaaaaaaaaah-ow-ooh!!!
>
> (207)

At the extreme edges on either side of ordinary human flesh, stand two antipathetic values: the priceless and the worthless. Under these circumstances, It is negotiable, even fungible. For Eliza, the magic behind Higgins's gift does not reside ultimately in her belief in God, effervescent as her response may be, but in the charmed force of "the Mammon of unrighteousness" (Luke 16:19), also known as "the invisible hand." Moreover, the price that Eliza's father later charges Higgins, shrewdly reckoning that the "Gentleman" will pay to have his unfettered way with her, is five pounds, the sum then reputed to be the market rate for underage girls sold into sexual slavery by their parents.[27]

When the moment of Eliza's transformation finally comes, following the labors of Hercules in diction and deportment for which Higgins willingly shares some credit with Colonel Pickering but not with Eliza herself, the two self-congratulatory gentlemen in *My Fair Lady* find an unintentionally ironic way of staking their claim to sole authorship to her newly sculpted vowel sounds. Insulting in their condescension, they treat her metamorphosis as a minor miracle:

ELIZA.    The rain in Spain stays mainly in the plain.
HIGGINS, *triumphantly*.    By George, she's got it! By George,
    she's got it!

(141)

Invoking the name of the dragon-slaying saint, England's holy patron, Higgins's exclamatory and repeated "it" ostensibly refers to the lesson they've been drilling into her head for weeks, but in Lerner's subtext, as more explicitly in Shaw's text, the "it" more aptly expresses an eloquence residing in Eliza's capacious aptitude, not one that Higgins has implanted, but one he's accidentally discovered. A supreme egoist, he never fully admits or even grasps the truth of the matter, but even *his* fascination with her cannot be reduced to his preening himself over the parrot he thinks he has created. At some level, even he has to intuit that "it" comes out in her not because of the way she has been taught to behave or because of the way in which she has been treated, but because she is gifted with the most remarkable gift of all—the gift of tongues.

As for the audience members at any performance of *Pygmalion*, they know from the beginning that Eliza has got It. Even at the premiere in 1914, they knew taking their seats what the characters themselves could never learn: underneath the squalor and grime, no less than the diadem and chiffon, there lay the real Eliza: Mrs. Patrick Campbell (1865–1940). Shaw conceived the role for her as early as 1897, when she reigned supreme as the neurasthenic bad girl of Pineroticism, playing fallen women elegantly and expertly in Arthur Wing Pinero's "sex problem" plays *The Second Mrs. Tanqueray* (1893) and *The Notorious Mrs. Ebbsmith* (1895).[28] By the time *Pygmalion* opened, "Mrs. Pat" had turned fifty, requiring big dollops of suspended disbelief and grease paint to represent Eliza's eighteen years. So irresistible did Shaw find her personal magnetism, however, that she carved one of the greatest roles for any actress of any time out of his putatively hardheaded theatrical imagination. In a passage that sums up the shaping experience of the true It-Effect on a susceptible soul and comes as close as words can to specifying the contents of the ever-elusive and all-powerful "*Something*," Shaw famously wrote to Mrs. Pat:

> I want my Virgin Mother enthroned in heaven. I want my Italian peasant woman. I want my rapscallionly fellow vagabond. I want my dark lady. I want my angel. I want my tempter. I want the lighter of my seven lamps of beauty, honour, laughter, music, love, life and immortality. I want my inspiration, my folly, my happiness, my divinity, my madness, my selfishness, my final sanity and sanctification, my transfiguration, my purification, my light across the sea, my palm across the desert, my garden of lovely flowers, my million nameless joys, my day's wage, my night's dream, my darling and my star.[29]

Religious imagery—of darkness and light, profaneness and sanctity, temptation and salvation—dominates the Shavian billet-doux. With his words tantalizingly on her lips as Eliza, he acquiesced in giving Mrs. Pat everything she wanted, including the right clothes, after which "*Pygmalion* threatened to become a play known for Mrs. Campbell's sexual appeal and dramatic costumes."[30] The It-Effect intensified by the Galatea-Cinderella scenario still affects spectators of the film version of *My Fair Lady* today, particularly in Eliza's descent down the staircase dressed to kill for the Embassy Ball, the way Nell Gwyn's angel ex machina in *The Virgin Martyr* affected Pepys. Lerner's stage direction reads simply: "Eliza *appears on the landing—a vision*" (156). Unforgettably, Cecil Beaton dressed Audrey Hepburn for the scene in a luminous gown modeled directly on the "Snow Princess" dress that Lucile (Lucy, Lady Duff Gordon) had designed for Lily Elsie's triumph in *The Merry Widow* (1907). Through the 1964 film of *My Fair Lady*, Hepburn's Eliza Doolittle (lip-syncing Marni Nixon's voice) became a culture-industry effigy.

The It-Effect recycles its idols widely and markets them relentlessly. Eliza's contemporary role-icon reappears in the "Barbie *My Fair Lady* Collector's Edition" of five dolls, costumed in different dresses and accessories to show the stages of her transformation from Covent Garden flower girl to overdressed fashion plate (fig. 22). Plastic, the modern substitute for wax in effigy-making, provides the ideal fleshlike material for Galatea-Cinderella because plastic is the medium par excellence of metamorphosis, as Roland Barthes explains in his essay on the material as a modern myth of popular culture and vernacular religion:

> So, more than a substance, plastic is the very idea of its infinite transformation, as its everyday name indicates, it is ubiquity made visible. And it is this, in fact, which makes it a miraculous substance: a miracle is always a sudden transformation of nature. Plastic remains impregnated throughout with this wonder: it is less a thing than the trace of a movement.[31]

The more things change, however, the more they stay the same: underneath the different dresses, the body of the doll always belongs to "Barbie," distinctively herself and infinitely reproducible, who began life as "Lilli," a sex toy for the German pornography market. The formidable Mrs. Higgins sternly reproaches her son and his collaborator as two grown men who only demean themselves by playing with "dollies" to feed their undernourished sex lives, but they don't allow this to take anything away from their sense of triumph at their Galatea's metamorphosis. Pickering and Higgins are astonished and relieved at Eliza's success, while the audience feels vindicated and perhaps spiritually uplifted by the spectacular realization, moved as if by an invisible hand, of an image transformed into an idea before their eyes: "By George, she's got *it!*"

As *Pygmalion* begins with a bouquet of flowers being cast into the mud, it ends with the ominous possibility that Eliza will be similarly discharged after she has blossomed briefly and faded. Having reached the high rank of accessory, she finds herself unemployed as the curtain falls. *My Fair Lady* finesses this awkward point by returning her to the Higgins household to fetch the Professor's slippers like a spaniel. In the world constituted by Shaw's play, however, she is left at last without appropriate options except to be sold into a brokered marriage, which she recognizes immediately

Fig. 22. "Barbie" as Eliza Doolittle in *My Fair Lady,* Collector's Edition.
Photo: Ruben D. Roman and Samantha K. Roman.

as a form of prostitution: "I sold flowers," she reminds Higgins
after the social triumph of the ball and the psychological fiasco of
its aftermath. "I didn't sell myself. Now you've made a lady of me
I'm not fit to sell anything else" (257). Shaw does not allow her to
entertain thoughts of the profession that a number of previous
Galateas had chosen, joining in the time-honored succession,
inaugurated in 1660 by Charles II, of working-class girls who
learned to pass as great ladies on the stage. Shaw's reticence on
this point seems puzzling because he explicitly recognized this
well-worn career path in his afterword to *Pygmalion,* citing Gwyn,
who sold oranges and spirits, where he might have mentioned
Abington, who sold flowers. Perhaps he does not want to let Eliza
off so easily, or more likely he sees in her stubborn innocence,
which stops just short of prudery, a sympathy-building character-
trait that a declaration for the stage would necessarily blight.

Ignoring the stage and ruling out prostitution except through
marriage, the unromantic ending of *Pygmalion,* which has dis-
satisfied audiences from the first production onward, leaves Eliza's
options narrowing to some form of "buy a flower off a poor girl."
Now homeless, she will either set herself up in a shop with funds

extracted as a gift from the guilt-ridden Colonel Pickering or go back to the streets. Beggary has symbolic merit as a fate in this context, however. Performing a role-icon that could hardly be more public or more intimate, beggars can acquire a celebrity all their own, even to the point of becoming generally known by their first names. Changing the precedence but not the reciprocity of *charismata* and *stigmata,* they must appeal successfully to the public or they disappear. Taking on accessory roles like actors or kings, in order to prove effective as symbols, they must become useless as producers. Beggars do not, however, thereby cease contributing to what Adam Smith called "the general Stock of Society." On the contrary, giving visible form to the "invisible hand," they help to depress the wage-price spiral by cowing passersby, fighting inflation by lowering the expectations of all those who can see themselves as only a paycheck or two away from a similar predicament. "Look at her," Higgins urges, "a pris-ner of the gutters" (109). All flesh being only grass, It works like charm.

# 6.

# bone

The king most worthily hath caused every soldier to cut his
prisoner's throat.

—*Henry V* (4.7.9–10)

On the afternoon of Shrove Tuesday, February 23, 1669, Samuel
Pepys violated the corpse of Katherine of France, Henry V's
queen. He records in his *Diary* entry for that day, his birthday, how
he came to be touring Westminster Abbey with members of his
family. He and Mrs. Pepys were entertaining out-of-town cousins,
to whom the shows of London beckoned on the last day before
Lent.[1] Having taken in the antics of the lunatics at Bedlam but
finding themselves disappointed by the postponement of the
opening of Thomas Shadwell's *Royal Shepherdess* at the Duke's Playhouse, the party settled on an alternative entertainment. Coming
upon a secular relic and minor tourist attraction in the Confessor's
Chapel, the partially mummified remains of Katherine of Valois,
Pepys picked up and fondled the torso and kissed on the lips the
cadaver of the woman whose life inspired Shakespeare to write the
character of "Queen of all, Katherine" in *Henry V:*

> Therefore I now took them to Westminster Abbey and there did
> show them all the tombs, very finely, having one with us alone
> (there being other company this day to see the tombs, it being
> Shrove Tuesday); and there did we see, by particular favour, the
> body of Queen Katherine of Valois, and had her upper part of

her body in my hands. And I did kiss her mouth, reflecting
upon it that I did kiss a Queen, and that this was my birthday, 36
year old, that I did first kiss a Queen. (9:456–57)

Cutting up for his tour group, which included his teenaged nieces
as well as his wife, and performing a makeshift love scene as if he
were an actor on a stage or a carnival masquerader (it was, after all,
Mardi Gras day), Pepys found quite a leading lady, celebrated in
her own time and remembered thereafter with a whiff of sex. As
the daughter of Charles VI of France, Katherine had served as a
bargaining chip in the dynastic showdown wherein Henry V of
England insisted on a suitable trophy in marriage as part of the
price of peace after Agincourt. As Shakespeare has the warlike
Harry say, wooing the demure princess with broken French but
unremitting purpose:

You have witchcraft in your lips, Kate; there is more eloquence
in the sugar touch of them than in the tongues of the French
council; and they should sooner persuade Harry of England
than a general petition of monarchs. (5.2.288–93)

Persuaded he was, and their son became Henry VI. Widowed early,
Katherine married Owen Tudor. Raphael Holinshed, one of
Shakespeare's sources for *The Life of Henry V,* put a transgressive
spin on this liaison, recording that the queen, bereaved but not
inconsolable, "being young and lustie, following more hir owne
wanton appetite than friendly counsel, and regarding more priu-
ate affection than princelike honour, tooke to husband priuilie a
gallant gentleman and right beautifull person, indued with manie
goodlie gifts both of bodie & mind, called Owen Teuther."[2] Their
grandson became Henry VII, the first monarch of the dynasty that
bore his family's name. She died in 1437 at the age of 36, precisely
the age of Samuel Pepys on the day of his assignation with her
remains 232 years later, on a holiday from his job at the naval
office, where, in the unsettled and unsettling twilight of sacral
monarchy, his remarkable efficiency helped to lay the foundations
of invisible government and the instrument of global maritime
empire.

The restless perambulations of Queen Katherine's corpse enact the turbulence of the intervening periods of history, from medieval dynasties to modern. When her sepulcher in the Lady Chapel was disturbed by renovations ordered by Henry VII, her body was placed in a coffin at the east end of the Confessor's Chapel at the side of the tomb of Henry V. There she rested (but not undisturbed) on view by "especiall favor" until at least the mid-eighteenth century, her most recent reburial dating from 1878 (Pepys 9:457n). By the time Pepys handled the fragile segments of this macabre heirloom, the torso had become detached from the pelvis and the legs.

A proper royal funeral effigy of Queen Katherine in wood polychrome, now displayed in the Westminster Abbey Undercroft near the wax and iron-wire effigy of Charles II, eerily doubles and fleshes out the defiled souvenir of her corpse, but the detail-oriented clerk of acts did not confuse this poignant icon with her actual remains: he proudly specifies that he "did kiss a Queen." Pepys, whose stolen backstage kisses from pretty actresses have made his diary so quotable to theater historians (8:27–28), dreamed of planting them on most of the player-queens; yet in his jolly necrophilia, the social climber betrays himself as even more giddily presumptuous than he did when he went backstage. His performance recalls Pygmalion's impertinence when he first makes love to the ivory Galatea in Ovid:

> He knows 'tis madness, yet he must adore,
> And still the more he knows it, loves the more:
> The flesh, or what so seems, he touches oft,
> Which feels so smooth, that he believes it soft.
> Fir'd with this thought, at once he strain'd the breast,
> And on the lips a burning kiss impress'd.[3]

Pepys, vicariously playing King Henry or Owen Tudor's part in his own impromptu historical drama, intimately but publicly osculated not only with the remains of the celebrity, but with the ghostly idea of her as well. Wanting witnesses to applaud the deed, he recruited a captive audience of little Babs, Betty, and Elizabeth Pepys, cast as ladies of the court over which the skeletal queen presides; she, the aging diva (remarkably for her years, having passed through so many hands) shows that two and a half centuries later there's still witchcraft in her lips.

For some who possess it as for others who seek it, It can mean the kiss of death. As Pepys's bizarre act of lèse-majesté dramatizes, charismatic attraction can cause a frisson of aversion, when the initiate seeks and finds the skull beneath the skin. One version of It, certainly, always produces a thrill of fear, as Elinor Glyn's ascription of the force of fatal attraction to alpha predators suggests. Inspired in part by Douglas Fairbanks's performance in the silent swashbuckler *The Black Pirate* (1926), Glyn, who was writing the novel *It* at the time, created as her central character the ruthless robber-baron John Gaunt, who fights his way to the top using other men "like pawns in his game" and has "all types and classes" of women "groveling at his feet." Although Glyn thought of It as fundamentally androgynous, mindful of the example of her idol Fairbanks swinging through the rigging with an earring in his ear and a cutlass in his teeth, she also believed that the kind of attraction that It exerts will transfix every sentient being in its path: "He had that nameless charm, with a strong magnetism which can only be called 'It,' and cats, as well as women, always knew when he came into a room."[4]

This final chapter will explore that category of attraction in the case of the role-icon of "pirate," which attained its modern form in the late seventeenth and early eighteenth centuries, during the era commonly called, often with insufficiently conscious irony, "The Golden Age of Piracy." Added to the already well-stocked role-icon of "outlaw," the images and actions derived from this period of terror on the high seas have provided subsequent generations with a fecund repertoire of characters, situations, and scenarios to revive, savor, and transmit.[5] A staple of popular culture and therefore of public dreams, these scenarios often turn on the irresistible allure of the criminal hero-villain, whose special brand of It ranks first in the hearts of many a man and, if Glyn's testimony is to be credited, every woman and cat.

What might be called the scenario of negative attraction, the lethal charm of the dangerous exerted on the curious and fearful, emerges with unrivaled durability from the eighteenth-century stage in the vehicle of John Gay's *The Beggar's Opera* (1728). Gay created the most popular criminal this side of Robin Hood, the dashing highwayman Captain Macheath. In *Polly* (1729), Gay's sequel to *The Beggar's Opera,* Macheath escapes to the West Indies and turns pirate—a pirate in blackface, in fact, disguised as a Jamaican Maroon. As an icon of nearly three hundred years of pop culture, the last eighty of which have been as mass culture, Macheath's character, radiating allure and menace, turns up in many adaptations and revisions, most famously as Mack the Knife in Brecht and Weill's *Threepenny Opera* of 1928, as the shark with pretty teeth in Louis Armstrong's pop-single cover of the theme song from that musical in Marc Blitzstein's Americanized version of 1954, and as the McDonald's TV and print advertisement circa 1992 depicting a Ray Charles look-alike action-figure smiling toothily in joyous anticipation of a "Big Mac Attack."

Even among favorite criminal subspecialties, the popularity of piracy is extraordinary. In addition to the continuously proliferating theatrical and cinematic iterations of pirate lore, high-culture venues, seeking wider audiences, get into the act: when the National Maritime Museum in London scheduled an exhibition called "Pirates: Fact and Fiction" to last four months, it proved such a hit that the museum had to keep it open for three years to accommodate the pirate-hungry public. Although the show provided a lot to think about, there wasn't actually that much to see: documents such as Captain Kidd's privateering commission from the Public Record Office; handsome but unremarkable portraits such as those of Robert Louis Stevenson and William Dampier from the National Portrait Gallery; the manuscripts of both Byron's *The Corsair* and Gilbert's *Pirates of Penzance;* a costume from the 1909 London production of J. M. Barrie's *Peter Pan;* and of course, it being the Maritime Museum, lots of old charts, logbooks, navigation instruments, and other salty impedimenta.[6] Nevertheless, it was a mob scene.

Pirates steal dreams, inducing people to remember them, in fear and fascination, by romanticizing their frightening legends—no humdrum, workaday vessel left unboarded, no timber left unshivered, no plank left unwalked, no bodice left unripped. Pirates also steal time, sifting silkily through the uncanny worm-holes that seem to open up between past and present, reemerging from history to answer the urgencies of the future, whether they be vindictive, erotic, prophetic, or, as they most often are, utopic, in the sense of combining all of the above and much more. "Pirate" provides the most vivid instance of a role-icon that charges the nominated incumbents with charismatic appeal prior to and in continuing support of whatever personal charms they bring to the performance. That icon is both strong and unstable. Because pirate crews were historically multinational, multilingual, and multiracial—as well as democratic (the pirate captain served by popular fiat and could be deposed by majority vote)—piratophiles have depicted them as proto-revolutionary, progressive social democracies before the letter. Because pirates seemed to live as they pleased in a confined wooden world of libidinous masculinity, historians of sodomy have looked to them in hopeful inference, the slender documentary evidence bearing on their onboard sex-ual practices generously supplemented by the spirit of common-sense deduction, tinting the Atlantic triangle pink. That at least two women in the Golden Age, Ann Bonny and Mary Read, famously passed as male pirates for a time and then continued to win honors among their startled shipmates after their sex had been unveiled, has excited the interest of feminist scholars (and not only feminist scholars).

Other historical data on pirates compel attention more in dread than admiration. That a handful of desperados, never at any one time numbering more than five thousand individuals, stymied the combined forces of the world's greatest empires, first Spain and Portugal in their time, then Great Britain, France, and the Dutch, the Moguls and the sultans in theirs, has no doubt piqued the curiosity of contemporary adversaries of the dominant world order. That pirates, despite their well-documented readiness to torture, murder, and gang-rape the helpless, persist in popular memory as dashing rogues prompts reflection on what can pass for romance in an atmosphere of blissful condonation under the aegis of the abnormally interesting. The law held pirates to be at war against the whole world, and many of them agreed that they were. They stood before ancient and modern statutes as *hostis humani generis*, "common enemies of mankind," and therefore were executed, if captured alive and convicted, after a juryless trial under admiralty law, not common law or civil code, on a special gibbet erected between the marks of high and low tides, so as not, even in the moment of their deaths, to reenter the society they had eternally foresworn.7 At the same time, English privateers like Sir Henry Morgan, operating under the sanction of letters of marque, served as imperial mercenaries, plundering the Spanish Main so rapaciously that they made Samuel Pepys fear the outbreak of general naval war while he and his colleagues had all they could handle (and sometimes more) contending with the Dutch: "That we have done the Spanyard abundance of mischief in the West Indys by our privateers at Jamaica; which they lament mightily, and I am sorry for it to have done it at this time" (8:75). Always living on the margins of society, pirates, sailing under the flag of King Death, have typically worked their way into the innermost perimeter of its fears and dreams.

One specific scenario that gives recurrent life to the glamour and terror of piracy is in some form known to everyone: the ghost ship. Usually invisible, the ghost ship remains nevertheless uncannily active, sailing around "out there" somewhere in the mists of time, but showing up periodically in search of moral redemption or new recruits. Manned by a spectral crew, which is restless to return, as if from a doomed state of exile, be it to the world of the dead or the undead, in order to lift some ancient curse or remedy some unavenged injustice, the ghost ship sets up an action that figures in many different performances. These run from Richard Wagner's *The Flying Dutchman* to Disney's theme-park joy-ride "Pirates of the Caribbean," which inspired the recent cinematic epic *Pirates of the Caribbean: The Curse of the Black Pearl* (2003) and *Dead Man's Chest* (2006), starring Johnny Depp as Captain Jack Sparrow (fig. 23). Depp, channeling Keith Richards, makes use of all three of the overlapping role-icons of "rake," "fop," and "pirate." As the Disney pirates ruthlessly but loveably search for the talisman that holds the key to releasing them from the terrible

Fig. 23. Johnny Depp as Captain Jack Sparrow (wax effigy), © Corbis.

curse under which they must otherwise cruise eternally in their marine Limbo, they appear to themselves as themselves, a literal "skeleton crew," only as they sail in and out of the velvety shadows of the tropical moon. But the business of ghosts, however much of it gets done, always seems to remain unfinished: hence the freedom with which scenarios of outlaw glamour navigate through time, setting sail in the 1720s and reappearing on the cultural horizon, skull and crossbones flapping in the breeze, two hundred years later.

In 1926 German composer Kurt Weill wrote an article called "Dancemusic: Jazz." Speaking in the first-person plural, Weill described how the citizens of a new interculturally produced sonic and kinesthetic space pledged allegiance to the mesmerizing rhythms that summoned their world into imaginary fullness of being. Referring to the music of the Atlantic world, Weill wrote: "The rhythm of our time is jazz. In it the slow but sure American-ization of all our physical life finds its most notable manifestation. The shimmy outweighs everything else."[8] Weill, whose composi-tions heretofore had experimented with atonalism, refers to the dance craze for the shimmy-shake, derived from the word *chemise,* which featured the shaking of the body from the shoulders down, preferably in a short, beaded dress—*contraposto* in dynamic motion. Fascinated with the explosive success of jazz via the newly developed technologies of the phonograph and the radio, as well as in the pro-liferation of jazz cabarets and nightclubs, he began to explore the fusion of Euro-symphonic and contemporary popular forms.

Two years later, Weill put his theory to the test, collaborating with Bertolt Brecht and others on *The Threepenny Opera,* which pre-miered in Berlin in August 1928, with book and lyrics adapted by Brecht and his collaborator Elisabeth Hauptmann from John Gay's *The Beggar's Opera* of exactly two hundred years earlier.[9] This transmission history represents a genealogy of performance in which the archive, in this case the extant playscripts, and the reper-toire, the performance traditions of at least three continents, unite in the perfection of a new version of a well-traveled scenario. Igor Stravinsky once said that the late quartets of Beethoven were always contemporary, and so it seems to be with *The Beggar's Opera.* The huge success generated by Gay's delicate romance of Captain Macheath and Polly Peachum played out against the background of the raunchy stews of London vice and crime led directly to the much-anticipated sequel, *Polly,* which was suppressed on political grounds. The original success, however, sustained the ballad opera through numerous revivals on the eighteenth-century and nine-teenth-century English stage, and launched four major twentieth-century adaptations of Gay's original: Brecht and Weill's; Václav Havel's *The Beggar's Opera: A Play in Fourteen Acts on John Gay's Theme* (written and suppressed, 1972; produced, 1975); Wole Soyinka's *Opera Wonyosi* (1977), with additional music by Israel Ijemanze; and Marathi playwright P. L. Deshpande's *Teen paishacha tamasha* (*The Three-Paisa Entertainment,* 1978).[10]

That Gay's sequel was silenced by Robert Walpole's government, that Havel's adaptation was forbidden by the "normalizing" regime of post-1968 Czechoslovakia, and that Soyinka has faced imprisonment and threats of death by hanging under several regimes—all attest to the enduring popularity of the material. So does its unacknowledged influence in more subtly subversive works, such as the echoes of the cross-dressed captive Polly in the adventures of Peter and Wendy among the Caribbean pirates and Indians in J. M. Barrie's *Peter Pan* (1904).

Coming up on three centuries after his debut, what is it about Captain Macheath and his gang of thieves and pirates that tends to stick not only in people's minds, but also in their craws? How is it that he sails through time, masked and disguised but always in one way or another as himself? The answer clearly has to do with the It-Effect, the mass desire inspired by glamorous and menacing people—the living, the dead, or the invented. The contradiction that makes them the most interesting, simultaneously alluring and alien, is their danger, balanced precariously at the tipping point of love and death. Whether this allure roots itself more in curiosity or in fear is hard to say, but it manifests itself as the experience of a relentlessly successful seduction on the mass-cultural scale.

In creating the character of Macheath, John Gay exploited the paradox he found in his source material, popular biographies of contemporary criminal masterminds such as Jack Shepherd, Jonathan Wild, and the even more ruthlessly "unbiddable" (though not unbribable) prime minister of Great Britain, Sir Robert Walpole. The more they got away with, the bigger their draw. "Of all animals of prey, man is the only sociable one," soliloquizes the jailor, Lockit, in act 3, scene 2 of *The Beggar's Opera:* "Every one of us preys upon his neighbor, and yet we herd together" (*BA* 1361). It was the paradox expressed in this single line that inspired Václav Havel to adapt *The Beggar's Opera* as a critique of the Czech puppet regime of the 1970s, elaborating a joke that circulated at the time: "Under capitalism, man exploits his fellow man, whereas under communism it's the other way around."[11] However misinformed Lockit's zoology (lions form prides, after all, and wolves packs), his social-scientific paradox has authority: as a warden, he should know about antisocial herds. His burden is made all the heavier by the difficulty of keeping the charming outlaw Macheath, at this point a roving land pirate, confined in Newgate Prison long enough to be hanged, when all the women in the play, including Lockit's own daughter, Lucy, who is also Macheath's "wife," long for his escape. All except for one: the femme fatale Jenny Diver betrays the bandit to the authorities, who arrest him in the brothel where he has sought solace in her arms. Like Achilles, the hero has a fatal vulnerability, but it is most definitely not in his heel.

Macheath unquestionably has "It," and so does the most beguiling of his other "wives," the lovely and resourceful Miss Polly Peachum, who turns out in the end to be a more ruthless pirate than her lover. In this success, the characters were amplified and abetted by the starring actors: Thomas Walker, who originally played Macheath, and the phenomenal Lavinia Fenton, who played Polly so vividly that she became "Polly" in the minds of an adoring public. The setting of *The Beggar's Opera* is metropolitan London, in the thieves' dens, lockups, and brothels that stand in for the halls of government and high society in this doubly inverted pastoral. The setting of *Polly* is colonial Jamaica, where the eponymous heroine escapes enslavement only by donning men's clothes and becoming a pirate herself, better to pursue Macheath, who has disguised himself in blackface as the Maroon buccaneer "Morano," about whom a crewmember says, "Though he is black, nobody has more the air of a great man" (*Polly* 2.2; *BA* 1565). John Gay mined extensively *The General History of the Pirates* (1724), a popular compendium of buccaneer lore of disputed authorship, but attributed by many to Daniel Defoe. Hovering on the cusp of news and fiction, *The General History* glamorized the pirates of the Caribbean, prominently among them "Calico Jack" Rackham, known by that sobriquet because of his distinctive underwear and his great romantic attraction. Both of the most famous transvestite pirates, Ann Bonny and Mary Read, served with Rackham: captured and condemned, the two women "pled their bellies" and escaped execution, while Rackham was hanged and left to rot in an iron cage between the tides.[12] In loving these rogues, Gay's audiences embraced the It-Effect of negative attraction, and the scenario's three-hundred-year run on stage and screen exemplifies the prescience of their early susceptibility to its charms in the deep eighteenth century.

Freud observed that most individuals suppress their instincts, but the rare one who does not "becomes a criminal, an outlaw, unless his social position or striking abilities enable him to hold his own as a great man, a 'hero.'"[13] Brecht said something very much like this in the 1930s when he remarked that a great man was a national calamity. Whenever that becomes the case, Brecht did not need to add, it does so because the great man is first a national attraction. For Wole Soyinka, in his African version of *The Beggar's Opera,* the term evokes the jovially murderous dictators "President for Life" Idi Amin and "Emperor for Life" Jean-Bedel Bokassa. The latter appears in *Opera Wonyosi* as "Folksy Boksy," who characterizes himself as a "black Napoleon" and whose hobnail boots serve the pre-choreographed purpose of stomping politically unreliable schoolchildren to death.[14] Gay makes ironic use of the "Great Man" epithet throughout *The Beggar's Opera* and *Polly,* the first time when Mrs. Peachum assures the aptly promising pickpocket, Filch: "If an unlucky session does not cut the rope of thy life, Boy, thou wilt be a great man in history" (*Beggar's Opera,* 1.6; *BA* 1338); the last time when Jenny Diver, Polly's foil, the darkly passionate pickpocket and whore who loves Macheath fiercely and betrays him repeatedly, taunts a member of the pirate crew: "You may talk of honor, as other great men do, but when interest comes in your way, you should do as other great men do" (*Polly,* 2.9; *BA* 1576). Historians agree that the topical reference hits at Sir Robert Walpole, the corrupt and highly effective prime minister, ironically and fearfully known as "the Great Man," but Gay splits the allegory between Macheath and Mr. Peachum, Polly's father, the ruthless thief-taker and fence, who appears only in *The Beggar's Opera* and says of his kind: "In one respect, indeed, our employment may be reckoned dishonest, because, like great statesmen, we encourage those who betray their friends" (*Beggar's Opera,* 2.10; *BA* 1354). What confused and angered moralists about the representation of Macheath, however, was not his depredations or his promiscuities and betrayals, but his prepossessing and widely celebrated attraction: "There is nothing moves one so much," says Lucy at the foot of the gallows, when Macheath is about to be hanged, "as a great man in distress" (*Beggar's Opera*, 3.15; *BA* 1371).

To some contemporaries, Macheath seemed as real as any living person, and of course, due to the magic of the It-Effect, created by the uncanny power of negative attraction, he was more so. In the cascade of pamphlets that followed the performance of *The Beggar's Opera* and the suppression of the production and unlicensed publication of *Polly,* one of the most interesting screeds to appear was the anonymous *Memoirs Concerning the Life and Manners of Captain Mackheath,* which takes the form of a moralizing (and titillating) criminal biography of the kind that real-life pirates and other criminals inspired. Citing the example of Etherege's rake-hero, Dorimant, the pamphleteer castigates John Gay for painting too alluring portrait of this miscreant. He then proceeds to lay out the facts of "Mackheath's" crimes, as if he is speaking of a real person notoriously known to everyone: "This Gentleman has been extremely misrepresented by the Author of the *Beggar's Opera;* he has indeed taken, I think, too great a Poetical License." The critic assures us that he writes the pamphlet out of a "Publick Spiritedness" that rises above ad hominem attack, "not to talk against the Man, but his Crimes." Rather, his intention is

> to undeceive my Fellow-Citizens, before whom he has been lately set upon the publick Stage as a Character of Heroism, if not of Virtue. The Dramatick Writer has indeed dress'd him out to Advantage, he stands erect in the first Piece of the Canvas, and has gained much popular Applause; he has made the Lover and the Warrior, he is the Darling of the Fair, and the Glory of the thievish Heroes who surround him: He is a perfect, polite, modern fine Gentleman, and *Dorimant* in *Sir Fopling*; tho a person of equal Morals, is not a more accomplished Rake.[15]

During the financial hallucination of the South Sea Bubble, the young Mackheath, the biographer explains, lost his way and was corrupted and dissipated by his quest for money and vicious pleasures. The pamphleteer finds the root of all evil, including the hero's, not in wealth per se but rather in its maldistribution, which issues an open invitation to its unauthorized redistribution by criminal means. Young Mackheath has the gift of charismatic eloquence, but his character eventually hardens into "Arrogance and Avarice." No sooner did he become chief "cashier" of the gang, taking charge of the lockbox, but he "embezzled some Part of this sacred Deposit."[16] What troubles the author of *The Memoirs of Mackheath* and his fellow pamphleteers more than anything else is the pervasive success of Macheath and Polly in insinuating themselves into the popular imagination of proper Englishmen and women, stealing not only their purses but their hearts.

*The Beggar's Opera* created a cult following and a brand, which spun off a product line of merchandise, such as Lavinia Fenton fans and aprons, forerunners to the official show-related T-shirts and coffee mugs hawked in theater lobbies today. Moralists fumed. In the anonymous *Thievery à la Mode: or, the Fatal Encouragement*, for example, the pamphleteer tells the cautionary tale of young Mellefont, who is seduced by the all-encompassing It-Effect of the show. Lured by a dissipated friend "to a whimsical entertainment at the Playhouse, very much in vogue, called *The Beggar's Opera*," Mellefont immediately begins to succumb to the land-pirates of Lincoln's Inn Fields and their outlaw glamour. The buzz surrounding the show, stimulated by the ubiquity of the spun-off products, finally seals his fate:

> Some few days after, passing by a great Picture shop, he saw the Prints of Captain *Macheath* and *Polly Peachum* hanging in the Windows with those of the first Quality of both Sexes in the Kingdom. And the same Evening happening to be at a Place where several Ladies were visiting, he observed that every one of them had the agreeable Highwayman and his two doxies painted on their Fans and Snuff-boxes. . . . In fine, [Mellefont] could go into no Company, hear no Discourse, but what was taken up with the Charming Characters of Captain Macheath and Polly Peachum.

Emulating Macheath's example, Mellefont predictably enough turns to a life of crime. Recognizing one of his robbery victims as a

fellow audience member at *The Beggar's Opera,* Mellefont jokes that
he is providing a "Sequel," adding, to the further consternation of
his outraged mark, "I hope that no Gentleman will be offended at
the Reality, who was delighted by the *Representation.*" Fatally
wounded in a botched stickup on his final caper, Mellefont calls
for a priest and confesses, making yet another contribution to a
well-stocked repertoire of foot-of-the-gallows penitence that eighteenth-century auditors and readers craved, especially from their
best-beloved highwaymen and pirates. His dying confession concludes "with a hearty Prayer, that he might be the only Person
seduced by the extravagant Applause the Town gave the Character
of a Thief in the *Beggar's Opera.*"[17]

The applause grew no less extravagant over the centuries as
Gay's masterpiece inspired a vogue for ballad opera and related
musical theater genres. Meanwhile, the erotic aura associated with
outlaw glamour intensified rather than diminished. As John
Brewer notes in *The Pleasures of the Imagination* (1997), *The Beggar's
Opera* became "a source of allusion as well known as the characters
in Shakespeare's plays and the poetry of Milton. Its thieves and
whores, songs and famous lines acquired a life of their own, separate from the stage performance."[18] They stole into some surprising places, taking aliases in their new lives. Conrad, the brooding
pirate captain and daring hero of Byron's *The Corsair,* seeks to pun-
ish all humankind, but, like Macheath, he loves too many women
at the same time. Devoted to Medora, his wife, who, like Polly,
remains the sentimental favorite, he falls in love with Gulnare, the
most beautiful captive in the Turkish pasha's harem, who, like
Jenny Diver, most resembles the dangerous hero in temperament.
At the end of the poem, Conrad sails off over the horizon to an
unknown fate, leaving behind an afterimage of pulse-quickening
mystery:

> He left a Corsair's name to other times,
> Link'd with one virtue, and a thousand crimes.
>
> $$(3.24.695-96)^{19}$$

The fate of Byron's poem, his publisher John Murray reports, was
to sell ten thousand copies on the first day of its issue, an unprece-

dented success, as remarkable in publishing history as the uninter-
rupted sixty-night run of *The Beggar's Opera* was at its moment of
theatrical history. Nineteenth-century stage melodrama lent itself
particularly well to pirate hero-villain scenarios, and the English
theater responded with shabby little shockers such as *Blackbeard, or
the Captive Princess* (1798), *The Red Rover, or The Mutiny of the Dol-
phin* (1829), and *Descart, the French Buccaneer* (1840). The silliness
of this material served up a wealth of opportunities for parodic
treatment, on which Gilbert and Sullivan capitalized in *The Pirates
of Penzance* (1879).[20]

Then, somewhere in the Never-Never Land between melodrama and parody, the nefarious Captain Hook took command of
the public imagination from the deck of his pirate ship as the best-
beloved villain in theatrical and cinematic history. But Barrie lets
the dark lore of the predators who sailed under the banner of King
Death seep in between the caulks of Hook's spectrally personified
vessel. The *Jolly Roger,* also known as "the cannibal of the seas," a
black brig lit from deep within by a dim green light, suits its captain. The script of *Peter Pan* provides a detailed stage direction to
match Hook's character to the poetical effigy of Charles II, evoking the combined role-icons of "king," "rake," and "fop" as
"pirate":

> Cruelest jewel in that dark setting is HOOK himself, cadaverous
> and blackavised, his hair dressed in long curls which look like
> black candles about to melt, his eyes blue as the forget-me-not
> and of a profound insensibility, save when he claws, at which
> time a red spot appears in them. He has an iron hook instead of
> a right hand, and it is with this he claws. He is never more sinis-
> ter than when he is most polite, and the elegance of his diction,
> the distinction of his demeanour, show him one of a different
> class from his crew, a solitary among uncultured companions.
> . . . In dress he apes the dandiacal associated with Charles II,
> having heard it said in an earlier period of his career that he
> bore a strange resemblance to the ill-fated Stuarts.[21]

Hook's black brig sails forever, "out there" somewhere in time, a
ghost ship, with the gourmet crocodile following relentlessly in its

wake, the alarm clock ticking, an ironic juxtaposition of the empty homogeneity of clock time opposed by the more richly textured cross-rhythms of patiently savored retribution. Barrie's physical characterization of Hook—swarthy face, black full-bottomed periwig, and menacing charm—conjures the rakish villain whose effigy thus continues to circulate in the minds of millions of viewers raised on the Captain Hooks of the Disney animated feature and the elegant interpretations offered up on stage and screen from Basil Rathbone's to Dustin Hoffman's. Like time, the scenario of negative attraction does not flow; it percolates.

Although the stage play *Peter Pan* bowed in 1904, Barrie withheld it from publication for nearly twenty years, making it contemporary with the wildly popular revival of *The Beggar's Opera* by Nigel Playfair at the Lyric Theatre Hammersmith in 1920, which caught the attention of the dramaturg Elisabeth Hauptmann, who began translating it and sharing her drafts with her collaborator, Bertolt Brecht, and he with his, musical prodigy Kurt Weill. Thus, when Gay's toe-tapping scenario collided with the emerging culture industry of the 1920s, two infectious rhythms, the action of the lady-killing highwayman turned blackfaced pirate and the massively popular phenomenon that Weill called "dancemusic: jazz" came together—the perfect Atlantic storm (fig. 24). Weill specified in notation the rhythms of the tango and the fox-trot; he marked the opening "Ballad of Mack the Knife" *Blues Tempo,* the "Ballad of the Easy Life" *Shimmy Tempo.* These appear in the score of the version translated and adapted by Marc Blitzstein, which opened off-Broadway in the Theatre de Lys in Greenwich Village on March 10, 1954, and ran for 2,611 performances. Brecht scholars will likely object that the more recent and now standard translation by Ralph Mannheim and John Willett, done under the imprimatur of the Brecht estate, is more faithful to the original; indeed, some might characterize it as deadly accurate. But Blitzstein's idiom is jazzier, his diction sleazier, his fingers snappier. Besides, Blitzstein's is the version of "Mack the Knife" that many listeners still recognize as the one that played week after week on "Your Hit Parade," with Dorothy Collins, Giselle Mackenzie, and Snooky Lanson, and which has now returned, like the

Fig. 24. *The Threepenny Opera,* Edison Theatre, Washington University in
St. Louis, 1984. Directed by Joseph Roach. Rhonnie Washingon
as Macheath. Suzanne Scates as Jenny. Author's photo.

repressed, through Kevin Spacey's channeling of Bobby Darin in
*Beyond the Sea:*

> Oh, the shark has pretty teeth, dear—
> And he shows them pearly white.
> Just a jack-knife has Macheath, dear—
> And he keeps it out of sight.[22]

The "Moritat," as it is known, is a lyric overture to the drama of
negative attraction that follows in the rest of *The Threepenny Opera,*
presaging the showstopping "Pirate Jenny."

In the Willett-Mannheim version, Polly sings this dark ballad, improbably, at her wedding feast, as she did at the premiere in 1928. In Blitzstein's version, Jenny, who is, after all, descended from the Jenny Diver in *The Beggar's Opera* who turns pirate moll in *Polly*, takes back her eponymous song as "Low-Dive" Jenny. Her moniker refers not only to her skill as a pickpocket, as most editions primly gloss it, but to her sexual specialty. Blitzstein started to work on his translation by experimenting with the lyrics for "Pirate Jenny." When he showed them to Kurt Weill and Lotte Lenya, who created the role of Jenny in the Berlin production of 1928, the couple encouraged him to translate the entire text of *Threepenny Opera*. First tried out at Brandeis University in 1952 with Leonard Bernstein conducting, the Blitzstein translation (which retained Weill's musical arrangements) became the longest-running version of this famously long-legged show, not least because Lotte Lenya revived her role from the premiere. On the one hand, it doesn't matter whether Polly or Jenny sings "Pirate Jenny," for both of them join Macheath-Morano's pirate crew and sail through time marked as the stage versions of Ann Bonny and Mary Read. On the other hand, for purposes of respectfully attending to the form of works shaped by popular reception, Lenya's interpretation of "Pirate Jenny" stood as definitive in its time, and it became, after "Mack the Knife," the show's signature number as well as hers. Though she was no It-Girl, Lenya certainly had It, the kind that radiated a breath-stopping aura of danger.

"Pirate Jenny" seethes with ornately fantasized revenge. It says that the downtrodden often secretly dream such vengeance against their oppressors, that outlaws dream it against the authorities, and that women dream it against men. Apostrophizing her absent customers while she pictures their demise, Jenny describes how she makes her living on her knees, metaphorically imagining herself as a domestic and thus educating the clueless to the fact that sex work is hard work:

> You gentlemen can watch while I'm scrubbin' the floors,
> And I'm scrubbing the floors while you're gawkin'
> And maybe once you tip me and it makes you feel swell,

> On a ratty water-front in a ratty old hotel,
> And you never guess to who you're talkin',
> And you never guess to who you're talkin'.

At the end of each verse, a chorus of refrain looks forward to the apocalyptic violence threatened by an approaching ship, a ghost ship, a mirage that she sees in her mind's eye with the vividness of sensation. This ominous scenario evokes, vindictively on the part of the singer, the feelings of sheer terror that must have seized the intended victims who lived in the rich treasure ports along the Spanish Main when they looked up at the horizon and saw the specter of a commandeered merchantman, which is what most pirate ships were, bristling with added guns and sailing toward them with the Jolly Roger nailed to the mast:

> And a ship, a black freighter, with a skull on the masthead will
>     be comin' in.

In next verse Jenny sings, "I'm countin' your heads while I make up the beds, 'cause there's nobody gonna sleep here," which brings her back to the refrain:

> And the ship, the black freighter, turns around in the harbor,
>     shootin' guns from the bow!

She then foresees, does this punk Cassandra, the flaming destruction of every building in the town except the one she's in, ending again:

> And the ship, the black freighter, runs the flag up its masthead
>     and a cheer rings the air!

Jenny's dark augury reaches its climax with the amphibious landing of the ghostly crew, who fan out to round up her abusers and bring them to her en masse for summary judgment and punishment:

> They're movin' in the shadows where no one can see,
> And they're chainin' up people and bringin' them to me,
> Askin' me, "Kill them now or later?"
> Askin' me, "Kill them now or later?"

Her answer, unsurprising as it is spine-chilling, is delivered in *Sprechstimme,* or cadenced, unpitched speech: "*Right now!*" In this same raspy whisper, she hastens to add the moral, "*That'll learn you!*" as the pile of bodies grows, and she closes with her fantasized escape aboard the ghost ship:

> Then a ship, the black freighter, disappears out to sea,
> And on it is—me.[23]

Her apparent destination is the mists of time, but everyone knows that she's actually going to find her way back into the repertoire soon.

It's never really a surprise when ghosts turn up from out of the past to represent displaced social relations, but pirate ghosts bear a double charge as the common enemies of mankind and exceptionally satisfying lovers. In *Polly,* everyone in Jamaica thinks that Macheath has died, but he has in fact come back in disguise, as ghost, as pirate, and as Maroon—and also as legend. As Polly says of her phantom lover, encapsulating the It-Effect in five words: "My imagination follows him everywhere" (2.1; *BA* 1563). The lecherous and acquisitive Mr. Ducat asks one of the Indians, who are allied with the English in their fight with the pirates and the Maroons: "Does Macheath command the enemy?" To which the Indian replies: "Report says he is dead. Above twelve moons are passed since we heard of him. Morano, a Negro villain, is their chief, who in rapine and barbarities is even equal to him" (1.12; *BA* 1560). Mrs. Ducat describes the arrival of Morano's pirates as an invasion, but clearly it is also an uprising. Polly, indentured to the unscrupulous Ducats, facing the choice between enslavement and joining the pirates, states the case for piracy as a war of resistance against intolerable injustices, even if that means a war with the rest of the world. She is passing as a young man at this point, when she is challenged by Morano, who does not recognize her in her male garb, as she does not recognize him in blackface. He asks, "What are you, friend?" She answers:

> A young fellow who hath been robbed by the world. And I came on purpose to join you, to rob the world by way of

retaliation. An open war with the whole world is brave and
honorable. I hate the clandestine, pilfering war that is
practiced among friends and neighbors in civil societies. I
would serve, sir. (2.5; *BA* 1570)

The stark alternative between slavery and piracy juxtaposes the two
institutions in a revealing way. The ghost ship and the slave ship
are specters of the past that remain under sail, "out there" somewhere, but always on their way back here. Their interlocking scenarios spill over into the interstices between high and popular culture, the eerie undersea walk of the animated skeletons who sail
with *The Back Pearl* in the climactic scene of *Pirates of the Caribbean*
doubling the master image of August Wilson's simultaneously produced *Gem of the Ocean* (2004), the penultimate play in that great
playwright's ten-play cycle of African-American history: that image
is "The City of Bones," a ghost metropolis on the ocean floor populated by the remains of drowned slaves.

History, like the sea, keeps giving up its dead; its sources seem
inexhaustible, even though they began bobbing up unbidden in
the wake left by the thoughts of casual interlocutors centuries ago.
In the course of his professional connection with maritime affairs,
Pepys had occasion to hear from Captain Christopher Myngs and
his colleagues, who shared their knowledge or at least their image
of a peculiarity they professed to have discovered in the burgeoning relationship of sea, flesh, and bone: "Among other things, he
and the other Captains that were with us tell me that Negroes
drownded look white and lose their blacknesse—which I never
heard before" (3:63). The enormity of the history indexed by this
offhand report might best be measured in connection with the
scope of the long-term plans for its consolidation: Charles II char-
tered the Royal Africa Company, "the favorite child of the Royal
house of Stuart," which operated slave-taking forts from Cape
Blanco to the Cape of Good Hope, for one thousand years, its
patent to expire in A.D. 2672.[24] In the event, this institution and
others like it proved shorter-lived, except for their consequences.

*It* in Latin is *id.* Freudians make expressive use of the ancient
word to dramatize the irreducibility of two fundamental uncon-

scious drives, the pleasure principle and the death wish. That pairing animates the scenarios of outlaw glamour and negative attraction. The stakes could not be higher, as Geoffrey Hartman explains, "The fateful question, then, is not whether what Freud identifies as a death drive can ever be overcome, for Thanatos is as immortal as Eros and genius partakes of both. The question is whether culture can diminish aggression and tilt the balance toward love."[25] Eros and Thanatos confabulate throughout Shakespeare's *Henry V,* in which the reduction of Harfleur and the slaughter of the unarmed prisoners of Agincourt by the "happy few" prepare the way, pragmatically and symbolically, for the king's wooing of Katherine, which is infantile in its language and uncircumscribed in its libidinous intent: "For I love France so well, that I will not part with a village of it—I will have it all mine. And, Kate, when France is mine and I am yours, then yours is France, and you are mine" (5.2.178–82). By Glyn's reckoning or by anyone's, Henry has It: his afterimage wafts through time as the "mirror of all Christian kings." He has unmatched confidence. His actions remain uninfluenced by others. He certainly possesses that "strange magnetism that attracts both sexes." He is powerfully "unbiddable." But on the score of "poignant antiphony," Shakespeare also continuously shadows Henry's attraction with the history that has not yet evaporated into romance. "Myth," as Barthes defines it, revealing its kinship to what Glyn called "romance" or "spiritual disguise," empties reality of history and fills it with nature: "it is, literally, a ceaseless flowing out, a haemorrhage, or perhaps an evaporation, in short a perceptible absence."[26] Like Pygmalion, but in a history, not a romance, Henry falls in love with the speechless effigy that his actions but not her intentions have summoned into being. Like Pygmalion, but in a history, not a romance, he claims her with a kiss that she cannot refuse. Like Pygmalion's, but in a history, not a romance, his vanity requires no response. In the end, the most enchanted and disturbing effigies will always prove to be the ones fashioned from flesh and blood.

Shakespeare's *Henry V* was not the stage version of the betrothal of Katherine of France performed during Pepys's lifetime, but the diarist's delight that he "did kiss a Queen" resonates equally in the one that he did see enacted, *Henry the Fifth* (1664), the version in rhymed couplets by Roger Boyle, Earl of Orrery. In it Mary Betterton ("Ianthe") played Katherine, for whose hand King Henry V, played by Henry Harris, and Owen Tudor, played by the great Betterton, are rivals. In it they sublimated history into romance, in the sense of Glyn's "spiritual disguise." Pepys records his enthusiasm for the play and the production, with but one significant reservation:

> And to the new play at the Duke's house, of *Henery the 5th*—a most notable play, writ by my Lord Orery; wherein Batterton, Harris, and Ianthes parts are most incomparably wrote and done, and the whole play the most full of heighth and raptures of wit and sense that ever I heard; having but one incongruity or what did not please me in it—that is, that King Harry promises to plead for Tudor to their mistress, Princess Katherine of France, more then when it comes to it he seems to do; and Tudor refused by her with some kind of indignity, not with the difficulty and honour that it ought to have been done in to him. (5:240–41)

Here Pepys sides with the self-fashioning new man in his wooing of Katherine in competition with King Henry. The intense appeal of this particular action to the diarist's longing for synthetic experience, demonstrated by his rave review, dominates his understanding of the characters and motivates his role in the necrophilic carnival he later stages at the Abbey. That he could not be satisfied with the king's efforts on behalf of Owen Tudor only goes to show the depth of his investment with both dynastic icons. Of course he could not go far wrong: either way, he steps into the shoes of the man who wins the hand of "Queen of all, Katherine." What King Henry actually says seems pretty generous to the impartial listener, delegating the perquisites of the sovereign to the new man vicariously:

> Madam, I have injurious been to him
> As far as ignorance could make a crime:
> I did employ him in my suit to you

But I declare (which some amends may be)
That he, at least, in all things equals me
Unless in title, but it's greater far
A crown to merit than a crown to wear.
Can title in that balance e'er prevail
Where love is merit and you hold the scale?
              (*Henry the Fifth*, 5.4.1–10; *BA* 32)

Music to the ears of mimetic desire this speech ought to have been, particularly in view of the subsequent history of Owen and Katherine, but the theater, while it appeals to private fancies, remains in the control of those accountable to the public at large. Not that the producers stinted on staging the parallels between the Lancastrian monarch and the Stuart. First, they cast the sympathetic Betterton as Owen Tudor, the dynastic founder. Second, they somehow persuaded King Charles II, the Duke of York, and Earl of Oxford to loan their coronation robes to the theater for this production, clothing the stage effigies in a remarkably authentic, if anachronistic way. The old prompter John Downes records that while Harris as Henry V wore the Duke of York's suit and William Smith as Burgundy wore Oxford's, King Charles's own robes were assigned to Betterton, an eye-filling preview of the eventual ascent of the Tudor (and perforce the Stuart) line.[27]

In this expansion of public intimacy, living effigies (the actors) continued to exert their considerable charm, as they still do today in the guise of tradition-bearing and tradition-inventing monarchs of many titles: beauty queens, queens of the silver screen, queens for a day, drag queens, welfare queens, and, most poignantly in recent memory, a queen of hearts. The image today often consists of the name, the face, and the scandal. But the true modern effigy is larger than that. Diana's shrine and museum at Althorp, for instance, and a traveling exhibition of memorabilia from it, continue to enchant the multitudes with the bits and pieces of her memory: the gingham frog soft-toy that she kept with her from childhood; the red blazer and knitted scarf from the Silfield School; the pastel portrait of Marmalade the Cat; the black leather tap shoes, and of course the floatlike wedding dress of silk taffeta and ivory tulle, with its twenty-five-foot-long train; the Gianni Versace suits and drop-dead evening gowns; the blast-resistant, mine-clearing outfit by Ralph Lauren; the many photos of her lovingly holding children of all races and, above all, the electrifying shots of her comforting the sick and dying, the lepers and the AIDS patients, laying her royal hands on them, as they look up gratefully into her eyes as if her touch could cure. And in some ways her touch, even at a mass-mediated remove, must still cure, for such an effigy now gives the world back the empathic image of its mind at the speed of light. As H. R. H. the Prince of Wales aptly said of Charles II and the other wax figures in the Abbey, Diana's after-image, which is the idea of her, continues to appear to the hallucinating public as "astonishingly lifelike," at least as much if not more so than his own.

In drawing attention to this quality, the Prince of Wales probably did not mean to refer to the more ancient but less prepossessingly lifelike effigies in the Abbey Museum, the medieval figures carved from single blocks of wood and painted in polychrome, which has flaked and faded through the centuries. Among them is the funeral effigy of Katherine of Valois, carved from one piece of oak for her funeral in February 1437 (fig. 25). As a conscript of the "Ragged Regiment," she has remained on display in Westminster Abbey ever since, eerily doubling the corpse with which Samuel Pepys staged his assignation. Her right arm and left hand are missing. Her face is plainly carved, probably from her death mask, with compressed features and drooping eyelids; yet for all that, across the vicissitudes of time, "The dead face has beauty as well as pathos."[28] Her image painted on wood is no doubt as close as physical vision can come to realizing her presence. Imagination can do more. Onstage in effigy, Katherine becomes the ventriloquized object of synthetic experience, refleshed at intervals by actresses from Mary Betterton to Emma Thompson, as in life her body, like Diana's, became the reusable vehicle of dynastic succession. In the end, it is Shakespeare's Henry V, not Orrery's, who captures in one summary speech the sense of the effigy's power to communicate itself vicariously to contemporaries and to generations yet unborn. Like Pygmalion, like Pepys, he seals the one-way bargain with a stolen kiss:

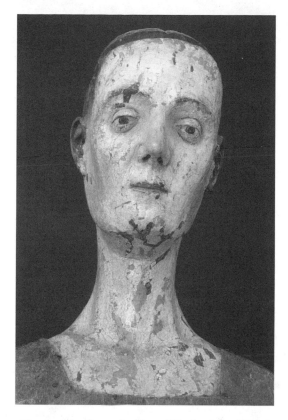

Fig. 25. Head of the funeral effigy of Katherine of Valois, 1437.
Photo: Malcolm Crowthers. © Dean and Chapter of Westminster.

O Kate, nice customs cu'sy to great kings. Dear Kate, you and I
cannot be confin'd within the weak list of a country's fashion.
We are the makers of manners, Kate; and the liberty that follows our places stops the mouths of all find-faults, as I will do
yours, for upholding the nice fashion of your country and
denying me a kiss; therefore patiently and yielding. *(Kisses her)*
(5.2.281–86)

King Henry might just as well have been speaking of the power of
the modern avatars of the It-Effect, mass-mediated makers of manners, which skilled artisans now model out of electrons as they
once made effigies of wood and wax. Like the figures of Westminster Abbey, his words are relics of an idea whose time has come.

# notes

## introduction

1. Brian Raftery, "Uma: Single White Female," *Gentlemen's Quarterly*, December 2003, 210–15.

2. Elinor Glyn, *It* (New York: Macaulay, 1927), 5–6.

3. *Oxford English Dictionary Online*, 2nd ed. (Oxford University Press, 1989), s.v. "it." Kipling's usage comes under "Sex appeal," but a rich set of examples may also be found under "it" in the "emphatic predictive use: the actual or very thing required or expected; that beyond which one cannot go; the *ne plus ultra;* the acme." Charles Lamb in *Dramatic Essays*, for instance, says "Lovegrove revived the character and made it sufficiently grotesque; but Dodd was *it,* as it came out of nature's hands." In 1906, the *Daily Chronicle* reported: "There is in America a curious use of the word 'it' conveyed by emphasis. Pre-eminently Roosevelt is 'it.' Next after Roosevelt an American would say 'Shaw is it.'"

4. For biographical details on Bow, I am indebted to Joseph Morella and Edward P. Epstein, *The "It" Girl: The Incredible Story of Clara Bow* (New York: Delacorte, 1976); and David Stenn, *Clara Bow: Runnin' Wild* (New York: Doubleday, 1988). Nicholas Daly has written an illuminating account of Glyn, Bow, and modernism in *Literature, Technology, and Modernity, 1860–2000* (Cambridge: Cambridge University Press, 2004), chap. 4, "'It': The Last Machine and the Invention of Sex Appeal," 76–109.

5. Michael L. Quinn, "Celebrity and the Semiotics of Acting," *New Theatre Quarterly* 22 (1990): 156. See also Bert O. States, "The Actor's Presence: Three Phenomenal Modes," in *Acting (Re)Considered: Theories and Practices,* ed. Phillip B. Zarrilli (London: Routledge, 1995), 22–42.

6. Marvin Carlson, *The Haunted Stage: The Theatre as a Memory Machine* (Ann Arbor: University of Michigan Press, 2001), 9.

7. Eugenia Perctz, "The 'It' Parade," *Vanity Fair*, September 2000, 313–82.

8. Max Weber, *On Charisma and Institution Building*, ed. S. N. Eisenstadt (Chicago: University of Chicago Press, 1968).

9. Eugenio Barba and Nicola Savarese, *A Dictionary of Theatre Anthropology: The Secret Art of the Performer* (London: Routledge, for the Centre for Performance Research, 1991), 184.

10. George Meredith, *Beauchamp's Career*, ed. G. M. Young (London: Oxford University Press, 1950), 331.

11. Stephen King, *It* (New York: Signet, 1981), 12.

12. Gordon Rogoff, "Burning Ice," in *Stanislavski in America: The "Method" and Its Influence on the American Theatre*, ed. Erika Munk (1966; New York: Fawcett, 1967), 264.

13. Alexander Pope, *An Essay on Criticism*, lines 299–300 and 298, in *The Poems of Alexander Pope*, vol. 1, *Pastoral Poetry and An Essay on Criticism*, ed. E. Audra and Aubrey Williams (New Haven: Yale University Press, 1961), 273. I am grateful to Jill Campbell for drawing my attention to this passage. On the relationship between performance and print, I am indebted to Julie Stone Peters's *Theatre of the Book, 1480–1800: Print, Text, and Performance in Europe* (Oxford: Oxford University Press, 2000).

14. See, for example, the essays collected in *The Global Eighteenth Century*, ed. Felicity A. Nussbaum (Baltimore: Johns Hopkins University Press, 2003).

15. Michel Serres and Bruno Latour, *Conversations on Science, Culture, and Time* (Ann Arbor: University of Michigan Press, 1995), 62.

16. The generative work on this subject for me and many others remains Jean-Christophe Agnew, *Worlds Apart: The Market and the Theater in Anglo-American Thought, 1550–1750* (New York: Cambridge University Press, 1986); especially chap. 3, "Artificial Persons," 101–48.

17. John Brewer, *The Pleasures of the Imagination: English Culture in the Eighteenth Century* (New York: Farrar, Straus and Giroux, 1997), especially 428–50.

18. Charles Lamb, "On the Artificial Comedy of the Last Century," in *The Essays of Elia* (New York: Wiley and Putnam, 1845), 185–86.

19. Thomas Babington Macaulay, *History of England from the Accession of James the Second*, ed. Douglas Jerrold (1848; New York: Dutton, 1966), 1:302.

20. Macaulay, *History of England*, 1:302.

21. Norman Holland, *The First Modern Comedies: The Significance of Etherege, Wycherley, and Congreve* (1959; rpt. Bloomington: Indiana University Press, 1967), 12.

22. Guided by Peter Holland's landmark study, *The Ornament of Action: Text and Performance in Restoration Comedy* (Cambridge: Cambridge University Press, 1979), 55–98.

23. Herbert Blau, *The Dubious Spectacle: Extremities of Theater, 1976–2000* (Minneapolis: University of Minnesota Press, 2002), 272.

24. Martin Harries, *Scare Quotes from Shakespeare: Marx, Keynes, and the Language of Reenchantment* (Stanford: Stanford University Press, 2000), 8–13. I am indebted to Harries, who has led me through the uses of the

word *reenchantment* in Susan Buck-Morss's reading of the Arcades project, in which Walter Benjamin troubles Max Weber's idea that the essence of modernization is demythification or disenchantment *(Entzauberung)* and offers instead his critique of production and consumption under capitalism as a "reactivation of mythic powers" or a "*re*enchantment": see Susan Buck-Morss, *The Dialectics of Seeing: Walter Benjamin and the Arcades Project* (Cambridge: MIT Press, 1981), 253–54. Simon During, in *Modern Enchantments: The Cultural Power of Secular Magic* (Cambridge: Harvard University Press, 2002) takes a historical approach to what he calls "the show business niche" of magic acts and shows leading up to and including cinema, which have "helped provide the terms and content of modern culture's understanding and judgment of itself" (1). My goal is similar, but I focus more than he does on the enchanted performer, less on enchanted technology, and I lend more credence than During does to the efficacy of the rites. Sue-Ellen Case usefully theorizes an alternative history of secular magic in *From Alchemy to Avatar: Performing Science and the Virtual* (London: Routledge, 2006), in which she explores the realms of cyber-generated simulations, which, as Baudrillard and Žižek prophesied, have become the most probative arenas of what's really happening.

25. David Aberbach, *Charisma in Politics, Religion and the Media: Private Trauma, Public Ideals* (London: Macmillan, 1996), x.

26. Joseph Roach, *Cities of the Dead: Circum-Atlantic Performance* (New York: Columbia University Press, 1996), 36: "Normal usage employs the word *effigy* as a noun meaning a sculpted or pictured likeness. More particularly, it can suggest a crudely fashioned image of a person, commonly one that is destroyed in his or her stead, as in hanging or burning *in effigy*. When *effigy* appears as a verb, though that usage is rare, it means to evoke an absence, to body something forth, especially something from the distant past *(OED)*. *Effigy* is cognate to *efficiency, efficacy, effervescence,* and *effeminacy,* through their mutual connection to ideas of producing, bringing forth, bringing out, and making."

27. Chris Rojek, *Celebrity* (London: Reaktion Books, 2001), 58. In addition to Rojek's very useful book, celebrities and their reception have been variously explored by Leo Braudy, *The Frenzy of Renown: Fame and Its History* (New York: Oxford University Press, 1986); Richard Dyer, *Heavenly Bodies: Film Stars and Society* (1986; New York: Routledge, 2004); Neal Gabler, *Life: The Movie: How Entertainment Conquered Reality* (New York: Vintage, 1998); and with special relevance here by the essays collected in *Theatre and Celebrity in Britain, 1660–2000,* ed. Mary Luckhurst and Jane Moody (London: Palgrave, 2005).

28. Emile Durkheim, *The Elementary Forms of Religious Life,* trans. Karen E. Fields (1912; New York: Free Press, 1995), 208. See the helpful cautionary note in *Social Performance: Symbolic Action, Cultural Pragmatics, and Ritual,* ed. Jeffrey C. Alexander, Bernhard Giesen, and Jason L. Mast (Cambridge: Cambridge University Press, 2006), introduction, 8–9.

29. Durkheim, *Elementary Forms,* 191, 217.

30. Roland Barthes, *Mythologies,* trans. Annette Lavers (1957; New York: Hill and Wang, 1972), 56–57.

31. Adam Smith, *An Enquiry into the Nature and Causes of the Wealth of Nations,* ed. R. H. Campbell, A. S. Skinner, and W. B. Todd (1776; Oxford: Clarendon Press, 1976), 1:476.

32. Smith, *Wealth of Nations,* 1:291. For informative accounts of the political economy of the theater and particularly the actress as symbolic credit and commodity, see James Peck, "Anne Oldfield's Lady Townly: Consumption, Credit, and the Whig Hegemony of the 1720s," *Theatre Journal* 49 (1997): 397–416; and Felicity Nussbaum, "Actresses and the Economics of Celebrity, 1700–1800," in Luckhurst and Moody, *Theatre and Celebrity,* 148–68.

33. Harries, *Scare Quotes from Shakespeare,* 14–18, 55, 151; see also Katherine Rowe's account of "the invisible hand" in *Dead Hands: Fictions of Agency, Renaissance to Modern* (Stanford: Stanford University Press, 1999), 15, 123–27.

34. "The Study of Poetry," in *Poetry and Criticism of Matthew Arnold,* ed. Dwight Culler (Boston: Houghton-Mifflin, 1961), 306.

35. Anita Loos, *A Girl Like I* (New York: Viking, 1966), 119.

36. The salient particulars appear in Lady Duff-Gordon's *Discretions and Indiscretions* (New York: Frederick A. Stokes, 1932) and Elinor Glyn's *Romantic Adventure* (New York: E. P. Dutton, 1937). For additional details and perspectives, see Anthony Glyn, *Elinor Glyn: A Biography* (London: Hutchinson, 1955); Meredith Etherington-Smith and Jeremy Pilcher, *The "It" Girls: Lucy, Lady Duff Gordon, the Couturiere "Lucile," and Elinor Glyn, Romantic Novelist* (London: Hamish Hamilton, 1986); and Joan Hardwick, *Addicted to Romance: The Life and Adventures of Elinor Glyn* (London: Andre Deutsch, 1994). In *The Cat's Meow* (Lion's Gate, 1994), Joanna Lumley elegantly plays Elinor Glyn to Kirsten Dunst's Marian Davies.

37. Lady Duff-Gordon, *Discretions and Indiscretions,* 149, 101, 28, 97–98.

38. Glyn, *Romantic Adventure,* 40. John Stokes has vividly evoked Bernhardt's reception in *The French Actress and Her English Audience* (Cambridge: Cambridge University Press, 2005).

39. Qtd. in Hardwick, *Addicted to Romance,* 122.

40. Cecil Beaton, in Elinor Glyn, *Three Weeks* (1907; London: Duckworth, 1974), introduction, xii–xiii.

41. Glyn, *Romantic Adventure,* 23.

42. Glyn, *Romantic Adventure,* 1. For the influence of Pepys on the later practice of diary-keeping, see Stuart Sherman, *Telling Time: Clocks, Diaries, and English Diurnal Form, 1660–1785* (Chicago: University of Chicago Press, 1996), 34–35.

43. Glyn, *Romantic Adventure,* 292.

44. *Vicarious* means that which has been delegated, as in *vicarious*

*authority;* also: that which is performed or suffered by one person as a substitute for another or to the advantage or benefit of another, as in *vicarious sacrifice* or *vicarious pilgrimage;* most familiarly, it means that which is realized through the imaginative or sympathetic consciousness of another, as in *vicarious experience, vicarious thrills,* and *vicarious humiliation;* or, tangentially but provocatively, that which occurs in an unexpected or abnormal part of the body—bleeding from the gums sometimes occurs in the absence of a normal discharge from the uterus, as in *vicarious menstruation (OED).*

45. Neil McKendrick, John Brewer, and J. H. Plumb, *The Birth of a Consumer Society: The Commercialization of Eighteenth-Century England* (Bloomington: Indiana University Press, 1982). See also Ann Bermingham, "The Consumption of Culture: Image, Object, Text," in *The Consumption of Culture, 1600–1800,* ed. Ann Bermingham and John Brewer (London: Routledge, 1995), 1–20. Feminist scholarship has mined a particularly rich vein of consumption history; see especially Elizabeth Kowaleski-Wallace, *Consuming Subjects: Women, Shopping, and Business in the Eighteenth Century* (New York: Columbia University Press, 1997); and Erin Mackie, *Market à la Mode: Fashion, Commodity, and Gender in the Tatler and the Spectator* (Baltimore: Johns Hopkins University Press, 1997). For a particularly illuminating account of consumption and fashion in the performance of everyday life, see Tita Chico, *Designing Women: The Dressing Room in Eighteenth-Century English Literature and Culture* (Lewisburg, Pa.: Bucknell University Press, 2005).

46. John Downes, *Roscius Anglicanus, or an Historical Overview of the Stage* (London: Printed for H. Playford, 1708), 27–28.

47. This is the central theme of the film *The Last King: The Power and Passion of Charles II* (BBC and A & E, 2004). For considered views of the intersecting theatrical and political contexts, see Susan Staves, *Player's Scepters: Fictions of Authority in the Restoration* (Lincoln: University of Nebraska Press, 1979); Nancy Klein Maguire, *Regicide and Restoration: English Tragicomedy, 1660–1671* (Cambridge: Cambridge University Press, 1992); and Paula R. Backscheider, *Spectacular Politics: Theatrical Power and Mass Culture in Early Modern England* (Baltimore: Johns Hopkins University Press, 1993).

48. *The Tempest; or, the Enchanted Island* (London: Printed by T. N. Herringman, 1674), prologue.

49. Warrant granted by Charles II to Killigrew and Davenant, August 21, 1660, in *Theatre in Europe: A Documentary History, Restoration and Georgian England 1660–1788,* ed. David Thomas and Arnold Hare (Cambridge: Cambridge University Press, 1989), 11.

50. Ronald Hutton, *Charles II: King of England, Scotland, and Ireland* (Oxford: Clarendon Press, 1989), 458.

51. Macaulay, *History of England,* 1:127.

52. Paul Hammond, "The King's Two Bodies: Representations of

Charles II," in *Culture, Politics and Society in Britain, 1600–1800,* ed. Jeremy Black and Jeremy Gregory (Manchester: Manchester University Press, 1991), 38, citing John Browne, *Charisma Basilicon; or, The Royal Gift of Healing Strumaes, or King's-Evil* (1684).

53. Charles Gildon, *The Life of Mr. Thomas Betterton, the Late Eminent Tragedian* (London: Printed for Robert Gosling, 1710).

54. Ernst Kantorowicz, *The King's Two Bodies: A Study in Medieval Political Theory* (Princeton: Princeton University Press, 1957). See Giorgio Agamben, *Homo Sacer: Sovereign Power and Bare Life,* trans. Daniel Heller-Roazen (Stanford: Stanford University Press, 1995), 91–103.

55. Glyn, *Romantic Adventure,* 283.

56. Downes, *Roscius Anglicanus,* 16.

57. Gildon, *Life of Thomas Betterton,* 10.

58. Anthony Aston, *A Brief Supplement to Colley Cibber,* in *An Apology for the Life of Mr. Colley Cibber* (1740), ed. Robert W. Lowe (London: John C. Nimmo, 1889), 2:299–300.

59. Rojek, *Celebrity,* 55.

60. Richard Steele, *The Tatler,* ed. Donald F. Bond (Oxford: Clarendon Press, 1987), 2:424.

61. *Hazlitt on Theatre,* ed. William Archer and Robert Lowe (1895; New York: Hill and Wang, n.d.), 94.

62. *Hazlitt on Theatre,* 93.

63. Edmund Burke, *Reflections on the Revolution in France,* ed. Conor Cruise O'Brien (1790; London: Penguin, 1968), 176.

64. Barthes, *Mythologies,* 33.

65. *Ovid's Metamorphoses, in Fifteen Books,* book 10, "The Story of Pygmalion and the Statue," trans. John Dryden (London: J. Tonson, 1719), 133–35. The opposite procedure, in which the speaker of a poem deconstructs the image of a woman piece by piece, occurs in Jonathan Swift's "A Beautiful Young Nymph Going to Bed"; see Claude Rawson, *Order from Confusion Sprung: Studies in Eighteenth-Century Literature from Swift to Cowper* (London: George Allen and Unwin, 1985), 160–63.

66. Virginia Postrel, *The Substance of Style: How the Rise of Aesthetic Value is Remaking Commerce, Culture, and Consciousness* (New York: HarperCollins, 2003), especially chap. 2, "The Rise of the Look and Feel," 34–65. See also Thomas Otten, *A Superficial Reading of Henry James: Preoccupations with the Material World* (Columbus: Ohio State University Press, 2006), especially chap. 8, "The Color of Air: New Materialism," 154–66.

## Chapter One

1. Anthony Harvey and Richard Mortimer, eds., *The Funeral Effigies of Westminster Abbey* (Woodbridge, Suffolk: Boydell Press, 1994), 79–94; foreword by H. R. H. the Prince of Wales.

2. Mark B. Sandburg, writing in a chapter titled "The Idea of Effigy,"

notes, "Our visual culture quite simply demands broad competency in effigies—not simply the mannequin kind but an entire range of recorded and digital bodies": *Living Pictures, Missing Persons: Mannequins, Museums, and Modernity* (Princeton: Princeton University Press, 2003), 3–4.

3. *The Complete Works of John Ruskin*, ed. E. T. Cook and Alexander Wedderburn (London: George Allen, 1904), 11:110–11.

4. Catherine MacLeod and Julia Marciari Alexander, *Painted Ladies: Women at the Court of Charles II* (London: National Portrait Gallery; New Haven: Yale Center for British Art, 2001). I am indebted to MacLeod and Alexander for producing the exhibition and the catalog, and especially to the latter for her helpful advice on the art historical issues of the period.

5. *The Complete Works of William Hazlitt*, ed. P. P. Howe (1932; New York: AMS Press, 1967), 10:38.

6. David Piper, *Catalogue of the Seventeenth Century Portraits in the National Portrait Gallery, 1625–1714* (Cambridge: Cambridge University Press,1963), 149.

7. Harvey and Mortimer, *Funeral Effigies*, 94.

8. Rob Walker, "Consumed," *New York Times Magazine*, December 12, 2004, 46.

9. Andrew Sofer, *The Stage Life of Props* (Ann Arbor: University of Michigan Press, 2003), 117.

10. T. S. Crawford, *A History of the Umbrella* (Newton Abbot, Devon: David and Charles, 1970), 88–91.

11. Glyn, *Romantic Adventure*, 11.

12. Glyn, *Romantic Adventure*, 21.

13. Glyn, *Romantic Adventure*, 24–25.

14. Lady Duff-Gordon, *Discretions and Indiscretions*, 21.

15. Glyn, *Romantic Adventure*, 16, 11.

16. Walter Bagehot, *The English Constitution*, ed. R. H. S. Crossman (1867; Ithaca, N.Y.: Cornell University Press, 1966), 86. On the Victorian context of Bagehot's views, see Margaret Homans, *Royal Representations: Queen Victoria and British Culture, 1837–1876* (Chicago: University of Chicago Press, 1998), 101–15.

17. Bagehot, *The English Constitution*, 248.

18. Bagehot, *The English Constitution*, 249.

19. Glyn, *Romantic Adventure*, 2.

20. Glyn, *Romantic Adventure*, 300–301.

21. Glyn, *Romantic Adventure*, 297–99.

22. Glyn, *Three Weeks*, 85.

23. Loos, *A Girl Like I*, 119, 120.

24. Elizabeth Howe, *The First English Actresses: Women and Drama, 1660–1700* (Cambridge: Cambridge University Press, 1992), 34.

25. Aphra Behn, dedication to *The Feigned Courtesans;or, A Night's Intrigue* (1679), in *The Works of Aphra Behn*, ed. Janet Todd (Columbus: Ohio State University Press, 1996), 6:86–87. Elin Diamond has illumi-

nated Behn's tactically gendered dramaturgy in *Unmaking Mimesis: Essays on Feminism and Theater* (New York: Routledge, 1997), chap. 3, "*Gestus,* Signature, Body in the Theater of Aphra Behn," 56–82.

26. Harold Weber, "Carolinean Sexuality and the Restoration Stage: Reconstructing the Royal Phallus in Sodom," in *Cultural Readings of Restoration and Eighteenth-Century Theater,* ed. J. Douglas Canfield and Deborah C. Payne (Athens: University of Georgia Press, 1995), 67–88. See also James Grantham Turner, "Pepys and the Private Parts of Monarchy," in *Culture and Society in the Stuart Restoration: Literature, Drama, History,* ed. Gerald MacLean (Cambridge: Cambridge University Press, 1995), 95–110.

27. *The Diary of John Evelyn,* ed. E. S. DeBeer (Oxford: Clarendon Press, 1955), 4:410.

28. Macleod and Alexander, *Painted Ladies,* 123, 157. Which player sat for the Magdalen is uncertain, complicated by the later tendency to identify any unknown female sitter as Nell Gwyn.

29. Macleod and Alexander, *Painted Ladies,* 124–25, 123, 129, 157.

30. For the most recent account, see Claire Tomalin, *Samuel Pepys: The Unequaled Self* (New York: Knopf, 2002), 191–210.

31. Thomas W. Laqueur, *Solitary Sex: A Cultural History of Masturbation* (New York: Zone Books, 2003), 180–81.

32. Macleod and Alexander, *Painted Ladies,* 171.

33. Qtd. Harvey and Mortimer, *Funeral Effigies,* 95, 97.

34. Bagehot, *The English Constitution,* 248.

35. Glyn, *Romantic Adventure,* 326.

36. Quoted in Stenn, *Clara Bow,* 208.

37. Hardwick, *Addicted to Romance,* 263.

38. Glyn, *Romantic Adventure,* 97

## Chapter Two

1. J. C. Flügel, *The Psychology of Clothes* (London: Hogarth Press, 1930), 117. See Jessica Munns and Penny Richards, eds., *The Clothes that Wear Us: Essays on Dressing and Transgressing in Eighteenth-Century Culture* (Newark: University of Delaware Press, 1999), especially the introduction by the editors and the afterword by Deborah C. Payne, 336–46; Aileen Ribeiro, *Art of Dress: Fashion in England and France, 1750–1820* (New Haven: Yale University Press, 2003).

2. John Harvey, *Men in Black* (Chicago: University of Chicago Press, 1995), 16.

3. Harvey and Mortimer, *Funeral Effigies,* 84–92.

4. Laurence Senelick, in *The Changing Room: Sex, Drag, and the Theatre* (London: Routledge, 2000), provides a comprehensive overview.

5. Peggy Phelan, *Unmarked: The Politics of Performance* (London: Routledge, 1993), 6.

6. Lady Duff-Gordon, *Discretions and Indiscretions*, 71.

7. Lady Duff-Gordon, *Discretions and Indiscretions*, 93. For context see Joel H. Kaplan and Sheila Stowell, *Theatre and Fashion: Oscar Wilde to the Suffragettes* (Cambridge: Cambridge University Press, 1994).

8. Roland Barthes, *The Fashion System*, trans. Matthew Ward and Richard Howard (New York: Hill and Wang, 1983). See also Allison Lurie, *The Language of Clothes* (New York: Henry Holt, 2000); Ann Hollander, *Seeing through Clothes* (New York: Viking Press, 1978); and especially Herbert Blau, *Nothing in Itself: Complexions of Fashion* (Bloomington: Indiana University Press, 1999).

9. Lady Duff-Gordon, *Discretions and Indiscretions*, 75.

10. Erica Rand, *Barbie's Queer Accessories* (Durham: Duke University Press, 1995).

11. Lady Duff-Gordon, *Discretions and Indiscretions*, 18.

12. Lady Duff-Gordon, *Discretions and Indiscretions*, 19–20.

13. Glyn, *Romantic Adventure*, 30.

14. Pope, *An Essay on Criticism*, line 301.

15. Lady Duff-Gordon, *Discretions and Indiscretions*, 18.

16. Glyn, *Romantic Adventure*, 31.

17. Barthes, *Mythologies*, 86–87.

18. Linda Mizejewski, *Ziegfeld Girl: Image and Icon in Culture and Cinema* (Durham: Duke University Press, 1999), 95–97.

19. Etherington-Smith and Pilcher, *The "It" Girls*, 178.

20. Lady Duff-Gordon, *Discretions and Indiscretions*, 249–50.

21. Sir James Frazer, *The Golden Bough*, 3rd ed., part 1, *The Magic Art and the Evolution of Kings* (London: Macmillan, 1966), 55.

22. David Freedberg, *The Power of Images: Studies in the History and Theory of Response* (Chicago: University of Chicago Press, 1989), 270–80.

23. *The Poems of John Wilmot, Earl of Rochester*, ed. Keith Walker (Oxford: Blackwell, 1984), 74.

24. Gillian Manning, introduction to *Libertine Plays of the Restoration* (London: Everyman, 2001), xxv. See also James Grantham Turner, *Libertines and Radicals in Early Modern London: Sexuality, Politics, and Literary Culture* (Cambridge: Cambridge University Press, 2001); Harold Weber, *The Restoration Rake-Hero: Transformations in Sexual Understanding in Seventeenth-Century England* (Madison: University of Wisconsin Press, 1986); and Maximillian E. Novak, "Marjorie Pinchwife's 'London Disease': Restoration Comedy and the Libertine Offensive of the 1670s," *Studies in the Literary Imagination* 10 (1977): 1–23.

25. Macaulay, *History of England*, 1:160.

26. John Harold Wilson, *A Rake and His Times: George Villiers, 2nd Duke of Buckingham* (New York: Farrar, Straus, and Young, 1954), 56–57.

27. Samuel Butler, *The Genuine Remains in Verse and Prose of Mr. Samuel Butler* (London: J. and R. Tonson, 1759), 735.

28. "A Short Discourse upon the Reasonableness of Men's having a

Religion" (1685), in *Buckingham: Public and Private Man. The Prose, Poems and Commonplace Book of George Villiers, 2nd Duke of Buckingham (1628–1687)*, ed. Christine Phipps (New York: Garland, 1985), 119, 236n.

29. Wilson, *Rake and His Times*, 6.

30. Expenditures for July 28 and August 3, 1674, Buckingham Papers (uncataloged), Osborn Collection, Beinecke Library, Yale University.

31. Winifred Burghclere, *George Villiers, 2nd Duke of Buckingham, 1628–1687: A Study in the History of the Restoration* (1903; rpt. Port Washington, N.Y.: Kennikat Press, 1971), 194–95.

32. *Bishop Burnet's History of His Own Time* (1723; London: William Smith, 1839), 33n; see Pepys 9:26–27.

33. Macleod and Alexander, *Painted Ladies*, 232–33.

34. Ruskin, "Academy Notes," in *Works*, 14:15.

35. "The Royal Academy Exhibition," *The Spectator*, May 6, 1855.

36. *The Reader: A Review of Literature, Science and Art*, January 9, 1864, 56.

37. *Moral Essays: Epistle to Bathurst*, in *The Poems of Alexander Pope*, ed. F. W. Bateson (New Haven: Yale University Press, 1951), 114–15.

38. Pope, *Epistle to Bathurst*, 115–16.

39. John Dryden, *Absalom and Achitophel*, lines 543–53, in *The Works of John Dryden*, ed. H. T. Swedenberg and Vinton A. Dearing (Berkeley and Los Angeles: University of California Press, 1972), 2:21. Claude Rawson, in *Satire and Sentiment 1660–1830: Stress Points in the English Augustan Tradition* (1994; New Haven: Yale University Press, 2000), 116, hears these lines echoed by Byron in *Don Juan* (7.55) and by Yeats in "In Memory of Major Robert Gregory."

40. Robert C. Elliott, *The Power of Satire: Magic, Ritual, Art* (Princeton: Princeton University Press, 1960).

41. Thomas Davies, *Dramatic Miscellanies* (London: Printed for the Author, 1783), 3:289.

42. Davies, *Dramatic Miscellanies*, 3:290.

43. Davies, *Dramatic Miscellanies*, 3:288.

44. Dryden, *Absalom and Achitophel*, lines 567–68.

45. Buckingham, "To Dryden," quoted in Phipps, *Buckingham*, 168. My reading of this poem is indebted throughout to John H. O'Neill, *George Villiers, Second Duke of Buckingham* (Boston: Twayne, 1984), 23–26.

46. Roger Lockyer, *Buckingham: The Life and Political Career of George Villiers, First Duke of Buckingham, 1592–1628* (London: Longman, 1981), 286.

47. Lockier, qtd. in O'Neill, *George Villiers*, 3; Fairfax, qtd. in Phipps, *Buckingham*, 3; Louis XIV, qtd. in Burghclere, *George Villiers*, 220–21; *Bishop Burnet's History*, 69; Clarendon, qtd. in *Bishop Burnet's History*, 33n; Walpole, qtd. in *The Complete Peerage*, ed. Vicary Gibbs (London: St.

Catherine's Press, 1910–59), 2:394; ballad, "No gallant peer," qtd. in Gibbs, *The Complete Peerage*, 2:395.

48. *The Prose Works of Andrew Marvell*, ed. Annabel Patterson, Martin Dzelzainis, N. H. Keeble, and Nicholas von Maltzahn (New Haven: Yale University Press, 2003), 2:43.

### Chapter Three

1. Harvey and Mortimer, *Funeral Effigies*, 92.

2. See the articles collected in *Eighteenth-Century Studies* 38, no. 1 (2004), the special "Hair" Issue edited by Angela Rosenthal.

3. Grant McCracken, *Big Hair: A Journey into the Transformation of Self* (Woodstock, N.Y.: Overlook Press, 1996), 130–31, 145.

4. Diane Simon, *Hair: Public, Political, Extremely Personal* (New York: St. Martin's Press, 2000), 7.

5. John Woodforde, *The Strange Story of False Hair* (London: Routledge and Kegan Paul, 1971), 29.

6. *The Poems of Alexander Pope*, vol. 2, *The Rape of the Lock and Other Poems*, ed. Geoffrey Tillotson, 2nd ed. (New Haven: Yale University Press, 1954), 144. Subsequent references to this volume are cited parenthetically.

7. "An Essay on the Hair, With the most proper Methods of dressing and preserving it," appended to *New London Toilet* (London: Printed for Richardson and Urquhart, 1778), 99.

8. Sir James Frazer, *The Golden Bough: A Study in Magic and Religion*, 3rd ed., part 2, *Taboo and the Perils of the Soul* (London: Macmillan, 1966), 252, 258.

9. Sigmund Freud, "Medusa's Head," in *The Complete Psychological Works*, ed. James Strachey (1922; London: Hogarth Press, 1955), 18:273–74.

10. Charles Berg, *The Unconscious Significance of Hair* (London: George Allen and Unwin, 1951).

11. Edmund Leach, "Magical Hair," *Journal of the Royal Anthropological Institute* 88 (1958): 147–64; Christopher R. Hallpike, "Social Hair," in *The Body Reader: Social Aspects of the Human Body*, ed. Ted Polhemus (New York: Pantheon, 1978), 134–46.

12. Gananath Obeyesekere, *Medusa's Hair: An Essay on Personal Symbols and Religious Experience* (Chicago: University of Chicago Press, 1981), 14–18.

13. Mizejewski, *Ziegfeld Girl*, 59.

14. Ruth Gordon, letter to the drama critic of the *New York Times*, dated December 21, 1971, qtd. in *Theatrical Letters*, ed. Bill Homewood (London: Marginalia Press, 1995), 256–57.

15. James Stewart, *Plocacosmos: or the Whole Art of Hair Dressing* (London: for the Author, 1782), 172, 175.

16. Stewart, *Plocacosmos*, 203–4.

17. See Ronald Paulson, *Hogarth's Graphic Works*, rev. ed. (New Haven: Yale University Press, 1970), no. 208, pp. 242–44.

18. John O'Brien, *Harlequin Britain: Pantomime and Entertainment, 1690–1760* (Baltimore: Johns Hopkins University Press, 2004), 136.

19. Addison, *The Spectator*, 2:178.

20. Cibber, *Apology*, 1:101; Steele, *The Tatler*, 1:493; *The Laureate or, the Right Side of Colley Cibber, Esq.* (London, 1740), in A. M. Nagler, *A Source Book in Theatrical History* (1952; New York: Dover, 1959), 219; Davies, *Dramatic Miscellanies*, 3:32; Aston, *Brief Supplement*, 300–301.

21. Rowe, quoted in Gildon, *Life of Thomas Betterton*, xiii–xiv.

22. Cibber, *Apology*, 1:99.

23. Dowes, *Roscius Anglicanus*, 21.

24. Thomas Betterton, *The History of the English Stage from the Restauration to the Present Time* (London: Edmund Curl, 1741), 84.

25. Betterton, *History of the English Stage*, 84.

26. Cibber, *Apology*, 2:35–36. Brett attended Cibber's *Love's Last Shift; or the Fool in Fashion* (1696).

27. *The Dunciad in Four Books* (1743), book 1, line 167, in *The Poems of Alexander Pope*, vol. 5, *The Dunciad*, ed. James Sutherland (New Haven: Yale University Press, 1953), 282.

28. Sir John Vanbrugh, *The Relapse; or Virtue in Danger*, ed. Curt A. Zimansky (Lincoln: University of Nebraska Press, 1970), 24.

29. Horace Walpole to William Cole, September 25, 1740, *The Yale Edition of Horace Walpole's Correspondence*, 48 vols., *Horace Walpole's Correspondence with The Rev. William Cole*, ed. W. S. Lewis and A. Dayle Wallace (New Haven: Yale University Press, 1937), 1:344.

30. William Barker, *A Treatise on the Principles of Hair-Dressing* (London: Printed by J. Rozea, [ca. 1780]), 63, 64.

31. Malcolm Gladwell, *The Tipping Point: How Little Things Can Make a Big Difference* (Boston: Little, Brown, 2000), 9–14.

32. *A Narrative of the Life of Mrs Charlotte Charke* (1755) in Fidelis Morgan, *The Well-Known Troublemaker: A Life of Charlotte Charke* (London: Faber and Faber, 1988), 5.

33. See Susan Staves, "A Few Kind Words for the Fop," *Studies in English Literature* 22 (1982): 413–28; Laurence Senelick, "Mollies or Men of Mode? Sodomy and the Eighteenth-Century London Stage," *Journal of the History of Sexuality* 1 (1990): 33–67; Kristina Straub, *Sexual Suspects: Eighteenth-Century Players and Sexual Ideology* (Princeton: Princeton University Press, 1992), 47–68, 127–50; and Thomas A. King, *The Gendering of Men, 1600–1750*, vol. 1, *The English Phallus* (Madison: University of Wisconsin Press, 2004).

34. *Memoirs of Richard Cumberland, Written by Himself* (London: Lackington, Allen, 1806), 59–60.

35. Peter Thomson, "Celebrity and Rivalry: David [Garrick] and Goliath [Quin]," in Luckhurst and Moody, *Theatre and Celebrity*, 127–47.

36. Stewart, *Plocacosmos*, 205.

37. Denis Diderot, "The Paradox of the Actor," in *Selected Writings on Art and Literature*, trans. Geoffrey Bremner (London: Penguin, 1994), 120.

38. Joseph Roach, *The Player's Passion: Studies in the Science of Acting* (1985; Ann Arbor: University of Michigan Press, 1993), 58–59.

39. Diderot, "Paradox of the Actor," 133, 129, 141, 106. See also William Ian Miller, *Faking It* (Cambridge: Cambridge University Press, 2003).

40. Margaret Thatcher, *Statecraft: Strategies for a Changing World* (New York: HarperCollins, 2002), 45.

41. Ian Baucom, *Out of Place: Englishness, Empire and Locations of Identity* (Princeton: Princeton University Press, 1999), 7–14.

42. Rhys Hughes, http://www.ookami.co.uk/html/rhys_huges_interviewed.html.

## Chapter Four

1. *The Reminiscences of Sarah Kemble Siddons*, ed. William Van Lennep (Cambridge: Widener Library, 1942), 17–18.

2. Charles Lamb, *Works*, ed. E. V. Lucas (1903; rpt. New York: AMS, 1968), 1:97.

3. Richard Dyer, *White* (London: Routledge, 1997), 1.

4. Cibber, *Apology*, 1:170–73.

5. Aston, in Cibber, *Apology*, 2:305.

6. Davies, *Dramatic Miscellanies*, 3:6.

7. Siddons, *Reminiscences*, 19.

8. Burke, *Reflections*, 176. I am here indebted to Christopher Reid, "Burke's Tragic Muse: Sarah Siddons and the 'Feminization' of the *Reflections*," in *Burke and the French Revolution* (Athens: University of Georgia Press, 1992), 1–27; Jonathan Bate, *Shakespearian Consititutions: Politics, Theatre, Criticism, 1730–1830* (Oxford: Clarendon Press, 1989), 88–89; and Rawson, *Satire and Sentiment*, 133–96.

9. Siddons, *Reminiscences*, 17–18.

10. Burke, *Reflections*, 194–95.

11. Burke, *Reflections*, 169.

12. Barker, *Principles of Hair-Dressing*, 32. Horace Walpole expressed mild distaste for this innovation: To Lady Ossory, *Walpole's Correspondence*, 33:359.

13. Heather McPherson, "Picturing Tragedy: Mrs. Siddons as the Tragic Muse Revisited," *Eighteenth-century Studies* 33 (Spring 2000): 401–30. See Pat Rogers, "'Towering Beyond Her Sex': Stature and Sub-

limity in the Achievement of Sarah Siddons," in *Curtain Calls: British and American Women and the Theatre, 1660–1820,* ed. Mary Anne Scholfield and Cecelia Macleski (Athens: University of Georgia Press, 1991), 48; see also Laura J. Rosenthal, "The Sublime, the Beautiful, 'The Siddons,'" in Munns and Richards, *Clothes that Wear Us,* 56–79; Shearer West, "Body Connoisseurship" in *Notorious Muse: The Actress in British Art and Culture,* ed. Robyn Asleson (New Haven: Yale University Press, 2003), 151–70.

14. James Boaden, *Memoirs of Mrs. Siddons* (Philadelphia: J. B. Lippincott, 1893), 280–81.

15. Thomas Campbell, *The Life of Mrs. Siddons* (London: Effingham Wilson, 1834), 2:355–57.

16. Robyn Asleson, "'*She Was Tragedy Personified*': Crafting the Siddons Legend in Art and Life," in *A Passion for Performance: Sarah Siddons and Her Portraitists,* ed. Robyn Asleson (Los Angeles: J. Paul Getty Museum, 1999), 57.

17. *Hazlitt on Theatre,* xi. For an understanding of Hazlitt's more representatively measured theatrical criticism, see the discussion of his response to Edmund Kean's Shylock in David Bromwich, *Hazlitt: The Mind of a Critic* (1983; New Haven: Yale University Press, 1999), 324–26, 402–4.

18. *Hazlitt on Theatre,* 17.

19. Boaden, *Memoirs of Mrs. Siddons,* 394.

20. Burke, *Reflections,* 175.

21. Glyn, *Romantic Adventure,* 101.

22. Boaden, *Memoirs of Mrs. Siddons,* 431.

23. Ellen Donkin, "Mrs. Siddons Looks Back in Anger: Feminist Historiography for Eighteenth-Century British Theater," in *Critical Theory and Performance,* ed. Janelle Reinelt and Joseph Roach (Ann Arbor: University of Michigan Press, 1992), 276–90.

24. Shearer West, *The Image of the Actor: Verbal and Visual Representation in the Age of Garrick and Kemble* (London: Pinter, 1991), 123–25.

25. Richard Wendorf, *Sir Joshua Reynolds: The Painter in Society* (Cambridge: Harvard University Press, 1996), 147–52.

26. Tom Brown, *Amusements Serious and Comical, Calculated for the Meridian of London, "with large improvements,"* 2nd ed. (London: Booksellers of London and Westminster, 1700), 51–52.

27. *Harris's List of Covent Garden Ladies; or, Man of Pleasure's Kalender for the Year 1793* (1793; rpt. Edinburgh: Paul Harris, 1982), s.v. "Abing—on, Mrs."

28. *Harris's List of Covent-Garden Ladies; or, Man of Pleasure's Kalender for the Year, 1788* (1788; rpt. New York: Garland, 1986), 84–85.

29. *Harris's List,* 1788, 84.

30. Glyn, *Romantic Adventure,* 15 and passim.

31. Addison, *The Spectator,* 2:178.

32. George C. D. Odell, *Shakespeare from Betterton to Irving* (1920; rpt. New York: Dover, 1966), 1:207.

33. David Román, *Performance in America: Contemporary U.S. Culture and the Performing Arts* (Durham: Duke University Press, 2005), 142–58.

34. Adrian Kear, "Diana Between Two Deaths: Spectral Ethics and the Time of Mourning," in *Mourning Diana: Nation, Culture and the Performance of Grief*, ed. Adrian Kear and Deborah Lynn Steinberg (London: Routledge, 1999), 170.

35. Charles Spencer, Viscount Althorpe, *Diana: A Celebration* (Princess of Wales Memorial Fund, n.d.), 75.

36. Glyn, *Romantic Adventure*, 97.

37. Burke, *Reflections*, 171.

38. Mica Nava, "Diana and Race," in Kear and Steinberg, *Mourning Diana*, 115.

39. Charles Spencer, Viscount Althorp, *Althorp: The Story of an English House* (New York: St. Martin's Press, 1998), 167.

*Chapter Five*

1. Richard D. Altick, *The Shows of London* (Cambridge, Mass.: Belknap Press, 1978), 91–93.

2. Harvey and Mortimer, *Funeral Effigies*, 84.

3. http://www.accel-team.com/pygmalion/; accessed November 18, 2004.

4. John Emerson and Anita Loos, *Breaking into the Movies* (New York: James A. McCann, 1921), 1.

5. Lady Duff-Gordon, *Discretions and Indiscretions*, 259–61.

6. Quinn, "Celebrity," 156.

7. Emerson and Loos, *Breaking into the Movies*, 17.

8. Gail Marshall, *Actresses on the Victorian Stage: Feminine Performance and the Galatea Myth* (Cambridge: Cambridge University Press, 1998), 16–19.

9. Bernard Shaw, *Pygmalion: A Romance in Five Acts* (1912), in *Selected Plays with Prefaces*, vol. 1 (New York: Dodd Mead, n.d.), 281–82. Subsequent references parenthetical.

10. For Nell Gwyn as Cinderella, especially on account of her small feet, see Thomas A. King, "'As if (she) were made to put the whole world into good Humour': Reconstructing the First English Actresses," *Drama Review* 36, no. 3 (1992): 78–102.

11. Jacky Bratton, *New Readings in Theatre History* (Cambridge: Cambridge University Press, 2003); Kathleen Wilson, "The Colonial Stage: Theatre, Culture, and Modernity in the English Provinces, 1720–1840" (in progress); Jane Moody, *Illegitimate Theatre in London, 1770–1840* (Cambridge: Cambridge University Press, 2000); Tracy Davis, *Actresses as*

*Working Women: Their Identity in Victorian Culture* (London: Routledge, 1991).

12. See Lewis Hyde, *The Gift: Imagination and the Erotic Life of Property* (New York: Vintage, 1979).

13. Marvin Carlson, *Places of Performance: The Semiotics of Theater Architecture* (Ithaca, N.Y.: Cornell University Press, 1989), 10–11.

14. Susan Foster, *Choreography and Narrative: Ballet's Staging of Story and Desire* (Bloomington: Indiana University Press, 1996), 1–12, 287 n. 66.

15. *The Covent Garden Jester; or, the Rambler's Companion* (1775; rpt. New York: Garland, 1986), dedication.

16. *My Fair Lady: A Musical Play in Two Acts,* adaptation and lyrics by Alan Jay Lerner, music by Frederick Lowe (New York: Coward-McCann, 1956), 30. Subsequent references parenthetical.

17. John Dunton, *The Night-Walker: or, Evening Rambles in search after Lewd Women, with the Conferences held with Them, To be publish'd Monthly, 'till a Discovery be made of all the chief Prostitutes in England, from the Pensionary Miss, down to the Common Strumpet* (London: Printed for James Orme, 1696), 13.

18. Charles Dickens, *Our Mutual Friend* (London: Penguin, 1997), 710.

19. Charles Dickens, *Little Dorrit* (London: Penguin, 2003), 181–82.

20. Brown, *Amusements Serious and Comical,* 56.

21. Dean MacCannell, *The Tourist: A New Theory of the Leisure Class* (1976; rpt. New York: Schocken, 1989), 41.

22. John Ruskin, "The Two Boyhoods," from *Modern Painters,* vol. 5, part 9, "Of Invention Spiritual" (1860), in *Unto this Last and Other Writings by John Ruskin,* ed. Clive Wilmer (London: Penguin, 1985), 146.

23. Addison, *The Spectator,* 4:99.

24. Addison, *The Spectator,* 2:534–35.

25. Ruskin, "The Two Boyhoods," 152.

26. Tracy C. Davis, in "Shaw's Interstices of Empire: Decolonizing at Home and Abroad," describes the relationship of female dependence of Eliza as that of "master and slave, colonizer and colonized." *The Cambridge Companion to George Bernard Shaw,* ed. Christopher Innes (Cambridge: Cambridge University Press, 1998), 225.

27. Celia Marshik, "Parodying the £5 Virgin: Bernard Shaw and the Playing of *Pygmalion,*" *Yale Journal of Criticism* 13 (2000): 321–41.

28. Joel H. Kaplan, "Pineroticism and the Problem Play: Mrs Tanqueray, Mrs Ebbsmith and 'Mrs Pat,'" in *British Theatre in the 1890s: Essays on Drama and the Stage,* ed. Richard Foulkes (Cambridge: Cambridge University Press, 1992), 38–58.

29. *Bernard Shaw and Mrs. Patrick Campbell, Their Correspondence,* ed. Alan Dent (New York: Alfred A. Knopf, 1952), 96–97.

30. Marshik, "Parodying the £5 Virgin," 337.

31. Barthes, *Mythologies,* 97.

## Chapter Six

1. Altick, in *The Shows of London,* 91–93, documents the different attractions exerted by the "Ragged Regiment" of medieval effigies made of wood and cloth, the waxwork figures of Charles II and others, and the shocking anomaly of Queen Katherine's mummy.

2. Raphael Holinshed, *Chronicles of England, Scotland, and Ireland* (1586; London: J. Johnson, 1808), 3:190.

3. *Ovid's Metamorphoses,* book 10, p. 134.

4. Glyn, *It,* 10–11.

5. Diana Taylor, in *The Archive and the Repertoire: Performing Cultural Memory in the Americas* (Durham: Duke University Press, 2003), still values the archive of written sources that scholars conventionally mine, but she also draws attention to the repertoire of performances that transmit works of embodied knowledge. Taylor locates her main object of study in "the scenario," as opposed to the text or the narrative: "Simultaneously *set-up* and *action*," she summarizes, "scenarios frame and activate social dramas" (28). I believe that it is the transmission of scenarios from generation to generation that makes time seem to percolate rather than flow.

6. David Cordingly, *Life Among the Pirates: The Romance and the Reality* (Little, Brown: London, 1995), xi.

7. Peter Earle, *The Pirate Wars* (London: Methuen, 2003), 206–8; Marcus Rediker, *Between the Devil and the Deep Blue Sea: Merchant Seamen, Pirates, and the Anglo-American World* (Cambridge: Cambridge University Press, 1989), 283; Peter Linebaugh and Marcus Rediker, *Many Headed Hydra: Sailors, Slaves, Commoners, and the Hidden History of the Revolutionary Atlantic* (Boston: Beacon, 2000).

8. Kurt Weill, "Dancemusic: Jazz," quoted in Douglas Jarman, *Kurt Weill* (Bloomington: Indiana University Press, 1982), 108–9.

9. Foster Hirsch, *Kurt Weill on Stage: From Berlin to Broadway* (New York: Alfred. A. Knopf, 2002), 32–54.

10. For helpful comparative insights, see Aparna Dharwadker, *Theatres of Independence: Drama, Theory and Urban Performance in India since 1947* (Iowa City: University of Iowa Press, 2005), 371–87.

11. Peter Steiner, introduction to Václav Havel, *The Beggar's Opera,* trans. Paul Wilson (Ithaca, N.Y.: Cornell University Press, 2001), xxiv.

12. See Diane Dugaw, *Warrior Women and Popular Balladry, 1650–1850* (Cambridge: Cambridge University Press, 1989).

13. Sigmund Freud, "Civilized Sexual Morality and Modern Nervousness," in *Sexuality and the Psychology of Love,* ed. Philip Rieff, *The Collected Papers of Sigmund Freud* (New York: Collin Books, 1963), 25. See Ian Kershaw, *Hitler* (London: Longman, 1991). I am grateful to Harold Weber and Lawrence Powell, respectively, for these references.

14. Wole Soyinka, *Opera Wonyosi* (Bloomington: Indiana University Press, 1981), 26.

15. *Memoirs Concerning the Life and Manners of Captain Mackheath* (London: Printed for A. Moore, 1728), 6–9.

16. *Captain Mackheath*, 22, 29.

17. *Thievery à-la-mode: or, the Fatal Encouragement* (London: Printed for J. Roberts, 1728), 13–24.

18. Brewer, *Pleasures of the Imagination*, 447–48.

19. Byron, *The Corsair*, in *Complete Poetical Works*, ed. Jerome J. McGann (Oxford: Clarendon Press, 1981), 3:214. Peter Thorslev, in *The Byronic Hero: Types and Prototypes* (Minneapolis: University of Minnesota Press, 1962), 67, suggests that Macheath may have served as a direct precursor to the Byronic hero. I am indebted to Paul Fry for this reference.

20. See Cordingly, *Life among the Pirates*, 37–38.

21. J. M. Barrie, *Peter Pan, or the Boy Who Would Not Grow Up* (New York: Charles Scribner's Sons, 1928), 54–55.

22. *Vocal Selections from The Threepenny Opera*, English adaptation by Marc Blitzstein (New York: Weill-Brecht-Harms, 1955), 5–6.

23. *Vocal Selections*, 14–19.

24. Angus Calder, *Revolutionary Empire: The Rise of English-Speaking Empires from the Fifteenth Century to the 1780s* (New York: E. P. Dutton, 1981), 265.

25. Geoffrey H. Hartman, *The Fateful Question of Culture* (New York: Columbia University Press, 1997), 14.

26. Barthes, *Mythologies*, 142–43.

27. Downes, *Roscius Anglicanus*, 27–28.

28. Harvey and Mortimer, *Funeral Effigies*, 41.

# index

Note: Page numbers in italic refer to illustrations.

260 index

Buckingham, 73, 88, 97–98,
99–102, 104–16; *The Country
Gentleman,* 109; *The Rehearsal,*
98, 100, 109, 112–13; "A Short
Discourse on the Reasonableness of Men's Having a Religion," 100; "To Dryden,"
114–15

Walker, Thomas, 215
Walpole, Horace, 115, 136, 154,
244n29
Walpole, Sir Robert, 214, 216
Weber, Harold, 240n26, 241n24,
249n13
Weber, Max, 7, 12, 233n8,
235n24
Weill, Kurt, 209, 212–13, 223; *The
Threepenny Opera,* 213, 221–25
Wendorf, Richard, 246n25
Wesley, John, 150

West, Shearer, 160, 246n13,
246n24
Westminster Abbey, 38, 45–46, 51,
55, 74, 83, 117, 134, 147–48,
150, 169, 171, 174–75, 205,
207, 228, 230–31
Whalley, Major General Edward,
2, 27
Wilkenson, Kathleen Mary Rose,
"Dolores," 94
Wilmot, John, Earl of Rochester,
98
Wilson, August, 226
Wilson, Kathleen, 247n11
Wollstonecraft, Mary, 153
Wycherley, William, 14, 98

Yates, Mary Ann, 137

Zeami, 7
Ziegfeld, Florenz, 22, 94–95, 126